EXPERIENCE SAMPLING IN MENTAL HEALTH RESEARCH

Experience Sampling in Mental Health Research provides comprehensive and user-friendly guidance on when and how to apply this methodology in the assessment of clinical populations.

Divided into three sections, the book offers step-by-step instruction on how to design, develop and implement an experience sampling study, as well as advice on how this approach might be adapted for common mental health difficulties. With an eye to the future of this type of research, the contributors also consider how experience sampling might be adapted for use as a form of clinical assessment and intervention.

Experience Sampling in Mental Health Research combines the knowledge and expertise of leading international experts in the field, and will be helpful for students, researchers and clinicians wishing to start or develop their understanding of this approach.

Dr. Jasper Palmier-Claus (BSc, MSc, PhD, ClinPsyD), Clinical Psychologist & Lecturer, Division of Psychology & Mental Health, University of Manchester & Greater Manchester Mental Health NHS Foundation Trust, Manchester, UK.

Professor Gillian Haddock (BSc, MClinPsychol, PhD), Head of the Division of Psychology & Mental Health, University of Manchester, Manchester, UK.

Dr. Filippo Varese (BSc, MSc, PhD, ClinPsyD), Senior Lecturer & Clinical Psychologist, Division of Psychology & Mental Health, University of Manchester, Manchester, UK.

EXPERIENCE SAMPLING IN MENTAL HEALTH RESEARCH

Edited by Jasper Palmier-Claus, Gillian Haddock and Filippo Varese

LONDON AND NEW YORK

First published 2019
by Routledge
2 Park Square, Milton Park, Abingdon, Oxon OX14 4RN

and by Routledge
52 Vanderbilt Avenue, New York, NY 10017

Routledge is an imprint of the Taylor & Francis Group, an informa business

© 2019 selection and editorial matter, Jasper Palmier-Claus, Gillian Haddock and Filippo Varese; individual chapters, the contributors

The right of the editor to be identified as the author of the editorial material, and of the authors for their individual chapters, has been asserted in accordance with sections 77 and 78 of the Copyright, Designs and Patents Act 1988.

All rights reserved. No part of this book may be reprinted or reproduced or utilised in any form or by any electronic, mechanical, or other means, now known or hereafter invented, including photocopying and recording, or in any information storage or retrieval system, without permission in writing from the publishers.

Trademark notice: Product or corporate names may be trademarks or registered trademarks, and are used only for identification and explanation without intent to infringe.

British Library Cataloguing-in-Publication Data
A catalogue record for this book is available from the British Library

Library of Congress Cataloging-in-Publication Data
[CIP data]

ISBN: 978-1-138-21285-5 (hbk)
ISBN: 978-1-138-21286-2 (pbk)
ISBN: 978-1-315-39834-1 (ebk)

Typeset in Bembo
by Taylor & Francis Books

To Erin Laverty Palmier-Claus

CONTENTS

List of illustrations	*ix*
List of contributors	*xi*
Preface	*xiii*

1	Why the experience sampling method? *Jasper Palmier-Claus, Gillian Haddock and Filippo Varese*	1
2	Designing and conducting an experience sampling study: Where to start? *Filippo Varese, Gillian Haddock and and Jasper Palmier-Claus*	8
3	The analysis of experience sampling data *Lesley-Anne Carter and Richard Emsley*	18
4	Experience sampling in the study of psychosis *David Kimhy and Julia Vakhrusheva*	38
5	Experience sampling in the study of autism spectrum disorders *Dougal Julian Hare and Yu-Wei Chen*	53
6	Experience sampling in the study of sleep and wakefulness *Lee Mulligan, Gillian Haddock, Donna Littlewood and* *Simon D. Kyle*	67
7	Experience sampling in the study of dyads and family dynamics *Debora Vasconcelos e Sa, Samantha Hartley and* *Christine Barrowclough*	81

viii Contents

8 Experience sampling in the study of self-harm 97
Daniel Pratt and Peter Taylor

9 Emerging applications of prediction in experience sampling 111
*Colin Depp, Christopher N. Kaufmann, Eric Granholm and
Wesley Thompson*

10 The development of ecological momentary interventions 124
Henrietta Steinhart, Inez Myin-Germeys and and Ulrich Reininghaus

11 Mobile cognitive testing using experience sampling 142
Joel Swendsen, Pierre Schweitzer and and Raeanne C. Moore

Index *156*

ILLUSTRATIONS

Figures

2.1 Conceptual representation of the chronological organisation of momentary and interval ESM items   12

3.1 Visual representation of the three-level random intercept model. Adapted from 'Module 11: Three-Level Multilevel ModelsConcepts' by Leckie, G. 2013. LEMMA VLE, University of Bristol, Centre for Multilevel Modelling. Accessed at https://www.cmm.bris.ac.uk/lemma/. Adapted with permission.   22

3.2 a) Random intercept model with solid line representing the average effect and dotted lines representing two subject-specific effects; b) Random coefficient model with solid line representing the average effect and dotted lines representing two subject-specific effects   23

3.3 a) Random coefficient model with positive covariance; b) Random coefficient model with negative covariance   23

3.4 Profile plots for paranoia. A random sample of 25 subjects, with red lines indicating day breaks.   33

3.5 Proportion of missing data for each beep   34

11.1 Cognitive decline in dementia and matching assessment methods   144

11.2 Nature of clinical and epidemiologic data demonstrating a correlation between physical activity and cognitive functioning   145

11.3 Assessment of lifestyles and cognitive functioning   145

Tables

3.1 ESM database structure with three paranoia items and baseline measure   19 x List of illustrations

3.2	Concurrent relationship between negative affect and paranoia; three level random intercept model	35
3.3	Negative affect by gender interaction; random intercept model	35
4.1	Examples of questions assessing momentary symptoms, mood, activities, and social cognition and context	46
5.1	Sample of ESM questions from Chen et al. (2016a, 2016b)	58
5.2	ESM question framework from Hare, Wood, Wastell & Skirrow (2015)	59
6.1	List of sleep–wake/circadian rhythm variables and definitions	72
7.1	Results of the Likert scale questions	87
7.2	Themes arising from content analysis of participant feedback	88
10.1	Summary of key questions and considerations researchers and clinicians should bear in mind across the EMI development process	136
11.1	Practice effects associated with the repetition of mobile cognitive tests	148
11.2	Association of neuropsychological tests with mobile cognitive test scores	148

CONTRIBUTORS

Christine Barrowclough: Division of Psychology & Mental Health, University of Manchester

Lesley-Anne Carter: Biostatistics Department, University of Manchester

Yu-Wei Chen: China Studies Centre, University of Sydney

Colin Depp: Department of Psychiatry, University of California San Diego & VA San Diego Healthcare System

Richard Emsley: Institute of Psychiatry, King's College London

Eric Granholm: Department of Psychiatry, University of California San Diego & VA San Diego Healthcare System

Gillian Haddock: Division of Psychology & Mental Health, University of Manchester

Dougal Hare: School of Psychology, Cardiff University

Samantha Hartley: Division of Psychology & Mental Health, University of Manchester

Christopher N. Kaufmann: Department of Psychiatry, University of California San Diego

David Kimhy: Department of Psychiatry, Icahn School of Medicine at Mount Sinai

Simon Kyle: Sleep and Circadian Neuroscience Institute (SCNi), University of Oxford

xii List of contributors

Donna Littlewood: Division of Psychology & Mental Health, University of Manchester

Raeanne C. Moore: Department of Psychiatry, University of California San Diego

Lee Mulligan: Greater Manchester Mental Health NHS Foundation Trust

Inez Myin-Germeys: KU Leuven, Department of Neuroscience

Jasper Palmier-Claus: Division of Psychology & Mental Health, University of Manchester & Greater Manchester Mental Health NHS Foundation Trust

Daniel Pratt: Division of Psychology & Mental Health, University of Manchester

Uli Reininghaus: Department of Psychiatry and Psychology, Maastricht University Medical Centre

Pierre Schweitzer: National Center for Scientific Research, University of Bordeaux

Henrietta Steinhart: KU Leuven, Department of Neuroscience & Department of Psychiatry and Psychology, Maastricht University Medical Group

Joel Swendsen: National Center for Scientific Research, University of Bordeaux

Peter Taylor: Division of Psychology & Mental Health, University of Manchester

Wesley Thompson: Department of Psychiatry, University of California San Diego & Institute of Biological Psychiatry, Roskilde, Denmark

Julia Vakhrusheva: Department of Psychiatry, Columbia University

Filippo Varese: Division of Psychology & Mental Health, University of Manchester

Debora Vasconcelos e Sa: Psychology Department, Anglia Ruskin University

PREFACE

This book has two purposes: first, to convince you that the experience sampling method (ESM) is an innovative and exciting research and clinical tool, and second, to provide guidance on how ESM might be applied to a variety of research questions and clinical populations. Hopefully, by the end, you will understand not only *why* ESM might useful, but also *how* it can be carried out. Our overall goal is to foster a passion for ESM and equip researchers, students and clinicians with the knowledge and skills for conducting this approach in their own work.

The first chapter of the book outlines the strengths of ESM and why it is a fruitful approach for studying mental health difficulties. Chapter 2 then provides general systematic guidance on how to develop an ESM study, which is followed by an outline of analytic procedures in Chapter 3. The subsequent five chapters then provide advice on how ESM might be adapted for the study of specific clinical problems, namely severe mental health difficulties, autism spectrum disorders, sleep disturbance, family dynamics, and suicidal ideation. Within these chapters, the authors provide ideas on how to modify and adapt ESM to meet the presenting needs of specific clinical populations. Lastly, a burgeoning area of interest is the use of ESM not only in research, but as a clinical tool, within health services. The final three chapters therefore offer guidance on using and developing ESM in assessment and predictive modelling, clinical intervention, and cognitive testing. This will help researchers to bridge the gap between research and clinical arenas.

Whilst the aim of this book is to provide a comprehensive guide to ESM, it is by no means an inflexible set of recommendations and readers should feel free to adapt and build on its contents. Additionally, we suggest that researchers seek supervision from appropriate experts (e.g. service users, statisticians) to develop the most appropriate study designs for their research questions.

We hope that you find this book useful. Good luck with your ESM research.
The authors.

1

WHY THE EXPERIENCE SAMPLING METHOD?

Jasper Palmier-Claus, Gillian Haddock and Filippo Varese

The experience sampling method (ESM) is a remarkably useful tool. It allows us to delve into the minutiae of human experience and provides insights into clinical phenomena inadequately captured through traditional data collection methods. This chapter will help to familiarise the reader with just some of the advantages and opportunities afforded by ESM. Our aim is to generate enthusiasm for this approach, whilst galvanising researchers, clinicians and students to build upon its capabilities and strengths. We also note the limitations of ESM to minimise their impact on future research.

What is ESM?

ESM was created by a group in the United States (Larson & Csikszentmihalyi, 1983), but was first pioneered in the field of mental health by researchers in Maastricht, Holland (Delespaul, 1995; deVries et al., 1986). Participants complete self-report questions at multiple times of the day in real-world settings when prompted by an electronic device. In the past, these devices have included sports watches and personal digital assistants, but increasingly more sophisticated technology, such as smartphone software applications and automated text solutions are being employed (Ainsworth et al., 2013). Regardless of the exact design, the intention in ESM is always the same: to assess phenomena close to the time that they naturally occur at multiple time points. Participants report on their experiences at or around the time of an alert or prompt. By taking numerous snapshots of a person's daily experiences, we are better able to appreciate the richness, fluidity, and dynamic nature of people's experiences (Myin-Germeys et al., 2009). This allows for a more developed and vivid picture of a person's thoughts, feelings and behaviours, and the events that might affect them.

The selection of the ESM is driven by knowledge of its many advantages, weighed against its limitations; there are certain questions that ESM is adept at answering, and awareness of these can help to produce effective and efficient study designs. Here we consider the reduced reliance on retrospective reporting and averaging, the high ecological validity of the data, the ability to sensitively measure change over time and temporal associations, and the insights into the instability of clinically important constructs.

Reduced reliance on recall and averaging

Questionnaire and interview assessments tend to deal in retrospective and global phenomena. That is, they assess how things are *generally* for the person or how things have tended to be over the previous day, week, or month. Conversely, ESM assesses phenomena at a specific moment (e.g. when an alert sounded) or within a discrete time period (e.g. the previous hour), which is referred to as momentary or ambulatory assessment data. Although global accounts have their advantages (for example, they can be very predictive of certain outcomes of interest), momentary assessment data is strengthened by a reduced reliance on retrospective recall and averaging (Palmier-Claus et al., 2011). These biases are often problematic in clinical research as they can cause key information to be lost. For example, when asked to recount how things have been generally over the previous week, it is possible that the participant will only recall extreme or recent instances of phenomena, and then generalise from them in their retrospective account, failing to account for the more humdrum of their everyday lives. Supporting this notion, research has sometimes demonstrated poor concordance between retrospective and momentary accounts (Stone et al., 1998). Ben-Zeev and colleagues (2012) found that individuals with mental illness overestimated the intensity of positive and negative emotions, and were limited in their ability to assess the variability of their mood and symptoms over time. Other studies have demonstrated that the strength of associations between momentary and interview measures of psychopathology vary considerably depending on the construct being assessed (Palmier-Claus et al., 2012a). It therefore appears that ESM provides different data and insights to conventional methods.

ESM allows researchers to assess individuals' experiences that were previously difficult or impossible to investigate through global, retrospective assessments. This includes brief or transient experiences that are not normally encoded into long-term memory, such as certain brief emotions, thoughts and behaviours. In some cases, time limited phenomena can be of the utmost clinical importance. One key example of this is suicidal thinking which may predict future risk of suicide (Young et al., 1998). Accurately measuring and understanding these thoughts could help to develop interventions and treatments that prevent escalation to self-injurious behaviour. Assessing multiple transient experiences at once could also help to provide insights into the triggers and factors precipitating key events of interest.

A real-world approach

ESM allows for assessment of phenomena across a wide range of times, situations, and environments. It can provide a more representative assessment of phenomena as they naturally occur in the real world (Palmier-Claus et al., 2011). To this effect, we can say that ESM data has high ecological validity; it represents a move away from more reductionist approaches, such as experimental design studies, that attempt to control the conditions surrounding a person's experiences, instead favouring the natural ebb and flow of experiences as they transpire in the individual's everyday life (Oorschot et al., 2009). ESM can also directly assess the impact of the situation on the phenomena of interest. It is typical in ESM research to include questions on the person's situation or environment. Many researchers will ask about whom the individual is with, where they are, and what they are doing (Delespaul, 1995). Coupled with information on the timing of the entry, this allows investigation of the context of people's experiences. It permits analysis of triggering, precipitating and protective factors, and the influence that the environment might be exerting on the phenomena of interest. For example, early ESM research simply attempted to explore the impact of social contacts on depressed mood, finding that optimal levels of affect could be seen in the presence of one to three people, but grew worse in larger numbers (de Vries & Delespaul, 1992).

Microlongitudinal assessment and temporal associations

By taking multiple recordings over a short time-frame, ESM can provide a sensitive and detailed assessment of change in phenomena. This can be helpful when measuring the impact of specific events on key variables, particularly when there is an immediate, but subtle, response. Possible applications include the measurement of early treatment effects (So et al., 2014), the impact of social context on symptoms (Brown et al., 2011), or the impact of stressful events on mood (Myin-Germeys et al., 2001). To illustrate the former example, there is now considerable evidence suggesting that antipsychotic medication can start to affect change within 24 hours (Kapur et al., 2005) and that early symptom change is a relatively good predictor of its long-term effectiveness (Kinon et al., 2010). Thus, ESM could be used to intensively monitor the course and trajectory of clinical experiences soon after administering medication, which could facilitate personalised treatment plans and improve outcome.

Microlongitudinal assessment allows researchers to explore the short-term temporal associations that exist between phenomena (i.e. is one variable related to another variable at a later time-point?), commonly referred to as a lagged association. This can help to explore the ordering of variables. ESM can examine proximal or distal lagged associations; they can be explored across time-points within a day, but also across days or weeks. Existing applications include research exploring the impact of craving on subsequent illicit substance use (Serre, Fatseas, Swendsen, & Auriacombe, 2015), ruminative self-processing on subsequent hallucinatory experiences (Palmier-Claus, Dunn, Taylor, Morrison, & Lewis, 2013), and sleep on subsequent functioning (Mulligan, Haddock, Emsley, Neil, & Kyle, 2016). Please note that longer-term temporal associations (e.g. months) are not well suited to ESM as participant burden, and likely dropout, may be too great. Researchers wishing to explore long-term changes should consider using global questionnaire or interview measures. Chapter 3 of this book provides an outline of how to analyse lagged associations in ESM data.

The importance of variability

ESM allows consideration of the natural variation that exists *within* individuals; we can examine the degree to which scores vary for a particular individual over time. This might include measuring fluctuations in mood within or across days, or the stability of constructs previously thought to be relatively constant over time (e.g. beliefs, symptoms). Measuring intra-individual variability can be very useful in clinical research. Indeed, at times, it can be a more meaningful predictor of dysfunction than the corresponding levels of intensity or severity, and provide novel insights into the mechanisms that underlie psychopathology. This is exemplified by our research on affective instability and suicidality. We found that the degree to which negative affect varied within individuals over time was a better predictor of suicidality, than the mean or average score (Palmier-Claus, Taylor, Gooding, Dunn, & Lewis, 2012b). We theorised that unstable affect caused greater activation of normally latent suicidogenic cognitive structures than continuously low mood, leading them to become more severe and entrenched over time (Palmier-Claus, Taylor, Varese, & Pratt, 2012c). Other research has suggested that variable appraisals of self-worth are indicative of fragile belief systems that can contribute to externalising attribution biases and paranoia (Thewissen, Bentall, Lecomte, van Os, & Myin-Germeys, 2008). It is likely that the study of intra-subject variability could have other meaningful applications in mental health research.

The limitations of ESM

It is important to consider the limitations of ESM in order to inform its use in clinical research. ESM is a relatively time-consuming and burdensome approach. Participants receive alerts and complete questions in their everyday lives, which can sometimes interrupt activities and cause frustration. Participants will also need to meet with the researcher or clinician before and after sampling, and talk with them over the phone during sampling (see Chapter 2). Although generally acceptable, some studies have noted moderate levels of dropout and non-compliance to ESM (Hartley et al., 2014) and researchers should be aware that they may need to over-recruit to studies to ensure adequate statistical power.

ESM can be expensive relative to traditional questionnaire approaches: researchers will need to procure electronic sampling devices, which can be lost, damaged or broken. One way of protecting against this problem is using text-message based alerts, but this has the limitation of the participant owning and being willing to use their own phone, and requires constant phone signal. Developing and updating new ESM platforms (e.g. software applications, websites) may require additional support from a software developer, which is prohibitive to small-scale studies. The nested structure of ESM data often complicates its analysis and we recommend that novice researchers have adequate support from a statistician.

Certain research questions are unsuited to ESM. This is particularly true when variables of interest relate to global constructs that are relatively stable over time (e.g. belief systems, personality traits), which yield similar responses across time-points and render repeated-assessment unnecessary (Kimhy et al., 2012). At these times, it might be worth refocusing on the momentary manifestations of these stable traits (e.g. appraisals or thoughts in specific situations) or choosing an alternative research methodology. Researchers should not employ ESM when studying rare events that might not occur in the sampling period (e.g. traumatic events, infrequent and sporadic symptoms). This could lead to considerable work with little insight into the phenomena of interest. Despite these limitations, ESM is still capable of being a valuable tool in mental health research. Generally, research to date has shown little reactivity to ESM (e.g. Hufford et al., 2002); the assessed symptoms and experiences tend not to change because of repeated momentary assessment.

Conclusions

ESM has several advantages in clinical research. This includes the ability to capture fleeting or momentary phenomena, reduce retrospective recall bias, sensitively monitor symptom change, and generate insights into the instability of clinical constructs. Subsequent chapters will explore its benefits to particular clinical difficulties and psychiatric populations. Taken together, these should provide the reader with sufficient understanding of *when* and *when not* to use ESM in clinical research. This book will inform the reader about *how* ESM can be applied in practice. It is the authors' opinion that ESM is underused in clinical research, despite offering an array of potential benefits. There is still a wide range of potential applications of ESM waiting to be tested.

References

Ainsworth, J., Palmier-Claus, J. E., Machin, M., Barrowclough, C., Dunn, G., Rogers, A., ... Wykes, T. (2013). A comparison of two delivery modalities of a mobile phone-based assessment for serious mental illness: native smartphone application vs text-messaging only implementations. *Journal of Medical Internet Research*, 15(4), e60.

Ben-Zeev, D., McHugo, G. J., Xie, H., Dobbins, K., & Young, M. A. (2012). Comparing retrospective reports to real-time/real-place mobile assessments in individuals with schizophrenia and a nonclinical comparison group. *Schizophrenia Bulletin*, 38(3), 396–404.

Brown, L. H., Strauman, T., Barrantes-Vidal, N., Silvia, P. J., & Kwapil, T. R. (2011). An experience-sampling study of depressive symptoms and their social context. *The Journal of Nervous and Mental Disease*, 199(6), 403–409.

de Vries, M. W., & Delespaul, A. E. G. (Ed.) (1992). *Variability in schizophrenia symptoms*. Cambridge: Cambridge University Press.

de Vries, M. W., Delespaul, A. E. G., Dijkman, C. I. M., & Theunissen, J. (1986). Advance in understanding temporal and setting aspects of schizophrenic disorder. In: F. Massimini & P. Inghilleri (eds.), *L'Esperienza quotidiana*, pp. 477–493. Milan: Franco Angeli.

Delespaul, P. (1995). *Assessing schizophrenia in daily life: The experience sampling method.* Maastricht, The Netherlands: Universitaire Pers Maastricht.

Hartley, S., Varese, F., Vasconcelos e Sa, D., Udachina, A., Barrowclough, C., Bentall, R. P., ... Palmier-Claus, J. (2014). Compliance in experience sampling methodology: the role of demographic and clinical characteristics. *Psychosis*, 6(1), 70–73.

Hufford, M. R., Shields, A. L., Shiffman, S., Paty, J., & Balabanis, M. (2002). Reactivity to ecological momentary assessment: An example using undergraduate problem drinkers. *Psychology of Addictive Behaviors*, 16(3), 205–211.

Kapur, S., Arenovich, T., Agid, O., Zipursky, R., Lindborg, S., & Jones, B. (2005). Evidence for onset of antipsychotic effects within the first 24 hours of treatment. *American Journal of Psychiatry*, 162(5), 939–946.

Kimhy, D., Myin-Germeys, I., Palmier-Claus, J., & Swendsen, J. (2012). Mobile assessment guide for research in schizophrenia and severe mental disorders. *Schizophrenia Bulletin*, 38 (3), 386–395.

Kinon, B. J., Chen, L., Ascher-Svanum, H., Stauffer, V. L., Kollack-Walker, S., Zhou, W., ... Kane, J. M. (2010). Early response to antipsychotic drug therapy as a clinical marker of subsequent response in the treatment of schizophrenia. *Neuropsychopharmacology*, 35(2), 581.

Larson, R., & Csikszentmihalyi, M. (1983). The experience sampling method. *New Directions for Methodology of Social & Behavioral Science*, 15, 41–56.

Mulligan, L. D., Haddock, G., Emsley, R., Neil, S. T., & Kyle, S. D. (2016). High resolution examination of the role of sleep disturbance in predicting functioning and psychotic symptoms in schizophrenia: A novel experience sampling study. *Journal of Abnormal Psychology*, 125(6), 788.

Myin-Germeys, I., Oorschot, M., Collip, D., Lataster, J., Delespaul, P., & van Os, J. (2009). Experience sampling research in psychopathology: opening the black box of daily life. *Psychological Medicine*, 39(9), 1533–1547.

Myin-Germeys, I., van Os, J., Schwartz, J. E., Stone, A. A., & Delespaul, P. A. (2001). Emotional reactivity to daily life stress in psychosis. *Archives of General Psychiatry*, 58(12), 1137–1144.

Oorschot, M., Kwapil, T., Delespaul, P., & Myin-Germeys, I. (2009). Momentary assessment research in psychosis. *Psychological Assessment*, 21(4), 498.

Palmier-Claus, J. E., Ainsworth, J., Machin, M., Barrowclough, C., Dunn, G., Barkus, E., ... Buchan, I. (2012a). The feasibility and validity of ambulatory self-report of psychotic symptoms using a smartphone software application. *BMC Psychiatry*, 12(1), 172.

Palmier-Claus, J. E., Dunn, G., Taylor, H., Morrison, A. P., & Lewis, S. W. (2013). Cognitive self-consciousness and metacognitive beliefs: Stress sensitization in individuals at ultra-high risk of developing psychosis. *British Journal of Clinical Psychology*, 52(1), 26–41.

Palmier-Claus, J. E., Myin-Germeys, I., Barkus, E., Bentley, L., Udachina, A., Delespaul, P. A. E. G., ... & Dunn, G. (2011). Experience sampling research in individuals with mental illness: reflections and guidance. *Acta Psychiatrica Scandinavica*, 123(1), 12–20.

Palmier-Claus, J. E., Taylor, P. J., Gooding, P., Dunn, G., & Lewis, S. W. (2012b). Affective variability predicts suicidal ideation in individuals at ultra-high risk of developing psychosis: An experience sampling study. *British Journal of Clinical Psychology*, 51(1), 72–83.

Palmier-Claus, J. E., Taylor, P. J., Varese, F., & Pratt, D. (2012c). Does unstable mood increase risk of suicide? Theory, research and practice. *Journal of Affective Disorders*, 143(1), 5–15. Serre, F., Fatseas, M., Swendsen, J., & Auriacombe, M. (2015). Ecological momentary assessment in the investigation of craving and substance use in daily life: a systematic review. *Drug and Alcohol Dependence*, 148, 1–20.

So, S. H. W., Peters, E. R., Swendsen, J., Garety, P. A., & Kapur, S. (2014). Changes in delusions in the early phase of antipsychotic treatment: an experience sampling study. *Psychiatry Research*, 215(3), 568–573.

Stone, A. A., Schwartz, J. E., Neale, J. M., Shiffman, S., Marco, C. A., Hickcox, M., ... Cruise, L. J. (1998). A comparison of coping assessed by ecological momentary assessment and retrospective recall. *Journal of Personality and Social Psychology*, 74(6), 1670.

Thewissen, V., Bentall, R. P., Lecomte, T., van Os, J., & Myin-Germeys, I. (2008). Fluctuations in self-esteem and paranoia in the context of daily life. *Journal of Abnormal Psychology*, 117(1), 143.

Young, A. S., Nuechterlein, K. H., Mintz, J., Ventura, J., Gitlin, M., & Liberman, R. P. (1998). Suicidal ideation and suicide attempts in recent-onset schizophrenia. *Schizophrenia Bulletin*, 24(4), 629.

2

DESIGNING AND CONDUCTING AN EXPERIENCE SAMPLING STUDY

Where to start?

Filippo Varese, Gillian Haddock and and Jasper Palmier-Claus

This chapter serves as an introduction for researchers wishing to conduct ESM research. The contents are relatively broad and provide general advice, which can then be tailored to the readers' area of interest. The chapter should be read in conjunction with the subsequent chapter on ESM data analysis by Carter and Emsley (Chapter 3), which outlines analytical considerations that might influence the ESM study design. Subsequent chapters in this volume further elaborate on many of the pragmatic issues covered here, but will clarify and expand on important applications and adaptations to specific clinical populations and settings. Many of the methodological recommendations outlined in this chapter build on the pioneering work conducted by leading ESM researchers based at the Maastrict University in the Netherlands, including Philippe Delespaul, Inez Myin-Germeys (now at KU Leuven, Belgium) and Jim van Os (now at Ultrecht University, Netherlands). Readers are also directed to other books (Delespaul, 1995; Hektner, Schmidt, & Csikszentmihalyi, 2007; Stone, Shiffman, Atienza, & Nebeling, 2007) and journal articles (Kimhy, Myin-Germeys, Palmier-Claus, & Swendsen, 2012; Palmier-Claus et al., 2011) offering general guidance on ESM from which this chapter necessarily borrows.

Choosing the most appropriate sampling strategy

Standard research methods generally sample *individuals*. That is, they assess people with a specific symptom or diagnosis supported by a particular healthcare service in a given geographical catchment, and then make inferences about that population based on their data. Conversely, ESM is most often concerned with the collection of multiple *momentary observations or experiences* to uncover findings that generalise to a broader "population of occasions" (Conner & Lehman, 2012). It is therefore essential that the rate of sampling (number of assessments per day or week) is representative of how things are for them generally. The natural counter-weight to this driver is the burden placed upon the researcher, participant and their system. Too intensive or frequent a sampling procedure could cause a participant to disengage with the research and, conversely provide less data over time. It could also cause significant disruption altering the phenomena of interest and invalidating the research findings. For example, the study procedure itself could start to influence the individuals' mood or disrupt the everyday activities that the researcher is interested in recording as they naturally occur. It is therefore essential that the sampling strategy is not too burdensome for participants, whilst allowing inferences and generalisability across time points. This is a careful balancing act that requires planning, preparation and piloting ahead of large scale research.

The sampling strategy should be largely influenced by the nature and expected frequency of the phenomena under study, in addition to the research aims and objectives. If the occurrence of the target phenomenon is relatively rare in the daily life of the individual, it is unlikely that it will be possible to capture it using the time-contingent sampling strategies employed in many ESM studies. In other words, if we ask people to complete self-report assessments at variable or fixed time intervals over the study duration period, we are likely to miss the phenomena of interest. In these circumstances, it might be more appropriate to employ *event-contingent sampling* (i.e. a data collection approach in which participants complete assessments once a pre-designated event has occurred, such as after a specific and relatively infrequent social interaction or symptom). The use of event-contingent sampling often requires longer study duration periods to allow for the collection of enough observations of the phenomena under scrutiny. Although this sampling strategy can maximise the ability to capture relatively infrequent target experiences, it provides limited or no information about experiences that occur outside the context of the target phenomenon (Palmier-Claus et al. 2011). This severely limits the ability of researchers to test potentially relevant processes that can lead to or moderate the occurrence of the target experiences. For this reason, when the phenomena of interest occur with a certain frequency in the daily life of research participants or when researchers are interested in examining the longitudinal contribution of specific explanatory variables influencing the occurrence of target phenomena, the use of time-based strategies is generally recommended. Two time-contingent sampling strategies are often employed in mental health ESM studies: interval-contingent sampling and signal contingent sampling.

Interval-contingent sampling

Interval-contingent sampling refers to an approach in which participants complete self-assessments after a pre-specified and generally regular time interval. This is exemplified by studies where participants complete hourly (e.g. Nowlis & Cohen, 1968) or daily self-reports (e.g. Wessman & Ricks, 1966). This sampling strategy presents several practical advantages over other ESM strategies: the study procedures are easily understood by study participants; the regularity of ESM assessment can decrease perceived participant burden; and data can be modelled to explore regular patterns in target variables (e.g. diurnal fluctuations in mood, fatigue, etc.). However, the regularity of the self-assessments can introduce a number of biases that may threaten the validity of the planned study, most notably expectancy effects and other involuntary anticipatory processes that may influence participants' ongoing experiences. It can strategically alter the participants' daily routine to minimise the burden caused by forthcoming assessments (e.g. participants might avoid certain activities or organise their schedules around pre-planned assessments).

Signal-contingent sampling

To overcome the considerable limitations of interval-contingent sampling, many researchers opt to use, whenever feasible, signal-contingent sampling. Signal-contingent sampling requires participants to complete self-reports when prompted by a signal delivered at random or quasi-random times. A prototypical example of signal-contingent sampling are studies where participants are instructed to complete brief self-assessment forms when prompted by an electronic device (e.g. an electronic wristwatch) programmed to "beep" multiple times per day (e.g. 10 times per day between 7.30am and 10.30pm) over several consecutive days (e.g. Udachina, Varese, Myin-Germeys, & Bentall, 2014). The seemingly unpredictable nature of the signals reduces expectancy effects and response biases. Furthermore, it has been argued that this form of sampling is more appropriate when the focus of the planned study concerns subjective experiences that are particularly susceptible to memory biases linked to retrospective reporting, as well as experiences that participants may otherwise attempt to regulate if the timing of ESM assessments was predictable (e.g. Conner & Lehman, 2012).

>An additional advantage of signal contingent sampling is the provision of additional opportunities to check the quality and validity of the data generated by research participants. Like most diary studies, ESM research (especially in its pen and paper version) is vulnerable to practices that could seriously undermine the validity of the data, such as 'data hoarding'. In this context, data hoarding refers to instances where participants might complete multiple assessments retrospectively rather than at specific times or following specific events as instructed. When the timing of signals is known (e.g. when the researcher is aware of the exact signalling schedule programmed in the electronic devices used in a given ESM study) and participants are required to 'time stamp' their assessments (e.g. by recording the exact time when they completed the assessment), it is possible for researchers to check that all data generated by participants are *bona fide* (i.e. they are produced within a timeframe that is sufficiently close to the prompt provided by the signalling device, usually within a 10-minute window), and take appropriate actions as required (e.g. the exclusion of 'invalid' data from any analyses). The need to conduct such 'manual' checking of data-points is, however, becoming increasingly obsolescent with the emergence of ESM facilitating technology (e.g. smartphone applications) which automatically log the time that each entry is completed.

One notable disadvantage of a signal-contingent sampling approach is its relative burden compared to event-contingent and interval-contingent sampling, a parameter that should be taken into account when designing ESM studies. Indeed, alarms or prompts can sometimes interrupt activities or draw attention to the participant. At times, researchers have adjusted the number of planned assessments within each day to ensure that the study procedures will not cause excessive inconvenience (e.g. when in class or at work), though this then potentially limits the validity and generalisability of the findings.

Continuous sampling

Due to the considerable advancements in the development and availability of wearable technologies in recent years, another data sampling strategy known as *continuous sampling* is becoming increasingly used in ESM research. Continuous sampling refers to the assessment of target phenomena and/or other variables of interest continually over the course of each day (as opposed to as part of consecutive discrete assessments completed multiple times per day). This sampling strategy is particularly suited to the assessment of variables (e.g. physiological states and activities) that can be recorded passively and automatically using bespoke sensors or devices (e.g. an activity tracker or actigraph), rather than requiring active self-reports by research participants. Continuous sampling can be used either in isolation in the context of ESM studies that aim to address medical and/or physiological research questions that do not require the collection of additional self-report information in the flow of daily life, or in conjunction with other data sampling procedures. For example, Mulligan and colleagues (2016) integrated multiple sampling strategies in a study investigating the association between sleep disturbances assessed via continuous motor activity recordings using a wrist actigraph unit and psychotic symptoms assessed using signal-contingent self-reports.

Development of ESM items and assessment batteries

Whenever an ESM study requires the collection of self-reported information, researchers should pay particular attention to the development of valid items that could be used to suitably assess participants' thoughts, feelings, symptoms, and experiences in the flow of daily life. Although the procedures used to generate ESM items resemble those used in the development and validation of questionnaire or survey studies, the moment-to-moment focus that characterises ESM research calls for specific considerations and adaptations. Most notably, whilst 'standard' cross-sectional survey research is often concerned with the assessment of trait-like variables (i.e. habitual cognitive, behavioural, and affective patterns that people tend to experience across a range of times, settings, and circumstances), ESM research is by definition focused on the assessment and examination of 'states' (i.e. experiences characterised by considerable intra-individual moment-to-moment variation). Researchers should therefore consider the 'momentary nature' of the phenomena one aims to measure, and develop items that accurately capture how people experience and/or describe such states over the course of their daily life.

ESM item wording

Previous researchers (e.g. Kimhy et al., 2012; Palmier-Claus et al., 2011) have recommended that the experiences captured by ESM items should be 'truly momentary' or experiences that potentially vary within individuals over small time frames (e.g. 'Right now I feel happy'), rather than global, schematic or reflective appraisals ('I am a happy person'). Of critical importance is the fact that items should reflect how individuals from the target population describe their own experiences and behaviours in the flow of daily life. In this respect, the experiences captured by specific ESM items should be self-explanatory and their meaning should be immediately apparent to the participant, and expressed using prosaic and 'colloquial' terms rather than technical jargon (e.g. 'hearing voices' as opposed to 'auditory hallucinations'). The specificity and frequency of the states assessed by ESM items also require careful attention. It is generally recommended that researchers should avoid items tapping into extreme states (e.g. 'Right now I feel livid') as these are less commonly experienced in the flow of daily life.

Despite the abovementioned recommendations for ESM items to be 'truly momentary', the wording can be adjusted to assess relevant experiences that might occur beyond the exact assessment points participants are asked to respond to as part of a sampling schedule. More specifically, as illustrated in Figure 2.1, the time-frame of ESM items can be amended to provide either a truly momentary assessment of participants' behaviours and experiences at a given time point (e.g. 'Just before the beep went off, I was feeling cheerful') or retrospective reports of experiences, behaviours and salient events that might have occurred *since the*

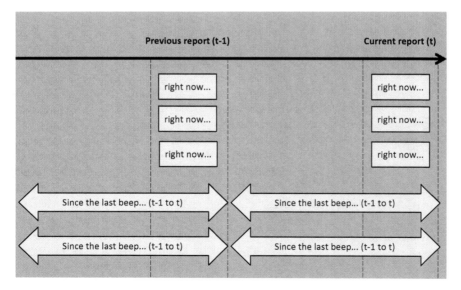

FIGURE 2.1 Conceptual representation of the chronological organisation of momentary and interval ESM items

previous report (e.g. 'Since the last beep/report I have used cannabis'). Whilst arguably the latter do not represent 'authentic' ESM items as they involve the retrieval and retrospective evaluation of previous experiences, 'since the last beep/report' items are often extremely useful due to their ability to capture relevant events that might not be possible to assess in time-contingent ESM studies because of their relatively low frequency/duration in the daily life of participants (e.g. the use of licit and illicit drugs). Furthermore, this type of item is often useful when researchers are interested in assessing psychological constructs that are intrinsically reflective (e.g. psychological processes such as cognitive and emotional avoidance: 'Since the last beep I have tried to push away negative thoughts and feelings'). Nonetheless, it has been noted that due to their retrospective nature the use of these items increases the risk of potential recall bias.

When starting to develop ESM items, it can be useful to review available questionnaire or interview measures assessing a certain construct of interest, whilst acknowledging that these will necessarily need to be adapted to measure a state-like construct at the time of assessment (e.g. 'I sometimes feel suspicious' would need to be reworded to 'Right now, I feel suspicious'). Consultation and careful piloting with members of the population of interest (e.g. people with lived experience of psychosis) are recommended to refine the wording of ESM items before their use in a larger scale study. Assessing the reliability of new item batteries is challenging as there is an expectation that appropriate ESM items will vary over time; test–retest or split half approaches are not always appropriate given that changes of time are actually desirable. Additionally, the validity of ESM items should not solely be judged on their ability to strongly correlate with questionnaire and interview assessments as the latter are testing more global constructs and appraisals that include the biases associated with recall and averaging multiple time-points (although one might expect a moderate associate if the items are similar enough).

Overall duration of ESM self-assessment forms and internal ordering

It is generally recommended that the overall duration of self-assessment forms should be kept to a minimum and that their completion should require no longer than two–three minutes at each assessment point. The brevity of self-assessment completion times is critical in two respects. Firstly, it reduces the inconvenience caused to study participants, therefore maximising compliance and retention. Secondly, it minimises the time lag between the participants' responses and the intended assessments of phenomena of interest (or events, if event-contingent sampling is employed), therefore minimising the influence of retrospective biases and reflective processes. In order to fit in more items and with the emergence of electronic diaries, research is now increasingly employing item branching to limit participant burden. In item branching, participants are presented with certain items only when they have responded to previous items in specific ways (e.g. participants who answered affirmatively to the question 'Right now, do you hear voices that other people can't hear?' can be asked further questions about their current voices/auditory hallucinations such as 'How distressing are the voices?'). Although this has the propensity to reduce completion times, researchers should be careful not to introduce response biases, as participants respond negatively to stop the activation of additional items and reduce the length of the assessment. Typically, it is sensible to be guided by the time taken to complete all of the ESM items so as not to disincentivise particular responses (e.g. reporting a symptom that would then lead to follow-up questions).

The order in which ESM items are presented within a specific self-assessment form is often guided by similar considerations aimed at reducing the influence of such biases. It is generally recommended (Kimhy et al. 2012) that either more transient experiences or those more likely to be influenced by recall and/or the interpretation of other experiences (e.g. mood and specific affective states, thoughts, and symptoms) should be prioritised and assessed early in the self-assessment form, followed by more stable experiences (e.g. current activities, social contexts and their appraisals) and finally more reflective or retrospective items (e.g. experiences or events that occurred in between the current and previous assessment point).

Equipment and technology

The choice of technology is largely led by the time, resources and finances available to the research team. Historically, researchers have employed electronic wristwatches that could be programmed with multiple alarms signalling when the participant should complete an entry in a corresponding paper booklet. Variants of this approach have included using text messages and phone reminders to signal when questions should be completed. Although this is a cost-effective data collection method with established validity and feasibility, it means that participants have to carry with them multiple, unwieldy objects (e.g. a watch, paper diary, pen, etc.). Additionally, entries tend not to be time-stamped, allowing for clustering or backfilling of responses. An alternative option is for entries to be completed electronically on an appropriately enabled handheld device (e.g. personal assistant, smartphone). These devices have the benefits of only allowing entries to be completed within certain time-windows, locking responses so that they cannot be changed. They also allow for more secure data-storage, branching of questions, and streamlined data transfer, obviating the need for manual data entry. Certain devices (e.g. smartphone applications) can also facilitate automatic wireless uploading of data to a central database in real time, which prevents data-loss caused by broken or missing handsets.

The primary drawback of using advanced technology to facilitate ESM is the associated costs. Equipment can be expensive and researchers should anticipate that at least 20 per cent of devices will go missing or be broken. With the development of smartphone technology comes the opportunity for participants to install software applications on their own smartphones, removing the need for additional equipment to be carried and allowing for the procedure to be better integrated into the person's daily life. This does, however, require the participant to: (i) own a smartphone; (ii) consent to their phone being used for research purposes; and (iii) be happy to use their data to download the required software/transfer data (note: typically this is later reimbursed by the research team). The former may become less problematic as smartphone applications become more commonplace, affordable, and advanced. Researchers can use one of several smartphone software applications now available (Palmier-Claus et al., 2012; Palmier-Claus et al., 2013) or develop their own. The latter is only advised if the team have support from a software development team, and this process can be expensive and time-consuming. There is also a need to ensure that the validity, acceptability, and feasibility of the technology are continually assessed and ensured, based on new iterations of its design. This can be labour intensive given the speed at which technology is advancing in the modern age.

Lastly, some ESM studies have used text message systems to facilitate ESM research. For example, Ainsworth and colleagues (2013) set up a text based system, where participants texted back their numerical responses that were recorded on a central system. This meant that even participants without sophisticated smartphones were able to use their handsets. The authors found that although responding in this way was more laborious and time-consuming than a software application, it was still a feasible and acceptable way for participants to provide data. The major limitation of text messages is that they require mobile-phone signal, a break in which can cause multiple prompts to appear at once outside of the intended time-points.

Pragmatic considerations to maximise recruitment and retention

Compared to simple questionnaire design studies, ESM research can be burdensome and time-consuming for participants. It is therefore vital that researchers effectively 'sell' the added benefits of this approach in terms of capturing the person's lived experiences. Sometimes it can be helpful to illustrate the limitations of recall by asking participants to try to recollect their thoughts or moods at specific times several days before (e.g. 'what were you thinking/how were you feeling on Tuesday at 2.34PM? This is very difficult to do!'). This neatly illustrates the importance of repeated assessments where the person has to recall information over shorter periods of time and how this can build up a more accurate picture of what's really happening for them.

The success of ESM research is often heavily dependent on the thoroughness of its briefing session (Palmier-Claus et al., 2011). The researcher will want to meet with the participant to pass on any equipment and complete baseline assessments, but this is also a good opportunity to encourage compliance to the procedure and address anticipated barriers to completion. The briefing session should be used to outline exactly what is expected of the participants and complete some practice entries, which can identify misunderstandings and prompt questions. It also allows the researcher to outline and directly model how to operate any software or technology, particularly if the participant is unfamiliar with such devices. At the end of the briefing session, the researcher should arrange time(s) where it is convenient to contact the participant during the sampling period to check and encourage compliance with the ESM procedure. It can be helpful to schedule this for two or three days into the sampling procedure so that the participant has had an opportunity to fill in the assessment forms, whilst not causing high levels of data loss if there are any problems. In the past, a briefing checklist has sometimes been used to ensure that the initial meeting is standardised and that all agenda items are covered (Palmier-Claus et al., 2011). It can be helpful to create a similar checklist for the mid-sampling phone call, and this should be updated based on common problems emerging during the study. The provision of contact details the participant could use to inform the research team of any problem (e.g. loss of equipment, software problem) could also benefit compliance and retention.

At the end of the sampling procedure, the researcher should conduct a debriefing session (Palmier-Claus et al., 2011). This can be helpful in determining the reasons for periods of non-compliance (i.e. uncompleted assessment forms), software or technology problems, and possible problems with the protocol that could be addressed in future research. When using paper diaries, it can also be helpful to check the clarity of participants' handwriting and ask them to clarify any ambiguities. In order to minimise initial burden on the participant and ensure that they are focused on how to complete the sampling procedure at briefing, many researchers wait until the debriefing session to administer longer, global assessments (e.g. interviews and questionnaires).

Conclusion

There are several important decisions when designing an ESM study: the sampling procedure, the wording and ordering of items, the choice of equipment and how best to engage and retain participants in the research. This chapter has provided very broad and general guidance on each of these key choices. In subsequent chapters, the authors will discuss how this approach can be applied to specific research questions, clinical difficulties, and populations. The final chapters will also consider how the aforementioned guidance might be adapted for use in healthcare settings as a clinical tool. Researchers should adapt and built on the guidance presented here, and through this book, to best meet the needs of their particular research question.

References

Ainsworth, J., Palmier-Claus, J. E., Machin, M., Barrowclough, C., Dunn, G., Rogers, A., … Wykes, T. (2013). A comparison of two delivery modalities of a mobile phone-based assessment for serious mental illness: native smartphone application vs text-messaging only implementations. *Journal of Medical Internet Research*, 15(4), e60.

Conner, T. S., & Lehman, B. J. (2012). Getting started: Launching a study in daily life. In M. R. Mehl & T. S. Conner (Eds.), *Handbook of research methods for studying daily life* (pp. 89–107). New York, NY: Guilford Press.

Delespaul, P. (1995). *Assessing schizophrenia in daily life: The experience sampling method.* Maastricht, The Netherlands: Universitaire Pers Maastricht.

Hektner, J. M., Schmidt, J. A., & Csikszentmihalyi, M. (2007). *Experience sampling method: Measuring the quality of everyday life*. Seven Oaks, CA: Sage.

Kimhy, D., Myin-Germeys, I., Palmier-Claus, J., & Swendsen, J. (2012). Mobile assessment guide for research in schizophrenia and severe mental disorders. *Schizophrenia Bulletin, 38* (3), 386–395.

Mulligan, L. D., Haddock, G., Emsley, R., Neil, S. T., & Kyle, S. D. (2016). High resolution examination of the role of sleep disturbance in predicting functioning and psychotic symptoms in schizophrenia: A novel experience sampling study. *Journal of Abnormal Psychology, 125*(6), 788.

Nowlis, D. P., & Cohen, A. Y. (1968). Mood-reports and the college natural setting: A day in the lives of three roommates under academic pressure. *Psychological Reports, 23*(2), 551–566.

Palmier-Claus, J. E., Ainsworth, J., Machin, M., Barrowclough, C., Dunn, G., Barkus, E., … Buchan, I. (2012). The feasibility and validity of ambulatory self-report of psychotic symptoms using a smartphone software application. *BMC Psychiatry, 12*(1), 172.

Palmier-Claus, J. E., Rogers, A., Ainsworth, J., Machin, M., Barrowclough, C., Laverty, L., … Lewis, S. W. (2013). Integrating mobile-phone based assessment for psychosis into people's everyday lives and clinical care: a qualitative study. *BMC Psychiatry, 13*(1), 34.

Palmier-Claus, J. E., Myin-Germeys, I., Barkus, E., Bentley, L., Udachina, A., Delespaul, P., … Dunn, G. (2011). Experience sampling research in individuals with mental illness: reflections and guidance. *Acta Psychiatrica Scandinavica, 123*(1), 12–20.

Stone, A., Shiffman, S., Atienza, A., & Nebeling, L. (2007). *The science of real-time data capture: Self-reports in health research*. Oxford, England: Oxford University Press.

Udachina, A., Varese, F., Myin-Germeys, I., & Bentall, R. P. (2014). The role of experiential avoidance in paranoid delusions: an experience sampling study. *British Journal of Clinical Psychology, 53*(4), 422–432.

Wessman, A. E., & Ricks, D. F. (1966). *Mood and personality*. Oxford, England: Holt, Rinehart, & Winston.

3

THE ANALYSIS OF EXPERIENCE SAMPLING DATA

Lesley-Anne Carter and Richard Emsley

Data structure

Multilevel data structures

Data collected using the experience sampling method (ESM) are a series of repeated measurements observed for each subject over a set period of time. This type of data is known as longitudinal or multilevel data. As several measurements are taken for each person, the data are correlated such that two measurements on the same person will be more similar to each other than two measurements taken on different people. This correlation means that some of the more traditional statistical methods such as linear regression cannot be used, because the observations are not independent. Non-independent observations can be accounted for in the analysis of multilevel data, but this requires the use of more complex statistical methods.

Throughout this chapter ESM will be considered to have a three-level data structure, with measurements at the lowest level, level 1, referred to as the moment or 'beep' level (Delespaul 1995) with reference to the alarm used in signal contingent designs, nested within the level 2 'day' level, nested within subject at level 3. Identifying the day level allows us to explore variation in symptoms day-to-day as well as moment-to-moment and person-to-person. Higher levels of data are also possible, such as participants nested within therapist or centre, and the ideas presented here can be easily extended to accommodate these higher levels.

The data obtained from an ESM study can be categorized by these levels. ESM diary items are level 1 or momentary-level variables. Any measures captured only once per day, such as sleep data, are categorized as level 2 or day-level data. Finally, any measures taken only once during the study, such as subject demographics or trait measures, are considered level 3 or subject-level variables.

Managing and entering data to represent the multilevel structure

In order to analyse ESM data using standard statistical software, the dataset must be set up correctly. ESM data will have many variables – one for each item – and many observations – one for each entry, for each person. This section will describe how to set up your database in terms of data structure and data coding. Extensions to this basic set up will be described in subsequent sections where additional data manipulation is presented.

Database structure

There are two approaches to formatting a database: wide format and long format. Wide format is typical with longitudinal or panel data, where each subject has one row of data and separate variables are used to record measures at each follow up point. Long format, on the other hand, has only one variable per measure and the repeated observations are recorded by allowing each subject to have multiple rows of data (see Table 3.1). For ESM data, software packages require the long format, where each row of the dataset will represent a different observation; for example, for six days of observation with 10 beeps a day, each subject will have 60 rows of data.

Three variables are always required: subject ID, a unique identification number for each participant; day number, which will equal $1, \ldots, n_2$; and

TABLE 3.1 ESM database structure with three paranoia items and baseline measure

ID	Day	Beep	Para1	Para2	Para3	Paranoia	Gender	Baseline Depression
1	1	1	1	1	1	1	Female	10
1	1	2	1	1	2	1.33	Female	10
1	1	3	4	3	4	3.67	Female	10
1	2	1	3	1	2	2	Female	10
1	2	2	2	3	2	2.33	Female	10
1	2	3	2	1	3	2	Female	10
1	...	...	...	...	...	...	...	...
2	1	1	7	6	7	6.67	Male	43
2	1	2	7	7	5	6.33	Male	43
2	1	3	6	5	6	5.67	Male	43
2	2	1	4	5	7	5.33	Male	43
2	2	2	5	2	5	4	Male	43
...	...	...	...	...	...	...	...	...

entry number, which will equal $1, \ldots, n_1$. You may also wish to have additional variables for the date and time at which the entry was completed. A separate variable is then required for each item or question in the ESM diary.

Often, researchers will wish to generate aggregated or final measures after data collection. For example, the diary may contain three paranoia items *para1, para2* and *para3*, which are then combined to create the average *paranoia* measure, which is the mean of the three separate items. Alongside the ESM data collected, the final database will likely also include demographic data and baseline measures. As these are subject-level variables and will not vary over the ESM period, to fit the long format database these values need to be repeated for each row of each subject. This is displayed in Table 3.1 where gender and baseline depression have been added.

Data coding

As much as possible, data should take numeric values. This is because statistical software can easily recognize numbers, but less so words. For example, Likert scales should be entered using their numeric coding, rather than 'Strongly disagree' to 'Strongly agree'.

Categorical variables should be numerically coded prior to data entry. For example, instead of recording 'Male' or 'Female', a gender variable *Female* should be coded 0 and 1, where the value 0 represents 'Males' and 1 represents 'Females'. This should be applied to all categorical variables, such as 'Ethnicity' or 'Employment status'.

Multilevel models

To analyse momentary variation, an analysis model is required that can accommodate repeated measurements for each participant and clustering at higher levels. Simple regression models are not suitable for analysing this type of data because these models assume that the residual errors are independent, which would not hold with nested ESM data. This means that basic statistical tests such as t-tests would also be invalid in ESM data. These types of analysis would underestimate the standard error of the estimate and may result in the incorrect finding of 'statistically significant' results and increased chances of a false positive finding.

As an alternative, random effect models (also known as multilevel or hierarchical models) are often used in ESM research and will be presented in this chapter. These models can be fitted using packages in standard statistical software such as Stata (StataCorp 2013), R (R Core Team 2016) and SPSS (IBM Corp. 2013), or in specialist multilevel software such as MLwiN (Rasbash et al. 2009), Win BUGS (Lunn et al. 2000) and Mplus (Muthén and Muthén 2007).

Multilevel models for concurrent analysis

Multilevel models allow for multiple levels of data to be considered without the need for aggregation and can be used to examine variation at each level of nesting (e.g. participant, day). They can accommodate the nested structure of ESM data, are valid for unbalanced data sets and can be extended to fit complex covariance structures arising in the data. This section will provide a general overview of multilevel models. For a more detailed introduction to multilevel models see (Goldstein 1995; Fitzmaurice et al. 2012).

Random intercept models

To understand random effects models, consider a two-level example where measurements are nested within subjects. This leads to a simple random intercept model:

$$y_{ik} = \beta_0 + \beta_1 x_{ik} + u_k + e_{ik}$$

In this model y_{ik} is the continuous response value for the ith measurement of individual k and x_{ik} is a moment level explanatory variable. The model can be split into two parts: the fixed part and the random part. The fixed part of the model, $\beta_0 + \beta_1 x_{ik}$, represents the population average effects. The intercept β_0 is the mean value of y_{ik} when $x_{ik} = 0$ and β_1 represents the change in y_{ik} for a unit increase in x_{ik}. This is the same interpretation as a simple linear model. Random effects models extend this by including a random component to allow for between-cluster variation. The random part of this model comprises of the subject-level random intercepts u_k, a normally distributed random variable with mean zero and variance σ_u^2, and residuals e_{ij}, a normally distributed random variable with mean zero and variance σ_e^2. These represent the unexplained variation in the outcome at each level of the data. The modelling procedure can estimate the variation in random intercepts σ_u^2, a measure of the between-subject variation, and the residual variance σ_e^2, a measure of the within-subject (or momentary) variation. Note that it does not provide an estimate of u_k for each individual k.

The two-level model can be extended to fit a three-level data structure where measurements i are nested within days j within participants k by including a random intercept for day v_{jk}

$$y_{ijk} = \beta_0 + \beta_1 x_{ijk} + u_k + v_{jk} + e_{ijk}.$$

In addition to the subject-level random intercept, the three-level model (see Figure 3.1) also has a day-level random intercept v_{jk} which is normally distributed with mean zero and variance σ_u^2. From this model the subject-level variation σ_u^2, the day-level variation σ_v^2 and moment-level variation σ_e^2 can be estimated.

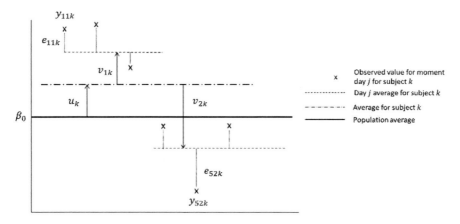

FIGURE 3.1 Visual representation of the three-level random intercept model. Adapted from 'Module 11: Three-Level Multilevel ModelsConcepts' by Leckie, G. 2013. LEMMA VLE, University of Bristol, Centre for Multilevel Modelling. Accessed at https://www.cmm.bris.ac.uk/lemma/. Adapted with permission.

Random coefficient models

A random intercept model assumes the relationship between x and y is fixed between participants. A random coefficient model on the other hand allows this relationship to vary between participants. A two-level random coefficient model has the form:

$$y_{ik} = \beta_0 + \beta_1 x_{ik} + u_{0k} + u_{1k}x_{ik} + e_{ik}$$

or, rearranging,

$$y_{ik} = (\beta_0 + u_{0k}) + (\beta_1 + u_{1k})x_{ik} + e_{ik}$$

where u_{0k} is the random intercept for individual k and u_{1k} is the random slope for x_{ik}. These random effects come from a multivariate normal distribution with:

$$\begin{bmatrix} u_{0k} \\ u_{1k} \end{bmatrix} \sim MVN\left(\begin{bmatrix} 0 \\ 0 \end{bmatrix}, \begin{bmatrix} \sigma_{u0}^2 & \sigma_{u0u1} \\ \sigma_{u0u1} & \sigma_{u1}^2 \end{bmatrix} \right).$$

As in the random intercept model, there is a subject-specific intercept, $\beta_0 + u_{0k}$, but now there is also a subject-specific effect of x, $\beta_1 + u_{1k}$. For example, using ESM to study psychosis one might hypothesize that increased anxiety leads to an increase in paranoia. Fitting a random intercept model we would assume that although subjects may start out with different levels of paranoia, accounted for by the random intercept u_{0k}, the effect of anxiety on paranoia is the same for each individual, resulting in parallel subject-specific slopes with fixed gradient β_1 (as in Figure 3.2a). In a random coefficient model, this relationship is allowed to vary between people, such that a unit increase in anxiety might have a stronger or weaker effect on paranoia for each subject k to account for their individual characteristics; their individual slope being $\beta_1 + u_{1k}$ (Figure 3.2b).

The covariance between the random intercept and random slope, σ_{u0u1}, is a measure of how the value of the intercept influences the slope for each individual. For a positive covariance, $\sigma_{u0u1} > 0$, a subject-specific line with a larger intercept value will have a steeper than average slope, while a subject-specific line with a smaller intercept will have a shallower than average slope (Figure 3.3a). Conversely, for a negative covariance, larger intercept values will lead to shallower slopes whereas a smaller intercept will lead to a steeper slope (Figure 3.3b). In terms of the psychosis example, a positive covariance would mean that for

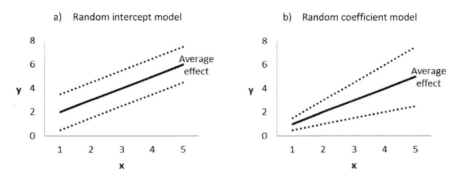

FIGURE 3.2 a) Random intercept model with solid line representing the average effect and dotted lines representing two subject-specific effects; b) Random coefficient model with solid line representing the average effect and dotted lines representing two subject-specific effects

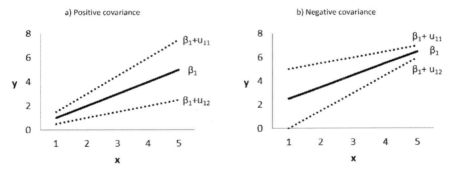

FIGURE 3.3 a) Random coefficient model with positive covariance; b) Random coefficient model with negative covariance

individuals who exhibit higher levels of paranoia for low levels of anxiety, anxiety will have a greater effect, whereas those with minimal symptoms for low levels of anxiety would see a much smaller increase in paranoia as anxiety increases.

For three-level data, it is possible to extend these ideas to have random slopes at level 3 and level 2. For ES data this corresponds to variation in subject-specific slopes when a random coefficient is included at level 3,

$$y_{ijk} = \beta_0 + \beta_1 x_{ijk} + u_{0k} + u_{1k} x_{ijk} + v_{jk} + e_{ijk}$$

or variation in day-specific slopes when included at level 2,

$$y_{ijk} = \beta_0 + \beta_1 x_{ijk} + u_k + v_{0jk} + v_{1jk} x_{ijk} + e_{ijk}.$$

Multilevel models for lagged analysis

When investigating momentary relationships you can choose to look at how two variables relate concurrently, in the same moment, or from one moment to the next. With the example of mood and paranoia, a concurrent relationship asks: 'how is a person's current mood associated with their current level of paranoia?' For this analysis both variables are entered into the model at the same time point, as has been presented in the previous section. If symptoms are expected to develop over time, a time-lagged analysis can instead be adopted. This type of relationship is sometimes referred to as a temporal relationship, and instead of entering both variables into the model at the same time point the predictor can be time-lagged so that the relationship between predictor at time point $t - 1$ and outcome at time t is investigated. In the example, this time-lagged analysis asks 'how is a person's current mood associated with their subsequent levels of paranoia?'

Time-lagged models can be useful when studying the effects of some exposure or event, the effect of which may take time to manifest, such as when investigating the effect of alcohol or drug use on symptoms. Both the concurrent and lagged relationships might be of interest here, but the interpretation of each would be subtly different. The concurrent relationship would test how the immediate use of drink or drugs affects symptoms, whereas the lagged relationship would look at the delayed effects of drink or drug use on symptoms.

Although a time lagged analysis can be an effective way of studying these lagged relationships, caution should be taken when drawing inference from the results: just because an ordering has been placed on these measures does not mean that one causes the other; a lagged analysis does not imply a causal process. As with the concurrent analysis, these models are just used to establish associations between two variables; there may be many confounders – both observed and unobserved – that explain the detected association.

Finally, there may be a temptation to control for previous values of the outcome by including the time-lagged outcome as an additional covariate. This should be avoided. Briefly, to include the time-lagged outcome as a covariate will break one of the assumptions of multilevel models that the covariates are independent of the

The analysis of experience sampling data   **25**

random effects and result in biased estimates of the model. Though the details of this are beyond the scope of this chapter, they are discussed in Rabe-Hesketh and Skrondal (2012) and Steele and colleagues (2013).

Data set up

To conduct a time-lagged analysis, the lagged variable must first be computed. This involves taking the old variable and shifting down the observations the desired number of time points. If interested in how negative affect at one time point affects symptoms at the next time point, the observations just need to be shifted by one row. If longer lags are of interest observations should be shifted down further.

It is important when creating a lagged variable to ensure that the lag occurs within a day only: lags should not be computed overnight. This is necessary for interpretation as it is assumed the effect of x on y occurs within a certain time frame; an overnight lag is typically of 8 hours or more and so does not represent the intended relationship. In the newly created lagged variable the first observation of the day will thus be blank.

Centring

For the models described above, interpretation of the regression coefficients is dependent on the scaling of the model variables. For the fixed effects, the intercept β_0 represents the population average value of y when all covariates are equal to zero. Inference on β_0 thus relies on an interpretable meaning of zero for x. For ESM research many of the questionnaire items are measured on a 1–7 Likert scale with the values representing an ordinal style measure of agreement, for example 1 = 'not at all', through to 7 = 'very much so'. For these measures, a value of zero makes no conceptual sense and as such in a model using these scales as covariates the fixed intercept would be uninterpretable. So it is often recommended that variables be rescaled to give meaningful zero values, a process known as centring.

Interpretation of random effects is also effected by the choice of centring. Random intercept and random slope variances are estimated at $x = 0$. In a random intercept model, subject-specific slopes stay constant so the choice of this zero value does not affect the intercept variance; however, in a random slope model, subject-specific slopes are allowed to vary, and so the random slope variance will depend on the choice of centring for x.

The simplest way to centre is by grand mean centring, where the overall mean of all observations for all subjects is subtracted from each observation in the variable. Alternatively, variables can be centred by cluster. In the three-level data structure for ESM, level 1 variables can be centred at levels 2 or 3. In a regression, centring at level 3 would provide a within-subject effect, averaged across days. Centring at level 2 would provide a within-day, within-subject interpretation. The choice of centring should thus be driven by the research question. Snijders and Bosker (1999) provide further details on centring in a longitudinal context.

Moderation

A popular research question in psychology is to explore if relationships are moderated by a third variable. This is not to be confused with mediation. Moderation and mediation, though often discussed together, are distinct questions. Moderation asks whether a relationship between two variables differs in relation to a third. For example, 'Does gender moderate the relationship between depression and paranoia?' Here, the inclusion of the moderator gender is asking whether the association between depression and paranoia is different for males compared to females. Mediation, on the other hand, looks at whether one variable affects another by acting through a third variable on a causal pathway. Moderation is quite straightforward to assess in ESM data by simply interacting the predictor and moderator, while mediation analysis is more complex. Bolger and Laurenceau (2013) provide an introduction to multilevel mediation and a discussion of some of the complexities of this type of analysis in an intensive longitudinal data setting such as ESM.

Extending the notation introduced above, a random intercept model investigating moderation can be specified as:

$$y_{ijk} = \beta_0 + \beta_1 x_{ijk} + \beta_2 m_k + \beta_3 x_{ijk} \times m_k + u_k + v_{jk} + e_{ijk}$$

where the relationship between level 1 predictor x_{ijk} and level 1 outcome y_{ijk} is allowed to differ by level 3 moderator m_k. In the example set above, $m_k = 0, 1$ is a binary moderator representing gender, x_{ijk} is momentary measured depression and y_{ijk} is momentary measured paranoia. The results of interest in the model are β_1: the effect of depression on paranoia when gender equals zero (e.g. males) and $\beta_1 + \beta_3$: the effect of depression on paranoia when gender equals one (females).

Moderation models could be extended to examine between-subject effects of the moderator by including a random coefficient for x_{ijk} at level 2. In the above example, including a random effect for depression at level 3 would result in $\beta_1 + u_{1k}$: the subject-specific effect of depression on paranoia for males and $\beta_1 + \beta_3 + u_{1k}$: the subject-specific effect of depression on paranoia in females.

Models with measurements at different levels

The analysis described so far has focused on associations between level 1 variables, or how momentary level variables (i.e. diary entries) are related. Other questions in ESM research might investigate how variables at different levels are associated. One area in which this applies is sleep studies, where the relationship between ESM measured symptoms and sleep quality is of interest.

An example research question might ask: how does sleep quality affect next day's paranoia levels? Here sleep quality is only measured once a day, in the morning, and is thus a level 2 measure. Paranoia is measured using an ESM diary, where multiple measures a day are taken, making it a level 1 measure. The question is how should the association be modelled? With a predictor at level 2 and an outcome at level 1, a model would be trying to map each value of the predictor onto each value of the outcome, attempting to quantify the relationship between sleep and paranoia at each time point the following day. Instead, what could be asked is how does sleep quality affect next day's average paranoia level? Here an average score of all available paranoia responses is used as the outcome.

Data set up

When analysing data at different levels, there are two options for the data set up. Option 1 is to transform the data set from a three-level configuration to a two-level configuration. This will reduce the number of rows of data to only one per day per participant. Alternatively, the data set can be left as three-level but it is specified in the model that only one row of data per day should be included, for example using only beep 1 data. In either case, first a new variable containing the day-level mean of the ES variable should be computed. This can be performed straightforwardly using statistical software, allowing the dataset to be collapsed to two-levels if required.

How to summarize multilevel data

Within-day and between-day variation

The first step to understanding ESM data is to summarize the variation captured by each measure. A helpful place to start is to simply plot the data to visually examine the variation. These are referred to as profile plots and can be used to identify whether there is greater variation between or within subjects.

Numerically, this can be described from the random part of the model by estimating the amount of variation in the outcome at the different levels of the data. To summarize the amount of variation, the variance partitioning coefficient (VPC) can be used which calculates the proportion of variance at each level.

The proportion of variance at level 3 is defined as the level 3 variance divided by the total variation

$$\rho_3 = \frac{Between\ subject\ variation}{Total\ variation} = \frac{\sigma_u^2}{\sigma_u^2 + \sigma_v^2 + \sigma_e^2},$$

with the proportion of variance at level 2

$$\rho_2 = \frac{Between\ day\ variation}{Total\ variation} = \frac{\sigma_v^2}{\sigma_u^2 + \sigma_v^2 + \sigma_e^2}$$

and the proportion of variation at level 1

$$\rho_1 = \frac{Residual\ variation}{Total\ variation} = \frac{\sigma_e^2}{\sigma_u^2 + \sigma_v^2 + \sigma_e^2}$$

similarly.

An alternative way of describing variation is the intraclass correlation coefficient (ICC). Rather than partitioning the variance, the ICC estimates the correlation between observations. In the ES structure this can be the correlation between two observations on different days

$$corr\left(y_{ijk},\ y_{i'j'k}\right) = \frac{\sigma_u^2}{\sigma_u^2 + \sigma_v^2 + \sigma_e^2}$$

when $i \neq i'$ and $j \neq j'$, or the correlation between two observations within the same day

$$corr\left(y_{ijk},\ y_{i'jk}\right) = \frac{\sigma_u^2 + \sigma_v^2}{\sigma_u^2 + \sigma_v^2 + \sigma_e^2}$$

when $i \neq i'$

For random intercept models this ICC is equal to the VPC. However, for random slope models this is not the case as the level 3 variation is now a quadratic function of x

$$var\left(u_{0k} + u_{1k}x_{ijk}\right) = var(u_{0k}) + 2cov\left(u_{0k}, u_{1k}x_{ijk}\right) + var\left(u_{1k}x_{ikj}\right)$$

$$= \sigma_{u_0}^2 + 2\sigma_{u_{01}}x_{ijk} + \sigma_{u_1}^2 x_{ijk}^2$$

The VPC at level 3 is thus

$$var\left(u_{0k} + u_{1k}x_{ijk}\right) = var(u_{0k}) + 2cov\left(u_{0k}, u_{1k}x_{ijk}\right) + var\left(u_{1k}x_{ikj}\right)$$

For random slope models, the VPC rather than the ICC should be used when discussing the proportion of variance at each level of the model.

Missing data considerations

Missing data can be particularly prevalent in longitudinal studies where participants are subject to multiple follow ups over time. ESM studies are especially vulnerable to this problem. Participants are required to complete questionnaires unsupervised, multiple times a day over several days, all while continuing with their usual daily routine. Complete data collection, where all the data is collected as intended, is unlikely, with prompts missed due to the demands of everyday life or as a result of the intensive sampling procedure becoming too burdensome. Although ESM study design typically includes an element of participant training in the data collection method and consent regarding the intensive sampling procedure, the self-reported design means that data quality is entirely subject to the participant's fidelity to the study protocol. Fewer observations available for analysis leads to a reduction in power to detect effects. Additionally, when subjects complete different numbers of observations, analysis methods which require balanced data cannot be used.

The analysis of experience sampling data **29**

Depending on the reason that data are missing, known as the missing data mechanism, and how the data are subsequently analysed, there is the potential for substantial bias in an analysis. Solutions to these problems will be discussed in this section.

Missing data mechanisms

The classification of missing data can be described by the missing data mechanisms as defined by Little and Rubin (1987): missing completely at random (MCAR), missing at random (MAR) and missing not at random (MNAR), also known as non-ignorable (NI) missingness. The standard definitions of these mechanisms state that all data intended to be collected, Y, can be partitioned into the observed data, the missing data and a binary missingness indicator, R. The three missing data mechanisms can then be defined as follows.

- MCAR occurs when the probability that data are missing depends on neither the observed data nor the missing data. In this case the observed data are simply a random subset of the sample.
- When data are stated to be MAR the probability that the data are missing depends on the observed data but not the missing data. The observed data are now no longer a random subset of the sample, but within strata are considered a random subset.
- The data are described to be MNAR when the probability of missingness depends on the values of the missing data.

Approaches to analysis with missing data

To fit the random effects models described in this chapter, statistical software uses maximum likelihood estimation (MLE). This benefits from being able to accommodate missing data without losing all information for that observation. One important assumption of maximum likelihood data is that the data are MAR. For valid inference we need to ensure this assumption is met. While missing data mechanisms are untestable, MAR can be investigated by looking to see whether any of the observed data predicts the probability the outcome data is missing. It has been shown that for multilevel data that compared to a simple multilevel model using MLE, multiple imputation provides no additional benefit in terms of estimation bias (Black et al. 2011). Moreover, multiple imputation can underperform compared to MLE alone when the imputation model is misspecified. As such, whilst no imputation method is required, the amount of missing data should be reported to provide the reader context regarding inference and power. This can be summarized as the number or proportion of missed diaries in the whole sample, or broken down into the average number of missed diaries at the day-level or beep-level to give a fuller description. A more detailed understanding of missing data within-subject can help the researcher to satisfy the MAR assumption, as will be demonstrated later in this chapter.

Statistical analysis plan

During the design phase of an ESM study a statistical analysis plan should be developed. A well-developed statistical analysis plan prior to data collection will help focus the study by defining specific research questions, and help to identify what data should be recorded.

The following four steps are recommended to prepare for statistical analysis. Steps 1 and 2 should be completed prior to data collection and steps 3 and 4 should provide structure for examining the ESM data after it has been checked and cleaned.

Step 1: Identify the research question

This is of primary importance and should be decided upon during the design process, to enable the whole study to be designed with a clear focus and purpose. In addition to the overarching objectives, specific hypothesis generation at this point will ensure all necessary data is collected. For example, if investigating predictors of poor sleep, is it objective or subjective measures of sleep that are of interest? How will each be measured? Alongside psychological factors of interest what else might influence sleep – alcohol or caffeine intake, for instance? These are known as confounders and will need to be controlled for in the analysis model. How would these best be measured – using ESM throughout the day or just once before sleep?

Step 2: Converting research questions into statistical models

Transforming a hypothesis into a valid statistical model is not always straightforward; what seems like a simple question can be difficult to define in a statistical model. First, consider the direction of the relationship of interest between two measures: which is the dependent variable, and which is the predictor, or independent variable? What covariates will need to be controlled for? This gives the basic structure. Next, how is the outcome measured? Typically, the outcome will be defined as continuous or binary. Other outcome types, such as binary or ordinal data, are also possible; however they are out of the scope of this chapter. Steele (2009; 2011) provides further details on analysis methods for these types of outcomes.

Next, identify the level at which each variable will be measured in the model. Are they all ESM measured variables or do they also include day- and subject-level measured variables? Although we recognize that the typical data structure of ESM is three-level, if only a day-level analysis is required then a two-level, rather than three-level data structure is all that will be needed.

Finally, consider the specific relationship that you wish to investigate. This may be a simple linear relationship or take a different shape: some relationships may be curved with a different sized effect at different levels of the predictor. Is the average effect of all participants of interest or do you suspect a different effect for each subject? A random intercept model is appropriate in the former, while the variation in subject-specific slopes can be captured using a random-coefficient model, as described in the centring section of this chapter.

Step 3: Data analysis

With all the levels of variation, summarizing this type of data numerically can be difficult to understand. Instead, profile plots can be used to visually examine the

The analysis of experience sampling data **31**

variation in the data both within and between subjects, and give an overview of the quantity of missing data, as well as flat responses (where there is no variation in score over time). For summary statistics, the VPC can be computed for each outcome to identify where the largest proportion of variation lies – within subject or between subjects. Finally, the main analysis model can be fitted.

Step 4: Interpreting the results

When fitting a multilevel model, the size and direction of the fixed effect is usually of primary interest. This is interpreted as the average effect on outcome for a unit increase in the predictor. So first of all, what is a 'unit'? If your predictor is measured on a Likert scale a unit will be 1 point on the scale, say moving from Strongly Disagree to Disagree. If your predictor is time measured in minutes, a unit will be one minute. Similarly, how is the outcome variable measured? Identifying the unit of measurement for each variable is essential to the interpretation of this coefficient.

You must then consider whether the size of the effect found is meaningful; a non-zero effect does not necessarily mean an important one. This should be established based on your expertise and knowledge, rather than looking at past research for estimates. If testing for a treatment effect, by how much should the intervention and control groups differ to be considered significant? If looking for an association, what strength of association would be important? This requires strong consideration, and a fair amount of time should be given to establishing this figure prior to data analysis.

As the effect is only an estimate, next consider how precisely it has been estimated. Look at the confidence interval. This gives the range of plausible values for this coefficient. If it contains a wide range of values the estimate is not very precise, and authors should be careful when drawing any conclusions from the size of the coefficient.

A word of caution on p values – typically coefficients with a p value of less than 0.05 are considered statistically significant. All this really means is that *statistically* the effect estimated is unlikely to be zero. It does not mean that the relationship is 'significant'. The size of the effect in relation to the scale of measurement needs to be interpreted to draw any conclusions on 'significance'. As such, the values of the coefficients should *always* be reported, not just p values, and confidence intervals should be reported in order for the reader to understand the range of plausible values that this could take.

Worked example:

Are momentary negative thoughts associated with psychotic symptoms such as paranoia?

This example will show how to implement the statistical analysis steps on an ESM dataset, and how to fit and interpret a simple three-level linear regression model.

The example dataset represents a fictional ESM study investigating the relationship between mood and symptoms in people with psychosis. A total of 100 participants were monitored for six days using ESM in this scenario, with 10 pseudo-random prompts per day. The diary captured momentary mood using a 7 point Likert scale, with items relating to negative mood phrased 'Right now I feel … anxious/satisfied/

32 Lesley-Anne Carter and Richard Emsley

irritated/sad/guilty'. Also monitored was paranoia using a 7 point Likert scale, 1 representing no paranoia and 7 representing severe paranoia.

Step 1: Identify the research question

The primary research question for this study asked whether negative affect was associated with higher levels of paranoia. The outcome variable was thus *paranoia*. To represent negative affect the five negative mood items were combined to form one composite score. This was achieved by taking the row mean of the items to give a final score *negative affect* in the same 1–7 range. At this stage, potential confounders were also identified. Additionally, when considering what would constitute a significant association, the authors decided that the relationship between mood and symptoms would be meaningful if for a unit increase in negative affect they saw half a unit increase in paranoia. The piece of research was also conducted with a secondary hypotheses in mind, namely, the researchers were interested in knowing whether the relationship between negative affect and paranoia was different for men and women.

Step 2: Turn research questions into statistical models

The two main considerations were whether the concurrent or time-lagged effect of negative affect was important and did the association differ substantially for each person. In this hypothetical example, we will say that the authors decided to focus on the concurrent relationship or the relationship between mood and symptom at the same moment. We will also say that they were only interested in the simple scenario of investigating the population average effects. The analysis models were thus random intercept models with momentary level variables measured at the same time point. For differences in the association by gender (a level 3 variable), they require an interaction of these variables with negative affect.

Step 3: Data analysis

To identify how variable paranoia was across participants, days and beeps, profile plots for a random subsample of 25 subjects are presented in Figure 3.4.

We can see that there is considerable variation moment to moment; however the magnitude of the variance appears small. Looking across days there appears to be very little day to day variation in symptoms, with the general shape of the graphs quite flat.

Missing data investigation

The data from this study, as with most ESM studies, were not complete. Approximately 9.85% of diaries were missing, indicating good overall fidelity to protocol. To confirm that the sampling scheme was appropriate for this population, we can investigate whether there were any patterns in missing data. Figure 3.5 displays a bar chart of the proportion of missing data for each beep, averaged across days. It is clear that there is a time trend in missed diaries, with earlier beeps more often missing. This suggests that the sampling time window was not appropriate for this population, who perhaps stay awake later into the night and sleep later the next day.

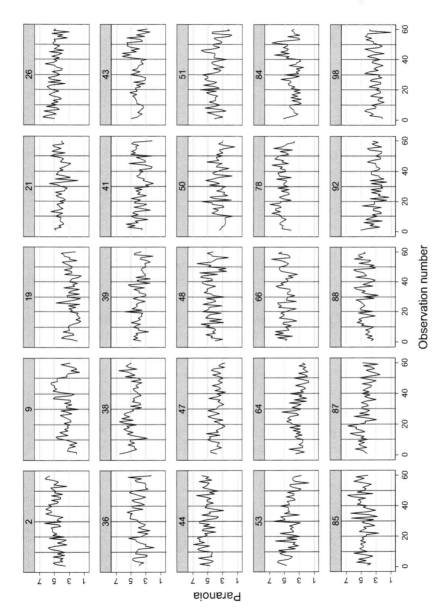

FIGURE 3.4 Profile plots for paranoia. A random sample of 25 subjects, with red lines indicating day breaks.

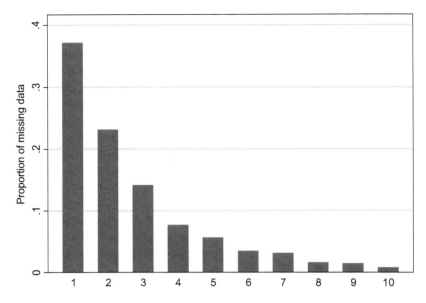

FIGURE 3.5 Proportion of missing data for each beep

Results of analysis model

As negative affect and paranoia were momentary level variables, a three level random effects model was used for analysis. This model contained random intercepts for subject and day.

The results of Table 3.2 show that negative affect is indeed related to concurrent paranoia, with a unit increase in NA associated with a 0.484 increase in paranoia. Comparing this estimate and its associated confidence interval to the meaningful effect of 0.5 defined prior to analysis, we can conclude that there is some evidence of a meaningful relationship between mood and paranoia. This result is based on 5409 out of the total 6000 observations, with beep number included to satisfy the MAR assumption of MLE of the random intercept model.

The random effects section of the table displays the amount of unexplained variation in paranoia scores at each level of the model. The highest amount of variation is at level 3, representing between-subject variation. So in this sample there is more variation in symptoms between people than within each person. These variances can be presented as proportions of total variance for easier interpretation. Using the previously presented formulae, we can see that approximately 63% of variation is between subjects, 10% is between day and 27% is between observations. As ICCs, we can see that the correlation between two observations from the same person measured on different days is 0.63, and the correlation between two observations within the same day, within the same person 0.73.

The analysis of experience sampling data **35**

TABLE 3.2 Concurrent relationship between negative affect and paranoia; three level random intercept model

Fixed effects	Coeff.	95% CI	P value	N
Intercept	3.636	(3.425, 0.846)	0.000	5409
Negative affect	0.484	(0.456, 0.511)	0.000	
Beep number	-0.001	(-0.007, 0.006)	0.814	
Random effects	Variance	SE		
Level 3 (Between-subject)	1.081	0.158		
Level 2 (Between-day)	0.178	0.015		
Level 1 (Within-day)	0.467	0.010		

Presenting the variance estimates alongside the fixed effect estimates is recommended so that readers can understand the variation in the sample. They are also important for calculating sample sizes in future research.

Does this relationship differ by gender?

To establish whether the association between negative affect and paranoia differs by gender, the previous model is fitted with the addition of a negative affect by gender interaction. This interaction variable was calculated by multiplying the negative affect and gender variables. The results of this analysis are presented in Table 3.3.

In this model, the coefficient for negative affect now represents negative affect when Female = 0, i.e. males. The coefficient of the interaction negative affect x Female is the additional effect of females. So the effect of negative affect on paranoia in males is 0.338 and in females is 0.338 + 0.303 = 0.641. As the additional

TABLE 3.3 Negative affect by gender interaction; random intercept model

Fixed effects	Coeff.	95% CI	P value	N
Intercept	3.515	(3.233, 3.797)	<0.001	5409
Negative affect	0.338	(0.300, 0.375)	<0.001	
Female	0.256	(-0.148, 0.659)	0.214	
Negative affect x Female	0.303	(0.249, 0.357)	<0.001	
Beep number	-0.001	(-0.008, 0.005)	0.721	
Random effects	Variance	SE		
Level 3 (Between-subject)	1.019	0.150		
Level 2 (Between-day)	0.175	0.014		
Level 1 (Within-day)	0.457	0.009		

effect for females is significant (95% CI (0.249, 0.357), $p < 0.001$) we can conclude that there is a differential effect of negative affect on paranoia by gender, with the effect almost twice as strong in women as in men.

Conclusion

The empirical example provided important aspects to present in the reporting of an ESM study. However, for further reporting guidelines see Stone and Shiffman (2002). Finally, not every aspect of ESM data analysis could be covered in this chapter. For further details of multilevel modelling, including random effects models for different response types, Steele and colleagues (VLA) provide a free, practical online course with examples in several statistical packages. For more complex ESM style questions, Bolger and Laurenceau (2013) give details on statistical analysis for intensive longitudinal data. The methods are described for two-level data but with the understanding from this chapter of how two-level models can be extended to three-levels, may be applied to ESM data.

This chapter has presented basic guidance for structuring and analysing ESM data: with multiple entries over multiple days, format your data as three distinct levels; use profile plots and summary measures to investigate variation at each level of the data; allow for between-subject and within-subject variation using random effect models; make sure the appropriate model is chosen for your research question and interpret results with care. The rich data source that ESM provides contains much potential for investigating new and complex problems, and allows us to gain insights into symptoms and behaviours previously out of our reach.

References

Black, A. C., Harel, O. & Matthews, G. (2011). Techniques for modeling intensive longitudinal data with missing values. In T. S. Conner & M. Mehl (Eds.). *Handbook of Research Methods for Modeling Daily Life* (pp. 339–356). New York: Guilford Press.

Bolger, N. and J. Laurenceau (2013). Intensive Longitudinal Methods: An Introduction to Diary and Experience Sampling Research, Guilford.

Delespaul, P. A. E. G. (1995). Assessing Schizophrenia in Daily Life: The Experience Sampling Method, Maastricht, The Netherlands: Universitaire Pers Maastricht.

Fitzmaurice, G. M., N. M. Laird, and J. H. Ware (2012). *Applied Longitudinal Analysis*, Hoboken: Wiley.

Goldstein, H. (1995). *Multilevel Statistical Models*, London: Hodder Arnold.

IBM Corp. (2013). *IBM SPSS Statistics for Windows*. Armonk, NY: IBM Corp.

Little, R. J. A. and D. B. Rubin (1987). *Statistical Analysis with Missing Data*, Hoboken: Wiley.

Lunn, D. J., A. Thomas, N. Best and D. Spiegelhalter (2000). WinBUGS – a Bayesian modelling framework: concepts, *structure, and extensibility. Statistics and Computing* 10(4): 325–337.

Muthén, L. and B. Muthén (2007). *Mplus* User's Guide, Los Angeles, CA: Muthén & Muthén.

R Core Team (2016). *R: A language and environment for statistical computing.* Vienna, Austria: R Foundation for Statistical Computing.

Rabe-Hesketh, S. and A. Skrondal (2012). *Multilevel and Longitudinal Modeling Using Stata, Volumes I and II*, Third Edition, College Station, Texas: Stata Press.

Rasbash, J., C. Charlton,W. J. Browne, M. Healy and B. Cameron (2009). MLwiN, Bristol: Centre for Multilevel Modelling, University of Bristol.

Snijders, T. A. B. and R. J. Bosker (1999). Multilevel Analysis: An Introduction to Basic and Advanced Multilevel Modeling, London: Sage Publications.

StataCorp (2013). *Stata 13 Base Reference Manual.* College Station, TX: Stata Press.

Steele, F. (2009) "Module 7: Multilevel Models for Binary Responses Concepts." [course material]

Steele, F. (2011) "Module 9: Single-level and Multilevel Models for Ordinal Responses Concepts." [course material]

Steele, F., J. Rasbash and J. Jenkins (2013). A multilevel simultaneous equations model for within-cluster dynamic effects, *with an application to reciprocal parent–child and sibling effects. Psychological Methods* 18(1): 87.

Stone, A. A. and S. Shiffman (2002). Capturing momentary, *self-report data: A proposal for reporting guidelines. Annals of Behavioral Medicine* 24(3): 236–243.

4

EXPERIENCE SAMPLING IN THE STUDY OF PSYCHOSIS

David Kimhy and Julia Vakhrusheva

The Experience Sampling Method (ESM) has been used for over three decades in studies of individuals with psychosis. Starting with the work of deVries and Delespaul in the 1980s (deVries, 1983; deVries et al., 1986; Delespaul & deVries, 1987; deVries & Delespaul, 1989), researchers have utilized ESM to characterize and elucidate multiple domains of psychotic symptoms, behavior, and functioning, as well as an underlying neurobiology. As the bulk of ESM studies of individuals with schizophrenia and related psychoses have centered on psychotic symptoms, primarily auditory hallucinations and persecutory delusions, we focused our review on these experiences.

ESM as a tool to assess the continuum of psychosis

While the bulk of literature has centered on the application of ESM in the context of those with full-blown psychotic disorders, a growing number of research studies indicate that ESM is a feasible and acceptable research method to study symptoms across the whole psychosis continuum, including individuals with psychotic-like experiences and/or subsyndromal symptoms. Specifically, several ESM studies have been conducted with individuals exhibiting schizoid and schizotypal personality features, groups that are often conceptualized as being at-risk for developing psychosis (Miller et al., 2002). For example, Chun and colleagues (2017) used ESM to examine the prevalence of schizoid, schizotypal, and paranoid personality traits in a non-clinical young adult population. Utilizing mobile devices, the participants were signaled randomly eight times per day over seven days to answer a self-report questionnaire. Participants were required to answer within five minutes of the signal, and were largely compliant with the protocol, responding to an average of 72% of the signals. In this non-clinical population, assessment using ESM methodology identified that all three personality traits were associated with decreased positive mood, rewarding experiences, and effective social functioning, as well as increased negative affect, somatic complaints, and subclinical psychosis. The study was also able to discriminate between the distinct daily experiences of individuals with each set of personality traits, leading to unique hardships. Schizotypal traits were more strongly associated with impaired functioning while paranoid traits were more associated with impaired cognitive performance.

Wigman and colleagues (2013) used ESM to investigate a novel method of psychopathology and symptom assessment in a sample of individuals with psychosis, their healthy twins, and unrelated controls. The authors drew on medical practices of monitoring daily changes in bodily functions to evaluate health and suggested that daily monitoring of mental well-being, and more specifically changing mental states in response to daily living, may be a helpful approach to evaluate an individual's progression towards health or illness. The authors found that higher levels of schizotypy in the twin sample predicted more frequent experiences of subclinical psychosis in daily life. These experiences were observed to be occurring more frequently in active psychosis, to a lesser degree in individuals with schizotypy, and much less frequently in individuals with no history of psychosis, lending credence to their hypothesis that frequency of subclinical psychotic experiences in daily life may be the "basic unit of psychosis." These findings contribute significantly to research aimed at accurate assessment of underlying predisposition to developing active psychosis.

Using ESM to assess specific symptoms of psychosis and contextual influences on symptoms

Auditory hallucinations

Recent reports provided additional support for the convergent validity of ESM. Kimhy and colleagues (2017) found that ESM assessment of auditory hallucinations displayed significant correlations with semi-structured clinical interview-based measures of auditory hallucinations including overall severity (PANSS; Kay et al., 1987), as well as frequency, duration, loudness, degree of negative content, and intensity of distress (PSYRATS; Haddock et al., 1999). ESM studies provided a rich view of the complexity of auditory hallucinations. Dynamic analyses of the time course of auditory hallucinations using experience sampling revealed a host of contextual influences. Specifically, in a sample of individuals with auditory hallucinations, hallucinatory experiences were present about 30% of the time, with episodes lasting on average 190 and 299 minutes (Delespaul, 1995; Delespaul et al., 2002). Such episodes were preceded by increased anxiety (Delespaul, 1995), delusional intensity (Oorschot et al., 2012), worry and rumination (Hartley et al., 2014), as well as distress and interference (Peters et al., 2012). Likewise, activities such as social withdrawal, inactivity, and working resulted in decreases in hallucinatory intensity (Delespaul, 1995; Delespaul et al., 2002). In contrast, leisure activities (e.g., watching TV) resulted in increased intensity of hallucinations

(Delespaul, 1995). Interestingly, Palmier-Claus and colleagues (2013) reported that among individuals at ultra-high risk for psychosis who reported strong beliefs about the need to control their thoughts, cognitive self-consciousness preceded the occurrence of hallucinatory experiences. These findings attest to the dynamic and multi-faceted nature of auditory hallucinations and the utility of using ESM to characterize their complex phenomenology.

Paranoia and persecutory delusions

Contextual influences have also been found to influence paranoia and persecutory ideation. Specific aspects of emotional experience have been found to impact the onset and persistence of paranoid episodes. Both an increase in anxiety and a decrease in self-esteem, as well as experiential avoidance, have been found to predict the onset of paranoid episodes (Thewissen et al., 2008, 2011; Udachina et al., 2009). In addition, the association between low self-esteem and paranoia was partially mediated by experiential avoidance, with the detrimental effect of experiential avoidance on self-esteem being more pronounced under high levels of activity-related stress (Udachina et al., 2014). Furthermore, the initial intensities of paranoia and depression were associated with longer duration, while anger/irritability with shorter duration, of paranoid episodes (Thewissen et al., 2011). In another study of community-dwelling participants diagnosed with schizophrenia or schizoaffective disorder, anxiety and sadness were significant predictors of subsequent paranoid ideation (Ben-Zeev et al., 2011), and among a subsample of participants with multiple paranoid ideations, anxiety was a significant predictor of conviction and associated distress, while sadness was only predictive of distress (Ben-Zeev et al., 2011). Parallel findings were reported by Hartley and colleagues (2014, 2015), who found that worry and rumination predicted greater levels of persecutory delusional ideation and thought control was significantly associated with persecutory delusions' severity and associated distress. Investigations of social context and its links to paranoia indicated differences in the effect of social company on momentary levels of paranoia and perceived social threat across the range of trait paranoia. Individuals with low and medium trait paranoia reported higher levels of perceived social threat when they were with less-familiar compared to familiar individuals (Collip et al., 2011). Those with medium level trait paranoia reported more paranoia in less-familiar company and those with high trait paranoia reported no difference in the perception of social threat or momentary paranoia between familiar and unfamiliar contacts (Collip et al., 2011). Altogether, these findings provided unique perspective on the variables that contribute to and correlate with episodes of paranoid ideation, providing a foundation of potential future interventions.

Using ESM to assess emotion functioning

Another area of inquiry that has received extensive interest in the research literature is emotional functioning and its potential impact on a range of clinical variables. Early work by Myin-Germeys and colleagues (2000) found individuals with a diagnosis of schizophrenia experienced higher intensity and more variability in negative emotions and lower intensity and variability in positive emotions, compared to healthy individuals. Furthermore, clinician-rated blunted and non-blunted participants reported similar emotional experiences, suggesting that individuals with schizophrenia are more emotionally active than has been assumed based on behavioral observations. Follow-up studies found that women experienced increased emotional reactivity to daily life stress compared with men, reflected in both an increase in negative affect and a decrease in positive affect (Myin-Germeys et al., 2004). In another study, individuals with schizophrenia reported lower levels of positive and higher levels of negative affect compared with controls (Oorschot et al., 2013). Specifically, high negative symptom individuals reported similar emotional stability and capacity to generate positive affect as healthy controls, whereas low negative symptom patients reported increased instability. All participants displayed comparable emotional responses to social company. However, the individuals experiencing psychosis, particularly those with more severe negative symptoms, displayed more social withdrawal and stronger preference to be alone. Potentially related to this finding, individuals experiencing psychosis have been found to display more environment-incongruent emotions, and such tendency is linked to neurocognitive functioning (Sanchez et al., 2014).

Emotion functioning in individuals with schizophrenia has also been investigated for its links to social and daily functioning. Kimhy and colleagues (2014b) found that compared to healthy controls, individuals with schizophrenia displayed significantly lower emotional granularity (i.e., the ability to differentiate among emotional states) for most emotions, but not negative states. Furthermore, hierarchical regression analyses indicated that emotional granularity significantly predicted social dysfunction, after controlling for relevant confounds (emotional awareness, symptoms, emotional intensity and variability). These findings suggest individuals with schizophrenia have a relatively intact ability to differentiate among negative emotions in everyday life. However, they experience significant difficulties differentiating between positive and negative emotions, and this may contribute to their social difficulties (Kimhy et al., 2014b). In another study, Brenner and Ben-Zeev (2014) examined whether individuals with schizophrenia can provide affective forecasts for an upcoming week. Participants expected more emotionally charged weeks than they actually experienced – both positive affect forecasts and negative affect forecasts were more intense than the average weekly ratings. Likewise, decreased positive emotions and enhanced negative emotions were associated with the perception that motivation for activity was external to subjects (e.g. they wished they were doing something else). Activities that required more exertion were related to enhanced positive emotion, whereas activities that subjects reported they wanted to do were associated with reduced negative emotions (McCormick et al., 2012). These findings support the view of emotional dysfunction as a core deficit in schizophrenia and related disorders.

Using ESM to assess neurobiology

In recent years, researchers have begun integrating ESM into studies investigating the underlying neurobiology of schizophrenia, particularly the role of stress sensitivity. For example, Kimhy and colleagues (2010) investigated the impact of autonomic regulation on stress during daily functioning. As part of this study, 20 patients with psychosis completed a 36-hour ambulatory assessment of stress and autonomic arousal employing ESM with mobile devices along with concurrent ambulatory measurement of cardiac autonomic regulation using a Holter monitor. The clocks of the devices and Holter monitors were synchronized, allowing the temporal linking of the stress and autonomic data. They then used power spectral analysis to determine the parasympathetic contributions to autonomic regulation and sympathovagal balance during five minutes before each experience sample. The authors reported that momentary increases in stress were preceded by decreases in cardiac vagal input (parasympathetic activity) and increased sympathovagal balance. A recent follow-up study using this methodology indicated momentary decreases in cardiac vagal input predicted transient increases in severity of auditory hallucinations among individuals with schizophrenia (Kimhy et al., 2017). Recent studies have also demonstrated efficacy of integrating ESM with mobile devices with various device-embedded sensors (accelerometers, microphone, global positioning system, WiFi, and Bluetooth), successfully capturing individuals' activity level, time spent proximal to human speech, and time spent in various locations (Ben-Zeev et al., 2016b).

Other research has integrated ESM with imaging studies. For example, Collip and colleagues (2013) investigated whether familial risk (the contrast between controls, patients and siblings of patients) moderated the relationship between hippocampal volume and emotional daily stress reactivity and whether familial risk moderated the relationship between hippocampal volume, cortisol and daily stress reactivity using ESM in 20 patients with schizophrenia, 37 healthy siblings with familial risk for schizophrenia, and 32 healthy controls. Multilevel linear regression analyses revealed a significant three-way interaction between group, hippocampal volume, and momentary stress in both the model of NA and the model of cortisol. Increased emotional stress reactivity was associated with smaller left hippocampal volume in patients and larger total hippocampal volume in controls. Similarly, siblings with small hippocampal volume demonstrated increased emotional and cortisol stress reactivity compared to those with large hippocampal volume. In another study, Lataster and colleagues (2011a) found significant interaction between experience of positive and negative affect, D_2 receptor occupancy estimates, and type of D_2 receptor bindings (loose vs. tight), with increasing levels of estimated D_2 receptor occupancy being associated with decreased feelings of positive affect and increased feelings of negative affect among tight-binding-agent users. No such association was apparent for loose-binding-agent users. Peerbooms and colleagues (2012) investigated the effect of COMT Val158Met × MTHFR interaction on resilience to stress in patients and controls. The MTHFR C677T genotype moderated the interaction between COMT Val158Met genotype and stress in patients, but not in controls; in patients with the MTHFR 677 T-allele, COMT Met/Met individuals displayed the largest increases in psychotic symptoms in reaction to ESM stress, whereas in patients with the MTHFR 677 C/C genotype no significant COMT Val158Met × ESM stress interaction was apparent. No moderating effect of MTHFR A1298C was found. Overall, the integration of ESM into studies of the neurobiology of schizophrenia offers unique perspectives about the impact of neurobiological variables on daily functioning in this population.

Incorporating ESM into treatment

Along with progress in studying of the phenomenological and neurobiological aspects of schizophrenia, a number of attempts have been made to incorporate ESM into treatment studies, either as a therapeutic tool or to monitor treatment progress. Early work in this area indicated preliminary feasibility and effectiveness – Kimhy and Corcoran (2008) described a case report of using ESM with a mobile device as part of a successful cognitive-behavior therapy of a patient at a clinical high-risk for psychosis with predominantly negative symptoms. Likewise, Granholm and colleagues (2011; Depp et al., 2010) reported on a project utilizing automated text messaging on mobile phones to obtain patient reported data on psychotic symptom severity, social interactions, and medication adherence in individuals with psychotic disorders. Fifty-five patients with schizophrenia or schizoaffective disorder were enrolled, out of which 42 completed the protocol successfully. Non-completers had more severe negative symptoms, lower functioning, and lower premorbid IQ. Among study completers, the average valid response rate was 86% and 86% of phones were returned undamaged. Results indicated medication adherence improved significantly, but only for individuals who were living independently. Likewise, the number of social interactions increased significantly and there was a significant reduction in hallucination severity. Finally, the probability of endorsing attitudes that could interfere with improvement in these outcomes was reduced significantly.

Oorschot and colleagues (2012) reported on use of ESM to examine symptomatic remission in 177 patients with schizophrenia. The 70 patients who met criteria reported significantly fewer positive and negative symptoms and better mood states compared with patients not in remission. Furthermore, patients in remission spent more time in goal-directed activities and had less preference for being alone when they were with others. However, the patient groups did not differ on time spent in social company and doing nothing. ESM has also been incorporated to studies of medication effectiveness. Lataster and colleagues (2011b) found that during antipsychotic medication switch to aripiprazole, more than half of all patients experienced exacerbation of psychotic symptoms. However, when symptomatically effective, the switch was accompanied by decreased feelings of both positive and negative affect in daily life, suggesting emotional dampening. More recently, Ben-Zeev and colleagues (2014) examined the feasibility of an extended mobile health (mHealth) intervention for people with schizophrenia-spectrum disorders up to six months following hospital discharge. During the first month, participants initiated 62% of use of the mHealth intervention, where 38% of use was in response to automated prompts. Baseline levels of cognitive functioning, negative symptoms, persecutory ideation, and reading level were not related to participants' use of the intervention. Examination of 342 individuals with schizophrenia-spectrum disorders over longer periods (up to six months) indicated that on average, participants engaged with the mHealth intervention for 82% of the weeks they had the mobile phone, with female gender, Caucasian race, younger age, and lower number of past psychiatric hospitalizations being associated with greater engagement (Ben-Zeev et al., 2016a). Altogether, these studies provide preliminary support for the feasibility and acceptability of integrating ESM into mHealth interventions for patients with schizophrenia and related disorders, including psychosocial and medication treatments (Bucci et al., 2015; also see Chapters 9 and 10 within this book for examples of implementation of ESM as part of mental health assessments and interventions).

Advantages of ESM

The use of ESM among individuals with schizophrenia and related disorders offers unique advantages over traditional retrospective assessment methods (see Chapter 1 in this book). However, perhaps one of the most important is the availability of "in-vivo" data on individuals' thoughts, feelings, symptoms, behavior, and social context. Traditional questionnaire and/or clinical interviews are typically retrospective and thus vulnerable to the influence of memory difficulties, as well as cognitive biases and reframing (Kimhy et al., 2006, 2012). This is true even in longitudinal studies in which prospective designs are used (e.g., conducting assessments prospectively every three months over a year). The assessments in such studies are still based on the participants' retrospective recollection. These issues are particularly challenging among individuals with schizophrenia and related disorders given the substantial episodic memory deficits experienced by many individuals with schizophrenia (Aleman et al., 1999), making the use of retrospective assessments problematic in this population. Consistent with this view, Ben-Zeev et al. (2012) examined in-vivo as well as retrospective 7-day affect in 24 individuals with schizophrenia and 26 non-clinical participants. Results indicated that participants from both groups retrospectively overestimated the intensity of negative and positive daily experiences. In the clinical group, overestimations for affect were greater than for psychotic symptoms, which were relatively comparable to their retrospective reports. In both samples, retrospective reports were more closely associated with the week's average than the most intense or most recent ratings captured with a mobile device. Similarly, a recent study comparing retrospective and ESM assessments of depressed mood among individuals with schizophrenia (Blum et al., 2015) found a significant correlation between the retrospective and ESM measures.

However, once variance due to long-term memory was controlled, the association between the retrospective and ESM measure was no longer significant, highlighting the potential impact of memory difficulties on outcomes assessed using retrospective measures.

Methodological issues

In addition to the generic methodological and pragmatic issues that researchers must consider while designing and conducting any ESM study (see Chapter 2 of this book), here we discuss how ESM can be specifically adapted to improve its feasibility, validity, and acceptability in people with psychosis.

The choice of equipment

Technological advances over the past decade allowed researchers to transition from paper-based ESM to the employment of mobile electronic devices. Evidence suggests that participation and completion rates in studies utilizing such devices are comparable to paper-based ESM (Kimhy et al., 2006, 2010; Swendsen et al., 2011). This is perhaps unsurprising given the high rates of mobile phone use in people with psychosis in the general population (Firth et al., 2015). However, lack of previous experience using mobile devices does not appear to significantly influence participants' ability to take part in ESM studies (Kimhy et al., 2012). Interestingly, use of smartphone devices with dedicated ESM software has sometimes been found to be advantageous compared to delivery via text messages (short message service, SMS; Ainsworth et al., 2013). Consistent with these findings, some studies have found there to be no significant differences between individuals with psychosis and healthy controls in their ability to understand the presented questions, type responses or operate the mobile devices, their stress level while using the devices, or their level of comfort carrying the mobile devices, as well as willingness to participate in future ESM studies. Contrary to this, participants with psychosis have sometimes characterized their participation in technology-facilitated ESM studies as significantly more challenging (Kimhy et al., 2006; Granholm et al. 2008).

Questionnaire development

In line with general methodological recommendations, the momentary nature of ESM implies that items should reflect momentary states rather than traits (see Chapter 2). It is important to note that putting "right now" in front of a trait-like item does not necessarily make it a momentary item. See Table 4.1 for an example of ESM questions that have been used in the assessment of psychosis and related difficulties. When constructing ESM items, it is crucial to employ "lay" language that reflects how people describe their own behavior and experiences, and avoid medically-related vocabulary (i.e., use "voices" rather than "auditory

46 David Kimhy and Julia Vakhrusheva

TABLE 4.1 Examples of questions assessing momentary symptoms, mood, activities, and social cognition and context

	Domains	Questions and Format
Psychotic symptoms	Visual hallucinations	I see things (that other people can't see)[1]
	Auditory hallucinations	I hear voices (that other people can't hear)[1]
	Suspiciousness	My thoughts are suspicious[1]
Mood	Sadness/depression	I feel sad/depressed[1]
	Irritation	I feel irritated[1]
	Panic	I fear I would lose control[1]
Cognition	Racing thoughts	My thoughts are going too fast[1]
	Preoccupation	I can't get rid of my thoughts[1]
	Difficulty expressing thoughts	My thoughts are difficult to express[1]
Activities	Current activities	I'm currently doing ...[2]
	Evaluation of activities	This activity is difficult[1]
	Competency	I'm feel competent doing this activity[1]
Social cognition & context	Loneliness	I feel lonely[1]
	Social context	I'm currently with ...[3]
	Social cognition	I like this company[4]

Note: Adapted from Kimhy et al., 2006; Question's format:[1] visual analog or Likert scale,[2] List of activities (select one from eating, watching TV, talking with other people, self-hygiene, nothing, etc.),[3] Checkbox (select as many as applicable from list – relatives, friends, acquaintances, strangers, etc.),[4] Yes/No.

hallucinations"; Palmier-Claus et al., 2011). Additionally, as individuals with schizophrenia may have truncated educational careers due to early illness onset, researchers may also want to adapt the language to a lower reading level (e.g. 8th grade reading level). General readability levels can be commonly obtained from word processing software (for example, see options for Readability Statistics in Microsoft Word).

In general, ESM research calls for particular consideration to the number of questions and/items included in a questionnaire, and the duration of each assessment. This is particularly crucial in the case of research with psychotic participants due to the attention and concentration difficulties frequently observed in this clinical group. In addition, it's important to be mindful of the frequency with which items are endorsed. Specifically, negatively formulated items tend to be endorsed less frequently, resulting in skewed distributions. In contrast, positively formulated items result in more normal-like distribution. Furthermore, ESM may be less useful for the assessment of experiences that occur very frequently or rarely. This will likely depend on the stage and severity of psychosis. For example, voice hearing experiences are relatively rare in people at risk of developing psychosis, but may be commonplace after transition to a first episode. Instead, research in the former group may wish to consider broadening the assessment to all auditory hallucinatory experiences (e.g. sounds, whispers). Finally, it is important to avoid reflective questions that link two distinct constructs, such as "in this social context, I feel down." Such questions require more reflection, rather than focus on momentary experiences. Furthermore, asking about mood and context independently and linking the outcome statistically after data collection would also limit the risk of socially desirable responses, as well as shed more light on patterns of reporting that participants are not consciously aware of. When creating a questionnaire, it is therefore recommended to first present questions relating to transient experiences (e.g., mood, thoughts, symptoms), followed by more stable items such as context, with retrospective items about recent experiences being presented last. It is also important to note, that when the latter are included, it is possible that current states may potentially impact recall or interpretation of previous experiences.

Time schedules

Researchers may want to take into account individual participants' daily schedule. While a uniform daily assessment schedule (e.g., 10am to 10pm) for all participants is methodologically more attractive, a flexible schedule adapted to each participant's unique timetable (for example, 1pm to 1am for a participant who regularly wakes up at noon and goes to sleep at 3am) may offer potentially higher compliance rates, particularly when patients feel sedated early in the day due to medication side effects or in the case of clients presenting considerable sleep disturbance (see Chapter 6). However, the use of individually variable schedules may limit the ability to conduct group comparisons of time of day related variables.

Recruitment and retention

The recruitment and retention of individuals with psychotic disorders can be challenging for researchers. For example, patients will often have competing demands (e.g. other appointments) and experiences (e.g. voice hearing) that cause appointments to be missed. Additionally, patients experiencing thought disorder may find it difficult to organize their thoughts and effectively complete the ESM tasks. Regarding age and gender, while younger participants may have better familiarity with mobile devices, age does not appear to play a significant role in participants' ability to successfully use such devices. Indeed, Granholm and colleagues (2011) completed a study of 145 schizophrenia patients living in the community with an average age of 46.5 years (SD = 11.2). Similarly, while some gender differences in specific domains of functioning have been documented in ambulatory monitoring studies (i.e., emotional responsiveness; Myin-Germeys et al., 2004), there are no reports of gender differences in compliance rates.

48 David Kimhy and Julia Vakhrusheva

Executing ESM procedures

Investigators may want to pay attention to ensuring that participants understand the study procedures and know how to operate the mobile devices and ESM software. Such procedures should include a tutorial on use of ESM, ideally, on the day of the assessment; it should be conducted individually; and should be relatively brief (less than 30 minutes). When psychotic experiences (e.g. voices) are present in the briefing session, it is important to check participants understand and repeat take-home messages. Allowing participants first-hand experience in completing the ESM questionnaire prior to start of data collection may be beneficial. Such a tutorial may reduce participants' stress and potential apprehension, ensure participants understand all questions, and increase the probability of successful task completion. Researchers may want to instruct participants not to respond to questionnaires under certain conditions that increase risk of harm (e.g., crossing a street, while driving). Finally, it is often advantageous to provide participants with contact information so that they could inform the investigators of potential problems that interfere with the study procedures (e.g. faulty equipment).

Outpatient vs. inpatient settings

Conducting ESM studies in inpatient psychiatric units may call for special preparations. First, successful implementation of such studies may require securing the cooperation of unit clinical staff. Specifically, such studies may require scheduling ESM assessments so as to minimize conflict with patients' clinical appointments (e.g., fMRI assessment outside the unit) and/or clinical activities on the unit (e.g., group therapy). Depending on the assessment schedule, it may also be helpful to inform the evening/night staff about patients' participation to minimize potential conflicts. Our group (Kimhy et al., 2006, 2010, 2015) has employed ESM with mobile devices in inpatient psychiatric units with minimal difficulties (Kimhy et al., 2015). This may be more difficult on forensic units where the use of technology is sometimes prohibited.

Conclusion and future directions

A review of the research and clinical literature on the use of ESM among individuals with psychosis and related disorders indicates rich and diverse implementation. However, at present, there are a number of issues related to the use of ESM in studies of these populations that are in need of further investigation. As researchers increasingly focus on longitudinal assessments involving integration of ESM into treatment studies and clinical applications (see Chapters 9 and 10), there is relatively scant information about the feasibility of using ESM continuously over extended periods of time. As most studies to date rarely included more than ten days of assessments, future studies should confirm the feasibility and validity of using ESM continuously in individuals experiencing psychosis over longer periods (i.e., months). Early work in the area has already commenced (Ben-Zeev et al., 2014,

2016a), indicating promising results. A different area of potential research involves a more multidimensional examination of psychotic symptoms. For example, the vast majority of studies on auditory hallucination used a single question to examine severity. Future studies would benefit from examination of different dimensions of the experiences under scrutiny. For example, in the case of auditory hallucinations, future ESM investigations may benefit from the multidimensional assessment of the different features of such experiences (e.g. location, loudness, degree of negative content, controllability, and amount and intensity of distress; Haddock et al., 1999). Likewise, for delusions the primary focus of most ESM investigations to date has been on paranoia. Future studies should examine additional types of delusions (e.g., reference or grandiose beliefs) or assess specific features of delusional beliefs (e.g. degree of conviction and associated distress). Technological advances have also made it feasible to integrate ESM with a range of sensors collecting simultaneous physiological, behavioral, and ecological data. Future studies should further examine the feasibility and validity of integrating such sensors and technologies to elucidate the underlying neurobiology of psychosis (Kimhy et al., 2017).

Finally, future studies should confirm the best way to integrate ESM into treatments. There is a need for demonstration of clinical effectiveness, therapeutic value, as well as studies of cost effectiveness. Initial research in this area suggests potential benefits for higher functioning individuals (Granholm et al., 2011). Additional information is also needed on the precise balance of face-to-face therapeutic contacts and augmented ESM interventions (Myin-Germeys et al., 2016). Furthermore, it is not clear what clinical domains (e.g., psychosis, mood symptoms, negative symptoms, social functioning) are most responsive to ESM interventions and whether this approach should be used continuously as part of treatment or is more appropriate for intermittent assessment of patients' progress.

References

Ainsworth J., Palmier-Claus J.E., Machin M., Barrowclough C., Dunn G., Rogers A., Buchan I., Barkus E., Kapur S., Wykes T., Hopkins R.S., Lewis S. (2013). A comparison of two delivery modalities of a mobile phone-based assessment for serious mental illness: native smartphone application vs text-messaging only implementations. *Journal of Medical Internet Research*, 15(4), e60.

Aleman A., Hijman R., de Haan E.H., Kahn R.S. (1999). Memory impairment in schizophrenia: a meta-analysis. *American Journal of Psychiatry*, 156(9), 1358–1366.

Ben-Zeev D., Ellington K., Swendsen J., Granholm E. (2011). Examining a cognitive model of persecutory ideation in the daily life of people with schizophrenia: a computerized experience sampling study. *Schizophrenia Bulletin*, 37(6), 1248–1256.

Ben-Zeev D., McHugo G.J., Xie H., Dobbins K., Young M.A. (2012). Comparing retrospective reports to real-time/real-place mobile assessments in individuals with schizophrenia and a nonclinical comparison group. *Schizophrenia Bulletin*, 38(3), 396–404.

Ben-Zeev D., Brenner C.J., Begale M., Duffecy J., Mohr D.C., Mueser K.T. (2014). Feasibility, acceptability, and preliminary efficacy of a smartphone intervention for schizophrenia. *Schizophrenia Bulletin*, 40(6), 1244–1253.

Ben-Zeev D., Scherer E.A., Gottlieb J.D., Rotondi A.J., Brunette M.F., Achtyes E.D., Mueser K.T., Gingerich S., Brenner C.J., Begale M., Mohr D.C., Schooler N., Marcy P., Robinson D.G., Kane J.M. (2016a). Health for Schizophrenia: Patient Engagement with a Mobile Phone Intervention Following Hospital Discharge. *JMIR Mental Health*, 3(3), e34.

Ben-Zeev D., Wang R., Abdullah S., Brian R., Scherer E.A., Mistler L.A., Hauser M., Kane J.M., Campbell A., Choudhury T. (2016b). Mobile behavioral sensing for out-patients and inpatients with schizophrenia. *Psychiatric Services*, 67(5), 558–561.

Blum L.H., Vakhrusheva J., Saperstein A., Khan S., Chang R.W., Hansen M.C., Zemon V., Kimhy D. (2015). Depressed mood in individuals with schizophrenia: A comparison of retrospective and real-time measures. *Psychiatry Research*, 227(2–3), 318–323.

Brenner C.J., Ben-Zeev D. (2014). Affective forecasting in schizophrenia: comparing pre-dictions to real-time Ecological Momentary Assessment (EMA) ratings. *Psychiatric Rehabilitation Journal*, 37(4), 316–320.

Bucci S., Barrowclough C., Ainsworth J., Morris R., Berry K., Machin M., Emsley R., Lewis S., Edge D., Buchan I., Haddock G. (2015). Using mobile technology to deliver a cognitive behaviour therapy-informed intervention in early psychosis (Actissist): study protocol for a randomised controlled trial. *Trials*, 16, 404.

Collip D., Oorschot M., Thewissen V., Van Os J., Bentall R., Myin-Germeys I. (2011). Social world interactions: how company connects to paranoia. *Psychological Medicine*, 41 (5), 911–921.

Collip D., Habets P., Marcelis M., Gronenschild E., Lataster T., Lardinois M., Nicolson N. A., Myin-Germeys I. (2013). Hippocampal volume as marker of daily life stress sensitivity in psychosis. *Psychological Medicine*, 43(7), 1377–1387.

Chun C.A., Barrantes-Vidal N., Sheinbaum T., Kwapil T.R. (2017). Expression of schizo-phrenia-spectrum personality traits in daily life. *Personality Disorders: Theory, Research & Treatment*, 8(1), 64–74.

Delespaul P.A., deVries M.W. (1987). The daily life of ambulatory chronic mental patients. *Journal of Nervous Mental Disease*, 175(9), 537–544.

Delespaul P. (1995). *Assessing Schizophrenia in Daily Life*. Maastricht, The Netherlands: Universitaire Pers Maastricht.

Delespaul P., deVries M., van Os J. (2002). Determinants of occurrence and recovery from hallucinations in daily life. *Social Psychiatry and Psychiatric Epidemiology*, 37(3), 97–104.

Depp C.A., Mausbach B., Granholm E., Cardenas V., Ben-Zeev D., Patterson T.L., Lebowitz B.D., Jeste D.V. (2010). Mobile interventions for severe mental illness: design and pre-liminary data from three approaches. *Journal of Nervous Mental Disorders*, 198(10), 715–721.

deVries M.W. (1983). Temporal patterning of psychiatric symptoms. World Psychiatric Association Congress, Vienna, Abstract.

deVries M.W., Delespaul P.A. (1989). Time, context, and subjective experiences in schizo-phrenia. *Schizophrenia Bulletin*, 15(2), 233–244.

deVries M.W., Delespaul P.A.E.G., Dijkman C.I.M., Theunissen, J. (1986). Advance in understanding temporal and setting aspects of schizophrenic disorder. In: F. Massimini & P. Inghilleri (eds.), *L'Esperienza quotidiana*, pp. 477–493. Milan: Franco Angeli.

Firth J., Cotter J., Torous J., Bucci, S., Firth, J.A., & Yung, A.R. (2015). Mobile phone ownership and endorsement of "Health" among people with psychosis: a meta-analysis of cross-sectional studies. *Schizophrenia Bulletin*, 42(2), 448–455.

Granholm E., Loh C., Swendsen J. (2008). Feasibility and validity of computerized ecolo-gical momentary assessment in schizophrenia. *Schizophrenia Bulletin*, 34(3), 507–514.

Granholm E., Ben-Zeev D., Link P.C., Bradshaw K.R., Holden J.L (2011). Mobile Assessment and Treatment for Schizophrenia (MATS): a pilot trial of an interactive text-messaging intervention for medication adherence, socialization, and auditory hallucinations. *Schizophrenia Bulletin*, 38(3), 414–425.

Haddock G., McCarron J., Tarrier N., Faragher E.B. (1999). Scales to measure dimensions of hallucinations and delusions: the psychotic symptom rating scales (PSYRATS). *Psychological Medicine*, 29(4), 879–889.

Hartley S., Haddock G., Vasconcelos e Sa D., Emsley R., Barrowclough C. (2015). The influence of thought control on the experience of persecutory delusions and auditory hallucinations in daily life. *Behaviour Research & Therapy*, 65, 1–4.

Hartley S., Haddock G., Vasconcelos e Sa D., Emsley R., Barrowclough C. (2014). An experience sampling study of worry and rumination in psychosis. *Psychological Medicine*, 44 (8), 1605–1614.

Kay S.R., Fiszbein A., Opler L.A. (1987). The positive and negative syndrome scale (PANSS) for schizophrenia. *Schizophrenia Bulletin*, 13, 261–276.

Kimhy D., Delespaul P., Corcoran C., Ahn H., Yale S., Malaspina D. (2006). Computerized experience sampling method (ESMc): assessing feasibility and validity among individuals with schizophrenia. *Journal of Psychiatric Research*, 40(3), 221–230.

Kimhy D., Corcoran C. (2008). Use of Palm computer as an adjunct to cognitive-behavioural therapy with an ultra-high-risk patient: a case report. *Early Intervention in Psychiatry*, 2(4), 234–241.

Kimhy D., Delespaul P., Ahn H., Cai S., Shikhman M., Lieberman J.A., Malaspina D., Sloan R.P. (2010). Concurrent measurement of "real-world" stress and arousal in individuals with psychosis: assessing the feasibility and validity of a novel methodology. *Schizophrenia Bulletin*, 36(6), 1131–1139.

Kimhy D., Khan S., Ayanrouh L., Chang R.W., Hansen M.C., Lister A., … Sloan R.P. (2015). Use of active-play video games to enhance aerobic fitness in schizophrenia: feasibility, safety, and adherence. *Psychiatric Services*, 67(2), 240–243.

Kimhy D., Myin-Germeys I., Palmier-Claus J., Swendsen J. (2012). Mobile assessment guide for research in schizophrenia and severe mental disorders. *Schizophrenia Bulletin*, 38(3), 386–395.

Kimhy D., Vakhrusheva J., Liu Y., Wang Y. (2014a). Use of mobile assessment technologies in inpatient psychiatric settings. *Asian Journal of Psychiatry*, 10, 90–95.

Kimhy D., Vakhrusheva J., Khan S., Chang R.W., Hansen M.C., Ballon J.S., Malaspina D., Gross J.J. (2014b). Emotional granularity and social functioning in individuals with schizophrenia: an experience sampling study. *Journal of Psychiatric Research*, 53, 141–148.

Kimhy D., Wall M., Hansen M.C., Vakhrusheva J., Choi J., Delespaul P., Tarrier N., Sloan R.P., Malaspina D. (2017). Autonomic regulation and auditory hallucinations in schizophrenia: An experience sampling study. *Schizophrenia Bulletin*, 43(4), 754–763.

Lataster J., van Os J., de Haan L., Thewissen V., Bak M., Lataster T., Lardinois M., Delespaul P.A., Myin-Germeys I. (2011a). Emotional experience and estimates of D2 receptor occupancy in psychotic patients treated with haloperidol, risperidone, or olanzapine: an experience sampling study. *Journal of Clinical Psychiatry*, 72(10), 1397–1404.

Lataster J., Myin-Germeys I., Wichers M., Delespaul P.A., van Os J., Bak M. (2011b). Psychotic exacerbation and emotional dampening in the daily life of patients with schizophrenia switched to aripiprazole therapy: a collection of standardized case reports. *Therapeutic Advances in Psychopharmacology*, 1(5), 145–151.

McCormick B.P., Snethen G., Smith R.L., Lysaker P.H. (2012). Active leisure in the emotional experience of people with schizophrenia. *Therapeutic Recreation Journal*, 46(3), 179–190.

Miller P.M., Lawrie S.M., Byrne M., Cosway R., Johnstone E.C. (2002). Self-rated schizotypal cognitions, psychotic symptoms and the onset of schizophrenia in young people at high risk of schizophrenia. *Acta Psychiatrica Scandinavica*, 105(5), 341–345.

Myin-Germeys I., Delespaul P.A., deVries M.W. (2000). Schizophrenia patients are more emotionally active than is assumed based on their behavior. *Schizophrenia Bulletin*, 26(4), 847–854.

Myin-Germeys I., Klippel A., Steinhart H., Reininghaus U. (2016). Ecological momentary interventions in psychiatry. *Current Opinion in Psychiatry*, 29(4), 258–263.

Myin-Germeys I., Krabbendam L., Delespaul P.A., van Os J. (2004). Sex differences in emotional reactivity to daily life stress in psychosis. *Journal of Clinical Psychiatry*, 65(6), 805–809.

Oorschot M., Lataster T., Thewissen V., Bentall R., Delespaul P.A., Myin-Germeys I. (2012). Temporal dynamics of visual and auditory hallucinations in psychosis. *Schizophrenia Research*, 140(1–3), 77–82.

Oorschot M., Lataster T., Thewissen V., Lardinois M., Wichers M., van Os J., Delespaul P., Myin-Germeys I. (2013). Emotional experience in negative symptoms of schizophrenia: no evidence for a generalized hedonic deficit. *Schizophrenia Bulletin*, 39(1), 217–225.

Palmier-Claus J.E., Myin-Germeys I., Barkus E., et al. (2011). Experience sampling research in individuals with mental illness: reflections and guidance. *Acta Psychiatrica Scandinavica*, 123, 12–20.

Palmier-Claus J.E., Dunn G., Taylor H., Morrison A.P., Lewis S.W. (2013). Cognitive-self consciousness and metacognitive beliefs: Stress sensitization in individuals at ultra-high risk of developing psychosis. *British Journal of Clinical Psychology*, 52(1), 26–41.

Peerbooms O., Rutten B.P., Collip D., Lardinois M., Lataster T., Thewissen V., Rad S.M., Drukker M., Kenis G., van Os J., Myin-Germeys I., van Winkel R. (2012). Evidence that interactive effects of COMT and MTHFR moderate psychotic response to environmental stress. *Acta Psychiatrica Scandinavica*, 125(3), 247–256.

Peters E., Lataster T., Greenwood K., Kuipers E., Scott J., Williams S., Garety P., Myin-Germeys I. (2012). Appraisals, psychotic symptoms and affect in daily life. *Psychological Medicine*, 42(5), 1013–1023.

Sanchez A.H., Lavaysse L.M., Starr J.N., Gard D.E. (2014). Daily life evidence of environment-incongruent emotion in schizophrenia. *Psychiatry Research*, 220(1–2), 89–95.

Swendsen J., Ben-Zeev D., Granholm E. (2011). Real-time electronic ambulatory monitoring of substance use and symptom expression in schizophrenia. *American Journal of Psychiatry*, 168(2), 202–209.

Thewissen V., Bentall R.P., Lecomte T., van Os J., Myin-Germeys I. (2008). Fluctuations in self-esteem and paranoia in the context of daily life. *Journal of Abnormal Psychology*, 117 (1), 143–153.

Thewissen V., Bentall R.P., Oorschot M., A Campo J., van Lierop T., van Os J., Myin-Germeys I. (2011). Emotions, self-esteem, and paranoid episodes: an experience sampling study. *British Journal of Clinical Psychology*, 50(2), 178–195.

Udachina A., Varese F., Myin-Germeys I., Bentall R.P. (2014). The role of experiential avoidance in paranoid delusions: an experience sampling study. *British Journal of Clinical Psychology*, 53(4), 422–432.

Udachina A., Thewissen V., Myin-Germeys I., Fitzpatrick S., O'kane A., Bentall R.P.. (2009). Understanding the relationships between self-esteem, experiential avoidance, and paranoia: structural equation modelling and experience sampling studies. *Journal of Nervous Mental Disease*, 197(9), 661–668.

Wigman J.T., Collip D., Wichers M., Delespaul P., Derom C., Thiery E., Vollebergh W.A., Lataster T., Jacobs N., Myin-Germeys I., van Os J. (2013). Altered transfer of momentary mental states (ATOMS) as the basic unit of psychosis liability in interaction with environment and emotions. *PLoS One*, 8(2), e54653.

5

EXPERIENCE SAMPLING IN THE STUDY OF AUTISM SPECTRUM DISORDERS

Dougal Julian Hare and Yu-Wei Chen

There is a small but growing body of research using the Experience Sampling Method (ESM) in people with Autism Spectrum Disorder (ASD). Such work holds great potential for the development of user-friendly and ecologically valid outcome measures for the intervention and support of people with ASD. As discussed elsewhere in this book, ESM is an approach that assesses moment-to-moment cognitive, emotional and behavioural events in daily life (Hektner, Schmidt & Csikszentmihalyi, 2007). It is useful for exploring idiosyncratic experiences and individual differences (e.g. thoughts, feelings, behaviour) in phenomena that vary across individuals, time and context. ESM typically involves individuals completing self-report questions in response to a signal (e.g. beep) at random or pre-determined intervals of time.

ESM has been used extensively in various formats (i.e. pen and paper, computerised) to explore the everyday experiences of individuals with anxiety and mood disorders, bipolar disorder, and psychosis (e.g. Palmier-Claus et al., 2011). However, there is also a small, but growing, body of research that has used ESM to investigate the daily lives of individuals with ASD (Hurlburt, Happé & Frith, 1994; Hintzen, Delespaul, Van Os & Myin-Germeys, 2010; Chen, Bundy, Cordier, Chien & Einfeld, 2016a, 2016b, 2015; Cordier, Brown, Chen, Wilkes-Gillan & Falkmer, 2016; Hare, Wood, Wastell & Skirrow, 2015). Such research has examined the use of ESM in the delivery of real-time intervention (e.g. Kramer, Simons, Hartmann et al., 2014) including small-scale pilot studies (Hare, Gracey & Wood, 2016). In this chapter, we will outline the specific differences in psychological and social functioning associated with ASD that indicate the need for research using ESM, summarise the extant findings from existing ESM studies and provide practical guidance to readers wishing to conduct their own research in this area.

Research in ASD

ASD, as currently defined in DSM-V (American Psychiatric Association, 2013), is a developmental disorder characterised by co-occurring and co-varying life-long impairments in social communication abilities and by the presence of repetitive, restricted and ritualistic behaviours. ASD occurs with and without intellectual impairments with the latter resulting in the presentation known as Asperger's Syndrome (AS)/high-functioning autism (HFA), which has facilitated much psychological research into ASD over the past 30 years. This is because it is possible to undertake research with this population and then 'back engineer' the findings to those people with ASD who are unable to communicate or participate in research.

The benefits of ESM in ASD

It is now well established that along with a range of difficulties in mentalisation, namely the understanding that other people have minds and that the content of others' minds differs from one's own mind, autistic people experience difficulties in *autonoetic functioning*. This refers to psychological processes that involve self-knowledge, particularly those involved in various aspects of autobiographical memory functioning (Lind, Williams, Bowler & Peel, 2014; Lind, Bowler & Raber, 2014; Hare, Mellor & Azmi, 2007) and the construction of an active subjective self (Jackson, Skirrow & Hare, 2012). In practice, these mean that many people with AS/HFA, as well as with other forms of ASD, can have difficulty in recalling their own actions and experiences. One potential way of over-coming these difficulties is to identify and develop research and clinical methodologies that mitigate, or even negate, the need for people with AS/HFA to draw upon autobiographical memory and potentially intervene in real time. The most obvious approach is to use ESM techniques, which raises specific questions about the use of ESM in people with AS/HFA, namely, (1) the feasibility of the broad ESM approach with this population, (2) the reliability of the ESM data collected in this population and (3) the nature of the questions that can be investigated. Given that at the time of writing (early 2017), the number of ESM studies conducted in people with AS/HFA is still very small, it is feasible to review the extant literature in order to address both questions.

The feasibility of ESM with people with ASD

All the published ESM studies to date have been with people with ASD all of whom have had average or above-average full-scale IQ scores ranging from 99 to 120, skewed toward the upper level, which possibly indicates that the use of ESM is more feasible in the high cognitively functioning people with ASD. This section comprises reviews of participants' compliance and acceptability of ESM, and the reliability and validity of the data it provides.

Compliance to ESM in ASD

Compliance with completing the ESM form can be seen in signal response rates, which refer to the proportion of signals for which responses are completed (Hektner et al., 2007). Researchers have identified average signal response rates in individuals with AS/HFA between 57% and 85% (Chen et al., 2014, 2016a, 2016b, Chen, Bundy et al., 2015; Chen, Cordier et al., 2015, Cordier et al., 2016; Hintzen et al., 2010, Khor et al., 2014a, Kovac et al., 2016), which are consistent with the compliance range identified in a review of studies using ESM in clinical populations (Hufford & Shields, 2002). However, the signal response rates were lower in children with AS/HFA (57%; Chen, Cordier et al., 2015; Cordier et al., 2016) than adolescents and adults (Chen et al., 2016a, 2016b, 2014; Chen, Bundy et al., 2015). This may be explained by the frustration of responding to signals identified in children when playing electronic games (e.g., computer or mobile games), which occupied the majority of their time (Chen, Cordier et al., 2015). Accordingly, the participants reported that they attempted to ignore the prompts in that situation. Further, some of the children reported that the ESM form (22 questions completed in an average of 2 minutes) was too long and repetitive. In addition to the effect of age on compliance, Khor and colleagues (2014a) found that adolescents with lower IQ scores tended to be less compliant with entry completion even though all participants had a diagnosis of AS/HFA. However, there was no relationship between compliance and ASD symptomatology or gender.

Acceptability of ESM in ASD

Past studies have suggested that people with AS/HFA generally enjoy involvement in ESM research and experience minimal interference with their daily routines. Although they are generally able to shift from everyday activities to completing the survey when signalled, they do report that this is sometimes frustrating (Hare et al., 2015). Regarding the acceptability of mobile technology, Hare and colleagues (2015) found that people with ASD experienced 'Palm Pilots', a now obsolete form of hand-held personal computer, to be user-friendly with minimal disruption to every activity. Similarly, both children and adults with AS/HFA considered the iOS devices and the *Participation in Everyday Life Survey Application* [PIEL App] (Jessup, Bian, Chen & Bundy, 2012) to be extremely easy and enjoyable to use (Chen et al., 2014, Chen, Cordier et al., 2015). Adults with AS/HFA indicated that signals prompted by the device interfered with their everyday life only slightly (Chen et al., 2014). One adult participant further appreciated being signalled to respond rather than relying on memory to complete the surveys. Chen and colleagues (2015) have suggested that an electronic device (i.e., iPod Touch) is a powerful means to keep the children engaged over the course of an ESM study.

The reliability and validity of ESM data in ASD

Chen and colleagues (Chen et al., 2014, Chen, Cordier et al., 2015) have examined whether momentary data collected from children and adults with AS/HFA are valid and reliable. First, they tested whether theoretically or logically linked variables were indeed significantly related in ESM data. They found that enjoyment was positively correlated with interest in a situation, but negatively associated with anxiety, supporting the internal validity of the data. The authors then explored the split half reliability of the data. Furthermore, no significant differences were found when comparing two halves of the week of subjective experience (e. g., perceived difficulty, interest in situations, and emotions), indicating that the data were internally reliable. Similar findings were identified in Kovac et al. (2016), where the split-half reliability was 0.87 and Cronbach's alpha was 0.88 across all measures of positive affect.

Authors have also explored the convergent validity of ESM data in people with ASD. Khor and colleagues (Khor, Gray, Reid & Melvin, 2014a; Khor, Melvin, Reid & Gray, 2014b) examined daily hassles and coping responses using both ESM and retrospective questionnaire measures, the latter completed by parents. As well as demonstrating the practicalities of such an approach, these studies showed that the ESM data was concordant with third-party parental reports, thus attesting to its validity.

Methodological developments

The choice of equipment and technology, reliable and valid items, and sampling rates are critical concerns faced by researchers when designing an ESM study for individuals with ASD. This section offers guidance, based on previous studies, for developing and carrying out an ESM protocol in this population.

Choosing methods and equipment

The method by which ESM is facilitated and delivered has varied considerably over the past two decades of research with people with AS/HFA, which largely reflects the substantial technological advancements over the same period. Early studies typically required participants to complete paper diaries when prompted by a digital wristwatch (Hintzen et al., 2010) or Hurlburt, Happé and Frith's (1994) unspecified 'digital beeping device'. Subsequent studies have utilised wholly electronic data collection. Hare and colleagues initially used Palm Pilots (OS R v3.1) running a bespoke ESM program (DeVries, Caes & Delespaul, 2001; Hurlburt et al., 1994) using free source code from the National Science Foundation [http://www.experience-sampling.org] (Hare et al., 2015) and then Palm Pilots (m500 Series) running a bespoke ESM program derived from their previous study and Intel Research iESP software (Hare et al., 2016). Palm Pilots were a very cheap and relatively easy means of prototyping ESM programs, but have become

Experience sampling in the study of autism **57**

increasingly obsolescent in the presence of more advanced mobile technology. Researchers are now increasingly using mobile-phone technology to facilitate data collection within ESM research. These devices have the benefits of wireless connectivity, a familiar user interface and considerable programming power (Ainsworth et al., 2013). There is research indicating high use of mobile phones in people with AS/HFA (MacMullin, Lunsky, & Weiss, 2016), which means that researchers may not need to purchase the devices for all participants, thereby substantially reducing up-front research costs. Some mobile applications/programs are free of charge and easily accessible. Additionally, data can be retrieved directly in a format ready for statistical analysis thus decreasing time and errors associated with data entry. Furthermore, signal schedules can be programmed and precise time stamps provided in each signal and response. This enables researchers to know exactly when the data were provided and prevents participants from providing retrospective responses, which might be contaminated by memory or false information. Khor and colleagues (2014a, 2014b) employed mobile phones running *mobiletype* program (Reid et al., 2009, 2011), whereas Chen and his colleagues (Chen et al., 2016a, 2016b; Chen et al., 2014; Chen, Bundy et al., 2015; Chen, Cordier et al., 2015; Cordier et al., 2016) utilised an iOS device (e.g., iPod touch or iPhone) running the PIEL App (Jessup, Bian, Chen & Bundy, 2012), which may be useful examples of research utilising a mobile-phone-based approach.

Item development

One advantage of ESM approaches is the flexibility to tailor the ESM form or diary (i.e. a sheet containing the ESM items) to the research questions being addressed. Over the last two decades, two research strands have been identified in the studies of using ESM with people with AS/HFA. The first has attempted to explore the relationships between subjective experiences and everyday contexts (Chen et al., 2016a, 2016b; Chen, Bundy et al., 2015; Cordier et al., 2016; Hintzen et al., 2010; Kovac et al., 2016). This research uses a conventional ESM approach to capture both the external and internal dimensions of experience. Accordingly, the ESM diary is comprised of a series of questions about the situation and participants' in-the-moment emotions, thoughts and motivation. For example, the ESM form used in Chen and colleague's (2016a, 2016b) studies in adolescents and adults with AS/HFA (see Table 5.1 for sample questions), which was patterned after previous research (Hektner et al., 2007), included questions to identify the participants' location, activity and quality of experiences and feelings. An alternative way to develop the ESM diary is to incorporate and adapt questions from psychometrically sound questionnaires. For instance, Kovac et al. (2016) combined the positive affect items from the Positive and Negative Affect Scale for Children (PANAS-C) (Laurent et al., 1999) with three open-ended context questions (i.e., *Where are you? What are you doing? Who are you with?*).

TABLE 5.1 Sample of ESM questions from Chen et al. (2016a, 2016b)

Questions	Response		Type
1. What was the main thing you were doing?	a. Nothing/ resting b. Personal care (in shower, dressing) c. Reading/ writing/ music/ web d. TV/ film e. Observing activity/ people f. Class/ work/ meeting	g. Talking/texting/ phone h. Electronic games i. Shopping j. Running/jogging/ fitness/sport k. Party/clubbing/ socialising l. Other	Multiple choices with one response
2. How interested were you?	Not at all ↔ Very much		Slider
3. How involved were you?	Not at all ↔Very much		Slider
4. Were you communicating with someone (in person, phone, or via internet)?	Yes No		Yes/no
5. Were you enjoying yourself?	Not at all ↔Very much		Slider

Given that people with ASD commonly have difficulty understanding abstract concepts and a tendency for literal and concrete interpretation of language (Klin et al., 2005), it is crucial to ensure that the wording of the questions is as straightforward and definite as possible. For example, Chen et al. (2016a, 2016b) avoided using the phrase '*being engaged*' because of its unclear and ambiguous meaning. Instead, '*being involved*', '*interest*' and '*enjoyment*' were used as part of the outcome of engagement. Meanwhile, the word '*interacting*' was replaced by a more explicit word '*communicating*'. Further, the situations where communication can take place (i.e., in person, phone, or via internet) were included to address the possible literal thinking.

The second research strand focuses on the assessment of emotional and cognitive processes in real time. In their pioneering study, Hurlburt, Happé and Frith (1994) used what they described as a 'descriptive experience sampling method' (DES) to explore the inner experience of three adults with AS/HFA. DES is a relatively unstructured approach, somewhat akin to ethnography, and which involves:

> … the subject wearing a small device that produces a beep at random intervals, which the subject hears through an earphone. The subject is instructed that his [sic] task is immediately to 'freeze the contents of his awareness' at the moment when the beep began and then to write down some notes about the details of that experience. The subject is later interviewed about this beeped moment, using his notes as a memory aid.
>
> *(Hurlburt, Happé & Frith, 1992, p. 386)*

The data thus obtained via DES was then categorised using Hurlburt's (1990) four-fold framework of *Verbal inner experience, Visual images, Feelings* and *Unsymbolised thinking* (i.e. 'pure' thought with no reported experience of words, images or symbolic forms). The most striking finding from Hurlburt, Happé and Frith's study was the predominance of visual imagery reported by the three participants with AS/HFA and their disinterest in or unawareness of other people's inner experience. More recent work on real-time exploration of emotional and cognitive processes in people with AS/HFA has utilised ESM rather than DES with a focus on understanding anxiety and coping strategies in this population (Hare et al., 2015, 2016; Khor et al., 2014a, 2014b). Table 5.2 shows a sample of an ESM question framework from Hare et al. (2015) developed for the examination of emotions, thoughts and behaviours.

TABLE 5.2 ESM question framework from Hare, Wood, Wastell & Skirrow (2015)

Question	Answer Type	Area of Interest	Coding Type
What were you thinking about just before the alarm sounded?	Text entry	Content of thought	Coded
How would you describe the thought you were having just before the alarm sounded?	Multiple Choice • confusing • annoying • worrying • practical • pleasurable • comforting • neutral	Appraisal of thought	Numeric/Coded (if other is selected)
What was the form of the thought you were having?	Multiple Choice • like written symbols • like written text • like someone was talking to me • like I was talking to myself • like an image • unsure	Form/Description of thought	Numeric / Coded (if other is selected)
Was this a normal thought for you?	Multiple Choice • yes • no • unsure	Whether thought was typical for the person	Numeric
How long had you been thinking about this before the alarm sounded?	Multiple Choice • < 1 min • 1–5 mins • 5–10 mins • over 10 mins	Amount of time concerned with thought	Numeric

(Continued)

60 Dougal Julian Hare and Yu-Wei Chen

Table 5.2 (Cont.)

Question	Answer Type	Area of Interest	Coding Type
How often do you think about this?	Visual Analogue • 1 = Never • 99 = Constantly	Regularity of thought	Numeric
How happy were you feeling just before the alarm sounded?	Visual Analogue • 1 = Very Sad • 99 = Very Happy	Mood	• Numeric
How nervous were you feeling just before the alarm sounded?	Visual Analogue • 1 = Very Relaxed • 99 = Very Nervous	Anxiety	Numeric
How many people were you with just before the alarm sounded?	Multiple Choice • I was by myself • I was with one other person • I was with two or more people	Whether anxious thinking is occurring more alone or in company	Numeric
How much did the alarm upset you?	Visual Analogue • 1 = Not at all • 99 = A great deal	Whether alarm caused distress	Numeric
Did the interruption to your thinking upset you?	Multiple Choice • Yes • No	Whether to thinking causes distress	Numeric
In what way did the interruption to your thinking upset you?	Multiple Choice • It made me feel nervous • I lost my train of thought • It annoyed me • Other (text entry)	Whether interruption was described as anxiety provoking or other	Numeric/Coded (if other is selected)
What were you doing just before the alarm sounded?	Text entry	Description of behaviour	Coded

To design ESM items for people with AS/HFA, there are specific cognitive parameters that need to be considered, given that this approach requires individuals to reflect on emotions and identify thoughts. As discussed earlier, it is crucial to ensure that the questions are straightforward, easily comprehended, and address only immediate experience. To do so, the ESM questions should be piloted on both the researchers and a small number of individuals who resemble the intended study population or have similar clinical conditions (Hektner et al., 2007, Chen et al., 2014, Chen, Cordier & Brown, 2015). For example, Chen and colleagues (2014) firstly consulted a group of clients with psychosis, who had similar social cognitive deficits to people with ASD (Couture et al., 2010), to examine whether the ESM questions and responses covered most of their daily routines and experience in real life. In addition, the researchers invited two psychiatrists who had extensive experience working with people with ASD and a manager from an autism-specific service provider to review the questions regarding the appropriateness of language use and wording, particularly in relation to those items pertaining to perceptions and feelings. After modifying the questions based on the suggestions and before piloting the ESM form in individuals with AS/HFA, Chen and colleagues trialled the ESM form in five neurotypical children and adolescents who were younger than the intended research population in order to ensure the questions were easily understood.

Researchers need to examine whether participants are able to comprehend the ESM questions easily before the formal trial. Suitable measures for this include the *Woodcock Reading Mastery Test – Third Edition (WRMT-III)* (Woodcock, 2011), as used by Chen and colleagues, and the *British Picture Vocabulary Scale II (BPVS II)* (Dunn, Dunn, Whetton et al., 1982) as used by Hare and colleagues. Chen and his colleagues confirmed the participants' reading comprehension level, as assessed by the WRMT-III, was equivalent to or higher than the required level to read and comprehend the ESM questions as determined by the Flesche-Kincaid readability test (Kincaid, Fishburne, Rogers & Chissom, 1975). Based on this information alterations to the questions may be necessary to meet the participants' needs. For example, Kovac and colleagues (2016) decreased language complexity of Likert scale anchors and added visual supports for the responses to items from the PANAS-C. On the other hand, Chen, Cordier and colleagues (2015) recorded the quality of experiences and emotions either dichotomously or using visual analogue scales with a reduced number of items. These alterations would be most beneficial to children/adolescents with AS/HFA or those who are less cognitively able.

Another decision that must be made in the design of an ESM study is the number of questions included in the ESM diary, which could in turn influence levels of compliance with completing the ESM form. While individuals with ASD often feel frustrated when transitioning from one activity to another (Lauritsen, 2013), researchers need to determine the length of each entry in order to get enough information to reliably answer research questions, but not overburden the participants (Hektner et al., 2007). In most published work in people with AS/HFA, the length of ESM diary has been either less than 20 questions (Hintzen et al., 2010; Hare et al., 2015, 2016; Kovac et al., 2016) or within two minutes for completion (Chen et al., 2014, Chen, Cordier et al., 2015). This finding is consistent with the recommendations of other authors (Hektner et al., 2007). Although the ESM form in Khor and colleagues (2014a) took 1–3 minutes to complete, the average signal response rates (61.81%) were still satisfactory. However, a shorter ESM form completed in less than two minutes is suggested especially for children with AS/HFA (Chen, Cordier et al., 2015).

Time schedules

Regardless of which mode of delivery is utilised, decisions on signalling schedule must be made in addition to the number of questions to be included in an ESM form as these will likely influence participants' compliance (Hektner et al., 2007). As suggested by Delespaul (1995), longer signalling periods are more feasible only if the ESM forms are short and/or if the frequency of signals per day is low. To date, ESM sampling periods in people with AS/HFA have been relatively short, ranging from three days (Hare et al., 2015, 2016) to two weeks (Khor et al., 2014a, 2014b), and the frequency of signals has varied depending on the purpose of the study and context of the study. For their research exploring everyday social experience of people with AS/HFA, Chen and his colleagues (Chen et al., 2016a, 2016b; Chen, Bundy et al., 2015; Cordier et al., 2016) asked participants to complete the ESM diary seven times per day randomly during waking hours for a week in order to yield a fairly representative sample of activities individuals participate in and to obtain multiple responses from these activities (Hektner et al., 2007). Conversely, Khor and colleagues (2014a, 2014b) collected the ESM data at random times once within each of the four stratified intervals (four signals/day) for two weeks. However, the policies at many schools prohibit the use of mobile phones at school, leading to the blocks for weekdays determined to be external to school hours. Consequently, the participants were asked to report the situations that had happened since the previous signal. This means that the recall bias was not completely eliminated, turning into a limitation of the study.

Executing the ESM procedure

Researchers should conduct an orientating meeting prior to the formal implementation of ESM. Despite the strength of using technology in individuals with AS/HFA, participants must be trained in all study procedures from the introduction of the study purpose, to how to use the device to complete the ESM diary. It is crucial for participants to be able to review the whole ESM diary and ask questions related to either the ESM questions or the use of the device, in order to avoid any confusion and misunderstanding. If necessary, researchers may further provide chances of practising the whole research procedure before the formal trial. For example, in their study of exploring everyday experience in children with AS/HFA, Chen, Cordier and colleagues (2015) and Cordier and colleagues (2016) asked participants to complete a three-day trial after the orientation meeting and before formal data collection. This step allowed for problems to be resolved before commencing data collection proper, thereby strengthening the rigour of the study. During sampling, regular contacts with the participant or their parents are necessary to ensure no technical malfunctions of the electronic device influenced the completion of ESM forms. As people with ASD often have restricted interests and resist changes of daily routines, researcher contact and/or encouragement from parents or caregivers may help them to maintain their interest and motivation during the data collection period. The researchers may also need to ask parents or caregivers to remind their children to respond to the signals, given that young people were found to easily forget to keep the device with them during waking hours (Chen, Cordier et al., 2015).

The importance of providing support before, during and after an ESM study with people with AS/HFA becomes even more important if there is an intervention component to the study. In particular, Hare and colleagues (2016) identified that they under-estimated the amount of face-to-face support required to use ESM to deliver a real-time stress management intervention and cautioned against presuming that all people with AS/HFA have a preference for minimal social interaction and so-called 'fit and forget' approaches that involve handing out electronic devices with little or no contact with researchers during the period of using the device.

Discussion and conclusion

From the research undertaken to date, it is evident that ESM can be effectively used in people with ASD if they have no other global intellectual impairments. In particular, ESM studies have shown that this group may experience the world in ways that are qualitatively and quantitatively different to the 'neurotypical' population. In order to advance this area of research, there are several lines of inquiry that could be fruitfully explored. The most pressing of these is to investigate the potentially iatrogenic effects of ESM in people with ASD/HFA, such as the effects of the signals interrupting activities. In addition, the potential use of ESM with less cognitively able people requires further exploration.

There is a need to modify and expand the types of data collected by ESM, which, so far, has almost always been verbal. For example, some research has extracted information from clinical reports (e.g. Hare 2015) and visual imagery (e.g. Hurlburt, Happé & Frith, 1994), which could be used alongside more traditional self-report measures. Visual methods are often idiosyncratic in nature, but may complement or even supplant verbal thought in some people with ASD. This may be related to the apparent absence of expected (verbal) cognitions (e.g. Hare et al., 2015) in this population.

With regard to future topics, there is scope for further exploration of both the internal psychological experience of people with ASD, including for example the experience ofinner voices, and the factors influencing everyday experience of the external social world (e.g., psychosocial functioning, severity of ASD and social anxiety). There is also need for ESM studies in specific settings such as schools, colleges and workplaces given the situation-specific demands that such environments might place on people with ASD (Flood, Hare & Wallis, 2011). Taken together, the use of ESM and contemporary mobile technology could lead to the development of effective and discreet real-time psychosocial support and intervention for people with AS/HFA. In many ways therefore, ESM is a tailor-made methodology for rapidly developing both research and interventions both for and

References

Ainsworth, J., Palmier-Claus, J. E., Machin, M., Barrowclough, C., Dunn, G., Rogers, A., & Hopkins, R. S. (2013). A comparison of two delivery modalities of a mobile phone-based assessment for serious mental illness: native smartphone application vs text-messaging only implementations. *Journal of Medical Internet Research*, 15(4), e60.

American Psychiatric Association. (2013). *Diagnostic and Statistical Manual of Mental Disorders* (5th ed.). Arlington, VA: American Psychiatric Publishing.

Chen, Y.-W., Bundy, A., Cordier, R. , & Einfeld, S. (2014). Feasibility and usability of experience sampling methodology for capturing everyday experiences of individuals with autism spectrum disorders. *Disability and Health Journal*, 7, 361–366.

Chen, Y.-W., Bundy, A., Cordier, R., Chien, Y.L., & Einfeld, S. (2015). Motivation for everyday social participation in cognitively able individuals with autism spectrum disorder. *Neuropsychiatric Disease and Treatment*, 11, 2699–2709.

Chen, Y.-W., Bundy, A., Cordier, R., Chien, Y.L. , & Einfeld, S. (2016a) The experience of social participation in everyday contexts among individuals with autism spectrum disorders: An experience sampling study. *Journal of Autism and Developmental Disorders*, 46, 1403–1414.

Chen, Y.-W., Bundy, A., Cordier, R., Chien, Y.L., & Einfeld, S. (2016b). A cross-cultural exploration of the everyday social participation of individuals with autism spectrum disorders in Australia and Taiwan: An experience sampling study. *Autism* Advance online publication.

Chen, Y.-W., Cordier, R., & Brown, N. (2015). A preliminary study on the reliability and validity of using experience sampling method in children with autism spectrum disorders. *Developmental Neurorehabilitation*, 18(6), 383–389.

Cordier, R., Brown, N., Chen, Y.-W., Wilkes-Gillan, S., & Falkmer, T. (2016) Piloting the use of experience sampling method to investigate the everyday social experiences of children with Asperger syndrome/high functioning autism. *Developmental Neurorehabilitation*, 19(2), 103–110.

Couture, S. M., Penn, D. L., Losh, M., Adolphs, R., Hurley, R., & Piven, J. (2010). Comparison of social cognitive functioning in schizophrenia and high functioning autism: more convergence than divergence. *Psychological Medicine*, 40(04), 569–579.

Delespaul, P. (1995). *Assessing Schizophrenia in Daily Life: The Experience Sampling Method*. Maastricht, The Netherlands: Universitaire Pers Maastricht.

DeVriesM. W., CaesC. I. M., and Delespaul, P. A. E. G. (2001). The Experience Sampling Method in stress and anxiety research. In E. J. L. Griez, C. Faravelli, D. Nutt, and J. Zohar, (eds), *Anxiety Disorders: An Introduction to Clinical Management and Research*. New York: John Wiley and Sons Ltd.

Dunn, L. M., Dunn, L. M., Whetton, C., et al. (1982). *The British Picture Vocabulary Scale*. Windsor: NFER-Nelson

Flood, A. M., Hare, D. J., & Wallis, P. (2011). An investigation into social information processing in young people with Asperger syndrome/high functioning autism. *Autism: International Journal of Research and Practice*, 15(1), 601–624.

Hare, D. J. (2015). Autism Spectrum Disorders in A. Carr, C. Linehan, G. O'Reilly, P. Noonan Walsh & J. McEvoy (eds), *Handbook of Intellectual Disability and Clinical Psychology Practice*. Oxford: Routledge.

Hare, D. J., Gracey, C., & Wood, C. (2016). Anxiety in High-functioning Autism: A pilot study of experience sampling using a mobile platform. *Autism*, 20(6), 730–743.

HareD. J., Mellor, C., & Azmi, S. (2007). Episodic memory in adults with autistic spectrum disorders: recall for self- versus other-experienced events. *Research in Developmental Disorders*, 28, 311–329.

Hare, D. J., Wood, C., Wastell, S., & Skirrow, P. (2015). Anxiety in Asperger's Syndrome: Assessment in real-time. *Autism*, 19(5), 542–552.

Hektner, J. M., Schmidt, J. M., & Csikszentmihalyi, M. (2007). *Experience Sampling Methodology: Measuring the quality of everyday life*. California: Sage.

Hintzen, A. M., Delespaul, P. A. E. G., van Os, J., & Myin-Germeys, I. (2010). Social needs in daily life in adults with Pervasive Developmental Disorders. *Psychiatry Research*, 179(1), 75–80.

Hufford, M. R., & Shields, A. L. (2002). Electronic diaries: Applications and what works in the field. *Applied Clinical Trial*, 11, 46–56.

Hurlburt, R. T. (1990). *Sampling Normal and Schizophrenic Inner Experience*. New York: Plenum Press.

Hurlburt, R., Happé, F., & Frith, U. (1994). Sampling the form of inner experience in three adults with Asperger syndrome. *Psychological Medicine*, 24, 385–395.

Jackson, P., Skirrow, P., & Hare, D. J. (2012). Asperger through the looking glass: An exploratory study of self-understanding in people with Asperger's Syndrome. *Journal of Autism and Developmental Disorders*, 42(5), 697–706.

Jessup, G., Bian, S., Chen, Y. W., & Bundy, A. (2012). *Manual of PIEL survey application. [iPhone/iPod Touch/iPad/iPad mini application]*. Sydney, Australia: The University of Sydney.

Khor, A. S., Gray, K. M., Reid, S. C., & Melvin, G. A. (2014a). Feasibility and validity of ecological momentary assessment in adolescents with high-functioning autism and Asperger's Disorder. *Journal of Adolescence*, 37, 37–46.

Khor, A. S., Melvin, G. A., Reid, S. C., & Gray, K. M. (2014b). Coping, daily hassles and behavior and emotional problems in adolescents with High-Functioning Autism /Asperger's Disorder. *Journal of Autism & Developmental Disorders*, 44, 593–608.

Kincaid, J. P., Fishburne, R. P., Rogers, R. L., & Chissom, B. S. (1975). *Derivation of New Readability Formula (Automated Readability Index, Fog Count and Flesch Reading Ease Formula) for Navy Enlisted Personnel*. Memphis, TN: Naval Air Station.

Klin, A., McPartland, J., & Volkmar, F. R. (2005). Asperger syndrome. In F. R. Volkmar, R. Paul, A. Klin, & D. Cohen (Eds.), *Diagnosis, Development, Neurobiology, and Behavior: Vol. 1. Handbook of Autism and Pervasive Developmental Disorders* (pp. 88–125). Hoboken, NJ: John Wiley & Sons Inc.

Kovac, M., Mosner, M., Miller, S., Hanna, E. K., & Dichter, G. S. (2016). Experience sampling of positive affect in adolescents with autism: Feasibility and preliminary findings. *Research in Autism Spectrum Disorders*, 29, 57–65.

Kramer, I., Simons, C. J. P., Hartmann, J. A., Menne-Lothmann, C., Viechtbauer, W., Peeters, F., Schruers, K., van Bemmel, A. L., Myin-Germeys, I., Delespaul, P., van Os, J., & Wichers, M. (2014). A therapeutic application of the experience sampling method in the treatment of depression: a randomized controlled trial. *World Psychiatry*, 13(1), 68–77.

Laurent, J., Catanzaro, S. J., Joiner, T. E., Rudolph, K. D., Potter, K. I., Lambert, S., Osborne, L., & Gathright, T. (1999). A measure of positive and negative affect for children: scale development and preliminary validation. *Psychological Assessment*, 11(3), 326–338.

Lauritsen, M. (2013) Autism spectrum disorders. *European Child &Adolescent Psychiatry*, 22, 37–42.

Lind, S. E., Williams, D. M., Bowler, D. M., & Peel, A. (2014). Episodic memory and episodic future thinking impairments in High-Functioning Autism Spectrum Disorder:

An underlying difficulty with scene construction or self-projection? *Neuropsychology*, 28 (1), 55–67.

Lind, S. E., Bowler, D. M., & Raber, J. (2014). Spatial navigation, episodic memory, episodic future thinking, and theory of mind in children with autism spectrum disorder: evidence for impairments in mental simulation? *Frontiers in Psychology*, 5, 1411.

MacMullin, J. A., Lunsky, Y., & Weiss, J. A. (2016). Plugged in: Electronics use in youth and young adults with autism spectrum disorder. *Autism*, 20(1), 45–54.

Palmier-Claus, J. E., Myin-Germeys, I., Barkus, E., Bentley, L., Udachina, A., Delespaul, P. A. E. G., Lewis, S. W., & Dunn, G. (2011). Experience sampling research in individuals with mental illness: Reflections and guidance. *Acta Psychiatrica Scandinavica*, 123(1), 12–20.

Reid, S. C., Kauer, S. D., Dudgeon, P., Sanci, L. A., Shrier, L. A., & Patton, G. C. (2009). A mobile phone program to track young people's experiences of mood, stress and coping: development and testing of the mobiletype program . *Social Psychiatry and Psychiatric Epidemiology*, 44(6), 501–507.

Reid, S. C., Kauer, S. D., Hearps, S. J. C., Crooke, A. H. D., Khor, A. S., Sanci, L. A., & PatternG. C. (2011). A mobile phone application for the assessment and management of youth mental health problems in primary care: a randomised controlled trial. *BMC Family Practice*, 12, 131–143.

Woodcock, R. (2011). *Woodcock Reading Mastery Tests (WRMT-III)* 3rd Edition. San Antonio, TX: Pearson Education.

6

EXPERIENCE SAMPLING IN THE STUDY OF SLEEP AND WAKEFULNESS

Lee Mulligan, Gillian Haddock, Donna Littlewood and Simon D. Kyle

What is sleep?

Sleep is a complex, universal behaviour described as "a reversible state of perceptual disengagement from, and unresponsiveness to, the environment" (Carskadon & Dement, 2011). Although the exact function of sleep remains elusive, it is fundamental for human health and wellbeing and necessary for the repair of numerous biological, psychological, emotional and cognitive processes (Colrain, 2011).

Two interacting processes govern sleep, which together regulate sleep and wakefulness. One process is the homeostatic drive for sleep, or "sleep pressure" (Borbély, 1982). In essence, sleep pressure begins at the onset of wakefulness and increases throughout the day, until the next onset of sleep. The other is the circadian system; our internal body clocks are synchronised to the earth's solar period (roughly 24 hours), which is regulated through exposure to day and night (Czeisler et al., 1999). This system facilitates the onset of sleep and wakefulness through the regulation of body temperature and production of sleep promoting hormones (i.e. melatonin).

Sleep and ESM

Given the interdependence of sleep and wake regulation, time-sampling research affords the opportunity to probe relationships between sleep processes and mechanisms known to contribute to mental health difficulties. Indeed, accumulating sleep pressure may affect several cognitive and attentional processes (Van Dongen & Dinges, 2005). Furthermore, there is a wealth of causal evidence that experimental sleep and circadian disruption engenders symptom change in a variety of populations (Pilcher & Huffcutt, 1996; Dinges et al., 1997; Petrovsky et al., 2014) and conversely, stress induction predicts subsequent sleep disturbance (Hall et al., 2007).

Therefore, mapping the dynamic bi-directionality between sleep and psychiatric symptoms over time holds significant promise in advancing our understanding of transdiagnostic processes underlying mental health problems (Harvey, Murray, Chandler & Soehner, 2011).

Despite the aforementioned research opportunities, few researchers have considered sleep in their ESM methodological designs or have studied sleep as a variable of interest (Mulligan, Haddock, Emsley, Neil & Kyle, 2016; Russell, Wearden, Fairclough, Emsley & Kyle, 2016; Hennig & Lincoln, in press; Short, Allan & Schmidt, in press). We now review the small number of studies that have utilised ESM to examine sleep and mental health, illustrate their respective strengths, and outline their novel contribution to our understanding of mental health problems. Specifically, we review studies published in the fields of major depression and psychosis.

Major depression

Disturbed sleep is both a feature of, and a risk factor for, a range of affective disorders, including major depression and bipolar disorder. Specifically, insomnia contributes to the onset, maintenance, and relapse of major depression (Baglioni et al., 2011; Franzen & Buysse, 2008). Given that sleep and affect can fluctuate both within and between days, ESM studies can capture the temporal features of this relationship, which other methodological designs may miss (Peeters, Berkhof, Delespaul, Rottenberg & Nicolson, 2006). However, to date, there exist only four studies in this area, reporting divergent results.

Firstly, Bouwmans and colleagues (2017) examined bi-directional relationships between subjective sleep quality and both positive and negative affect in 27 people with depression and a gender and age matched sample of healthy controls. Participants completed daily self-report measures of sleep quality on waking, and affect three times per day for 30 days. Changes in sleep quality (identified through deviations in mean score) significantly predicted changes in both positive and negative affect, independent of group. However, the reverse relationship was not significant; changes in positive and negative affect failed to predict changes in sleep quality.

These findings are in contrast to an earlier study conducted in adults with major depression ($n = 35$), minor depression ($n = 25$) and healthy controls ($n = 36$), which indicated that diagnoses may moderate the association between sleep and affect (Bower, Bylsma, Morris & Rottenberg, 2010). In this study, subjective sleep quality was measured once at baseline, and only the ratings of positive and negative affect were included in the sampling design, collected ten times per day, across a three-day period. Results showed a significant association between sleep quality and both positive and negative affect. However, when controlling for diagnosis, the relationship between sleep quality and negative affect was no longer statistically significant. This is consistent with results from an earlier ESM study investigating diurnal mood variation in people with depression, which indicated that neither sleep duration, nor sleep quality, predicted subsequent daily affect (Peeters et al., 2006).

Lastly, Cousins and colleagues (2011) examined relationships between diagnoses (i.e. "anxiety disorder", "major depression" and "no diagnosis"), affect and sleep in a sample of 94 young people. The authors used actigraphy to estimate objective sleep parameters and participants completed ratings of affect up to 24 times across two four-day assessment periods. They found that negative affect predicted subsequent sleep (specifically, less time awake) in the "major depression" group, but found no other main effects of sleep parameters in predicting subsequent affect, or vice versa, in other diagnostic groups. The authors also reported a number of significant interaction effects between diagnosis and parameters of sleep (i.e. sleep onset latency, total sleep time and wake-time after sleep onset) in predicting levels of affect, and levels of affect in predicting subsequent sleep (i.e. sleep onset latency and wake-time after sleep onset). However, the pattern of these interaction effects differed depending on diagnoses (i.e. "anxiety disorder" or "major depression").

Psychosis

Researchers have used ESM to examine biopsychosocial predictors of psychotic symptoms (Oorschot, Kwapil, Delespaul & Myin-Germeys, 2009). Sleep disturbance is highly prevalent in people who experience psychosis (Wulff, Dijk, Middleton, Foster & Joyce, 2012), and a wealth of cross-sectional studies demonstrate an association between sleep and psychotic symptoms across the psychosis continuum (Davies, Haddock, Yung, Mulligan & Kyle, 2016; Reeve, Sheaves & Freeman, 2015). However, cross-sectional studies are vulnerable to recall bias and are unable to examine relationships on a micro-scale. ESM studies integrating sleep measures have the potential to clarify the dynamic relationship between sleep and psychosis, and provide opportunities to examine potential mechanisms, which could inform novel targets for intervention.

Despite this considerable promise, only two published studies have integrated ESM and sleep measures in individuals experiencing psychosis. Firstly, Waters and colleagues (2011) investigated the relationship between objectively estimated sleep parameters (via actigraphy) and composite psychosis scores, across 28 days, in a small sample of people experiencing psychosis ($n = 6$). They found preliminary evidence that reduced sleep efficiency and total sleep time predicted increased next-day psychosis severity. Nevertheless, it is unclear how this paper accounted for the multilevel structure of its data, which could render these findings invalid.

In a larger and more robust study, Mulligan and colleagues (2016) recruited 22 individuals with an established schizophrenia-spectrum diagnosis. The authors screened participants for sleep disorders, other than insomnia, and excluded those who endorsed any other sleep-wake problem (i.e. sleep apnoea, circadian rhythm disturbances, hypersomnia). All participants provided objective (via actigraphy) and subjective (via sleep diary) recordings of sleep, alongside momentary ratings of affect, psychotic symptoms and functioning for seven days and nights. This study showed that subjective and objective sleep disturbance significantly predicted next-day psychotic symptoms and functioning. Moreover, levels of negative affect upon wakening mediated these relationships.

By integrating sleep measures and ESM, the aforementioned studies are the first to illustrate ecologically valid, temporal relationships between sleep parameters, psychosis and functioning. Not only do these findings provide empirical support for clinical conceptualisations of psychosis (Freeman, Garety, Kuipers, Fowler & Bebbington, 2002), but they also imply that interventions targeting sleep could also have the potential to enhance recovery outcomes for people with schizophrenia (Freeman et al. 2015).

Practical considerations of studying sleep using ESM

Despite this being a novel, exciting and burgeoning area of research interest, there have been no published guidelines to inform future work. The following section fulfils this important gap in the literature and provides the first guidance on how to implement an ESM sleep study. This includes practical considerations when conducting ESM sleep research, covering issues such as methodological design, variable choice, equipment, time schedules, and procedural adaptations. However, researchers should keep in mind their own specific research questions when choosing which aspects of this guidance to follow or adapt.

Designing an ESM sleep study

When designing an ESM sleep study, two cyclical periods of assessment require consideration: (1) the assessment of daytime processes (measuring daytime level variables); and (2) the assessment of night-time processes (measuring night-time level variables).

Daytime level variables

Daytime level variables comprise those most typically assessed within ESM studies taking place during the day or within waking hours. For instance, these might include measures of mental state (e.g. mood, mental health symptoms) and functioning (e.g. cognitive, social, personal) with the expectation that such variables could fluctuate within and between days. In a similar way, researchers can include a number of daytime level sleep variables in their ESM diaries to examine proxy measures of sleep and the consequences of disturbed sleep operating across the day. Indeed, it is often helpful to measure variables such as "napping", "fatigue", "tiredness" and "sleepiness" at multiple time points each day, given their variability and potential impact on both concomitant variables (e.g. affect, mental health symptoms, functioning) and prospective night's sleep (Werth, Dijk, Achermann, & Borbely, 1996).

Night-time level variables

To complement daytime level variables, researchers can also examine night-time level variables (i.e. assessments of processes occurring during the night) to provide a direct and informative measure of the sleep–wake cycle. Night-time level sleep variables can be subjective or objective in nature (Miller, Kyle, Melehan & Bartlett, 2014). However, the integration of subjective and objective methods is important to ensure adequate and valid examination of the sleep–wake cycle and permit the examination of discrepancies between subjective and objective sleep variables (Buysse, Ancoli-Israel, Edinger, Lichstein & Morin, 2006).

Subjective sleep methods

Subjective sleep measures provide information about sleep patterns and sleep quality, and do so without great time or expense. Sleep diaries, which retrospectively measure sleep data over time, provide the most comprehensive measure of sleep and are fundamental to understanding the subjective complaints of participants. With their low cost and ease of administration, sleep diaries are less influenced by recall bias and allow for the examination of weekday and weekend data. Consequently, sleep diaries are the "gold standard" subjective measure of sleep (Carney et al., 2012) and are ideal utilised within ESM protocols (for an example, see Mulligan et al., 2016).

Sleep diaries permit the recording of several subjective sleep variables (for a full list and definitions, see Table 6.1). These include measures of sleep onset latency (SOL), wake-time after sleep onset (WASO), sleep efficiency (SE), total sleep time (TST), time spent in bed (TIB) and a numerical estimation of overall sleep quality. Typically, participants complete sleep diaries in the morning to provide subjective and temporal approximations of the previous night's sleep. However, participants can also complete an evening diary to provide measures of caffeine intake and physical activity, variables often associated with prospective night sleep (Kredlow, Capozzoli, Hearon, Calkins & Otto, 2015).

When developing their ESM diary, researchers may wish to consult the existing sleep diary literature to inform their choice of night-time level subjective sleep items. Until recently, sleep diary items have remained largely unstandardised, which has made comparison between studies and translation to clinical practice especially difficult. However, we recommend using items taken from the Consensus Sleep Diary (CSD; Carney et al., 2012), as these have been developed through expert consensus in an attempt to standardise subjective sleep measurement. Nevertheless, the CSD items still require validation, testing and refinement. We also suggest presenting sleep diary items to participants in the morning, prior to the formal ESM sampling period, to ensure temporally relevant subjective approximations of previous night's sleep.

TABLE 6.1 List of sleep–wake/circadian rhythm variables and definitions

Sleep Parameters (as measured by sleep diary or actigraphy)

Sleep Efficiency (SE)	Actual sleep time expressed as a percentage of time in bed, with higher percentages indicating greater efficiency of sleep
Sleep Fragmentation (SF)	An index of time spent mobile during the sleep period, with higher values indicating greater fragmentation and sleep discontinuity
Sleep Onset Latency (SOL)	An indication (in minutes) of the length of time from "lights out" to the onset of sleep
Sleep Quality (SQ)	A numerical, subjective estimation of overall sleep quality, ranging from 1 (very poor) to 5 (very good)
Time spent In Bed (TIB)	An indication (in minutes) of the length of time from "lights out" to "lights on"
Total Sleep Time (TST)	An indication (in minutes) of the amount of sleep time during a sleep episode. TST is equal to TIB minus the awake time
Wake-time After Sleep Onset (WASO)	An indication (in minutes) of the amount of wake time, following the first initial onset of sleep

Circadian Rhythm Metrics (as measured by actigraphy)

L5 (least 5 average)	Average level of activity during the least active five hours within the 24-hour period. Higher values indicate more restlessness during sleep
L5 start time	The start time of L5, indicating the start of the five least active (most restful) hours
M10 (most 10 average)	Indicates level of activity during the most active 10 hours of wake, with higher values indicating a greater level of activity
M10 start time	The start time of the M10, indicating the start of the 10 most active hours
Inter-daily stability (IS)	The degree of stability in the sleep–wake rhythm across days. The IS has a range of zero to one, where zero indicates the absence of any discernible rhythm and one indicates perfectly stable rhythmicity
Intra-daily variability (IV)	The level of fragmentation in rest-activity periods within the 24-hour cycle. The IV has a range of zero to one, where higher values indicate more fragmented periods of rest activity. For example, if an individual experiences a single consolidated sleep period and a single wake period, the IV value will be close to zero. Conversely if sleep is highly fragmented throughout the 24-hour cycle, the IV value will be closer to one
Relative amplitude (RA)	Amplitude denotes the difference in activity level between the L5 and the M10. E.g. if an individual has restful sleep periods and active wake periods, amplitude will be higher. If sleep periods are restless and wake periods inactive, the amplitude will be lower. The RA is calculated as an average across days of measurement

Objective sleep methods

In comparison to subjective sleep measures, objective sleep measures can facilitate the direct measurement of sleep activity (including electrical brain activity) and sleep–wake patterns. Overnight polysomnography (PSG) remains the gold standard measure of sleep; however, its laboratory-based procedures are resource-intensive, lack ecological validity and are impractical for home implementation. To include objective sleep measures within ESM protocols, we suggest using measures that profile daily sleep–wake patterns, prospectively, over time.

Actigraphy utilises an accelerometer device to record patterns of light, sleep and wake behaviour. Actigraphs are watch-like devices worn continuously by participants to provide 24-hour recordings of rest-activity across several days, weeks or months (Ancoli-Israel, Cole, Alessi, Chambers, Moorcroft & Pollak, 2003). To maximise validity, participants can use an event marker on the watch device to signify periods in bed and number of awakenings throughout each night. All data are downloadable to a computer software package and validated algorithms can estimate objective sleep–wake parameters (Miller et al., 2014).

The use of actigraphy permits the estimation of several night-time level, objective sleep parameters. These include SOL, WASO, SE, TST, TIB and sleep fragmentation (SF). Because actigraphy records rest-activity rhythms throughout each day, calculation of circadian rhythm metrics (e.g. timing and amplitude of sleep–wake cycle) is also possible (see Table 6.1). As such, actigraphy presents a viable method for the objective recording of sleep and circadian rest-activity in naturalistic settings. This is widely recognised as its main strength comparative to PSG (Ancoli-Israel et al., 2015) and currently the most suitable objective measure to utilise within ESM studies.

Choosing methods and equipment

Recent developments in sleep monitoring equipment have led to the generation of novel methods that provide the integrated function of administering and recording momentary assessments, alongside objective measures of sleep. This potentially overcomes some of the practical issues of incorporating additional sleep equipment alongside traditional ESM devices (such as diaries, phones, watches or palm held computers). The Patient Reported Outcome (PRO) Diary is a compact wristwatch that combines both actigraphy and ESM assessments on a single device (CamNtech, Cambridge). The PRO-Diary can be programmed to present multiple questions at regular intervals across a given time period. In a similar way to traditional ESM methods, participants complete entries when prompted by an electronic alarm, using the slider and select keys on the watch display. Therefore, the PRO-diary provides a platform for the administration and recording of ESM assessments, alongside the continuous assessment of sleep–wake patterns. Preliminary studies utilising the PRO-diary have demonstrated high feasibility in a range of clinical and non-clinical samples (Jungquist, Pender,

Klingman & Mund, 2015; Mulligan et al., 2016; Kratz, Ehde, Bombardier, Kalpakjian & Hanks, in press).

Time schedules

Several ESM guidance papers describe the implementation of a sampling window comprising ten assessments per day, usually between the hours of 07:30am and 22:30pm (Palmier-Claus et al., 2011). However, there is recent evidence that people complete significantly fewer assessments in the morning (Edwards, Cella, Tarrier & Wykes, 2016), possibly due to discord between the sampling window and sleep patterns of individual participants. This is particularly true of certain samples, such as those experiencing psychosis, where wake time can be markedly delayed (Benca, 1992). Therefore, sleep–wake patterns may be an important moderator of compliance issues associated with ESM.

If researchers wish to examine sleep using ESM, they should consider the individual sleep–wake patterns of participants and contemplate adjusting their sampling windows accordingly. This is especially important in instances where the assessment window could inadvertently confound both sleep and ESM variables, and where, consequently, the study design could distort the recorded data or alter the habitual sleeping patterns of participants. Whilst some researchers have considered this issue (e.g. Ben-Zeev, Ellington, Swendsen & Granholm, 2011), only one has personalised the ESM assessment windows to correspond with the approximate times of sleep offset and onset of individual participants (Mulligan et al., 2016). Notably, comparative to other ESM studies investigating those with a diagnosis of schizophrenia, this study reported a superior adherence rate (74%), potentially demonstrating an additional benefit of adjusting ESM windows based on individual sleep–wake patterns.

Although the authors acknowledge this represents a departure from conventional ESM guidance, there is currently no available evidence to suggest a significant disadvantage of personalising ESM assessment windows (Kimhy, Myin-Germeys, Palmier-Claus & Swendsen, 2012), especially given its theoretical and scientific rationale in ESM studies examining sleep–wake patterns or processes operating across the 24-hour period. Indeed, investigating the pattern of symptoms across the day may give us insight into the circadian dys(regulation) of symptoms and help to develop novel, real-time interventions (Murray, 2007).

Executing the ESM procedure

Briefing

As described in Chapter 2 of this book, ESM procedures begin with a briefing phase in which the method of data collection is explained to participants. We recommend that during this phase, researchers should also introduce and socialise participants to the sleep method(s). For subjective sleep diary items, confusion about sleep recordings can be minimised if researchers share an example of a completed sleep diary (or complete a "dummy" sleep diary with participants, based on their previous night's sleep). Researchers should also explain the importance of completing the subjective sleep items each morning and collaboratively generate solutions to any identified obstacles. Exploring the morning routine of each participant could identify suitable places to keep the ESM diary to prompt completion upon wakening. For actigraphy, we suggest giving participants sufficient time to become familiar with the watch, its interface and display. We also recommend providing explicit instructions to participants (e.g. not to wear the device during "water activities") to mitigate the risks of significant data loss or damage to study equipment. Furnishing participants with written and accessible instructions can provide an important reference point throughout the study period.

Follow-up calls

The authors often employ follow-up calls to highlight and solve problems arising during sampling and to explore and resolve compliance issues with the ESM and sleep method(s). In the context of ESM sleep research, we suggest employing a larger number of contacts throughout the study period (with participant consent), given the concurrent measurement of both ESM and sleep variables and the potential for significant data loss.

Debriefing

The debriefing session gives researchers the opportunity to check the ESM and sleep methods and ensure that the minimum numbers of entries were completed. If not, the researcher can request participants complete one further day and night of assessment (assuming that this procedure was previously approved by an appropriate research ethics board). Researchers can also prompt completion of the sleep diary items for the previous night's sleep, if these were not completed. Any open-ended questions should also be reviewed to ascertain any ambiguities in responses (e.g. because of illegible handwriting).

Challenges of studying sleep using ESM

As outlined in this chapter, ESM sleep studies represent a novel approach to examine the dynamic and bidirectional links between sleep and mental health problems. However, these study designs can pose a number of challenges. The authors now consider these challenges and offer guidelines for overcoming them.

Compliance

Compliance is a challenge shared by all ESM studies and predictors of compliance remain largely elusive (Hartley et al., 2014). However, compliance difficulties are not exclusive to ESM research and are equally prevalent in longitudinal studies of sleep. For instance, evidence suggests the completion of sleep diaries can be variable in both clinical and non-clinical samples (Jerome et al., 2009; Wichniak et al., 2011). Reasons for poor compliance include participants forgetting to complete their diary each day (possibly completing several days at one time) and confusion regarding the sleep parameters being estimated (Meltzer, Mindell & Levandoski, 2007). Moreover, actigraphy watches are prone to data loss, most often due to non-compliance (i.e. people not wearing the device), technical difficulties, or unintentional breakages (Sadeh & Acebo, 2002). Consequently, actigraphy studies have variable completion rates (range 40%–80%; Gorczynski, Faulkner, Cohn & Remington, 2014), especially in groups with severe and enduring mental health diagnoses (Tahmasian, Khazaie, Golshani & Avis, 2013).

Researchers can use a number of strategies to maximise compliance and minimise data loss (Ward, Evenson, Vaughn, Rodgers & Troiano, 2005). By carefully considering sleep items and study equipment, and by making adaptations to the time schedules and execution of the ESM procedure (see practical considerations above), researchers can maximise the rigour of their ESM sleep studies, as there is preliminary evidence that implementing these strategies can result in high rates of compliance (Mulligan et al., 2016).

Statistical power

Unlike other independent or dependent variables, self-report sleep parameters can only be reliably measured at one time point (e.g. upon waking) whilst objective sleep parameters are composite scores pertaining to one sleep episode (i.e. each night). This has important implications for statistical power, as meaningful relationships between sleep and daytime variables can only be examined at the day-level (i.e. level two) and not at the beep-level (level three; see Chapter 3 for more information). Although not a limitation per se, researchers can overcome this shortfall in statistical power by ensuring they conduct an appropriate a priori power calculation. This ensures that their sample size is sufficient to examine statistical significance. Nonetheless, if adequately powered, multi-level modelling performed at the day-level is still superior to traditional cross-sectional statistical analyses, as it can maximise data availability by tolerating missing data without excluding whole cases (Snijders & Bosker, 2000).

Specifying the nature of sleep difficulty

The implementation of sleep methods and ESM items allow for the examination of sleep disruption. However, the causes of such disruption are heterogeneous, as several sleep difficulties could account for the measurement of disturbance (e.g. insomnia, circadian rhythm disturbances, parasomnia, periodic limb movement disorder or sleep apnoea). In order to test specific hypotheses regarding the relationship between sleep and mental health, researchers should ensure they specify the nature of sleep disturbance and control for the presence of other sleep disorders. This is a considerable challenge as sleep disorders can only be reliably determined via PSG, often co-occur, and exist on a continuum (Miller et al., 2014). However, the implementation of screening measures could help to minimise the heterogeneity of sleep complaints within a particular sample and control for the level of other sleep difficulties. This would help specify the nature of sleep disturbance within a particular group, minimise additional error variance (as the presence of other sleep disorders has the potential to interact with sleep and other ESM variables, in unpredictable and potentially opposing directions, which is likely to reduce signal-to-noise contrast) and permit a more valid examination of a priori hypotheses.

For any ESM study examining sleep, and in the absence of PSG, we suggest using the Brief Screen for Sleep Disorders (Wilson et al., 2010), an interview measure designed to identify the presence and level of underlying sleep disorder. This would allow researchers to identify "possible" signs of sleep disorder pathology, which they could control for, or use to inform decisions regarding study exclusion.

Conclusion

ESM is a potentially powerful research methodology with the unique capacity to examine bidirectional relationships between sleep–wake patterns and daytime variables. There is promising evidence for the feasibility of conducting ESM sleep studies, including high completion rates in difficult to engage populations experiencing psychosis (Mulligan et al., 2016) and major depression (Bouwmans et al., 2017). In this chapter, the authors have presented the first guidance on how to implement an ESM sleep study, paying close attention to issues such as methodological design, measurement of daytime level and night-time level sleep variables, equipment choice, time schedules and execution of the ESM procedure. They have also considered the challenges of implementing ESM sleep research and potential solutions. We hope that this chapter will serve as a catalyst for future ESM sleep studies, as this area holds significant promise in advancing our understanding of sleep and mental health processes operating across the whole 24-hour period. Our view is that as wearable devices undergo further refinement, we will possess the ability to integrate high-resolution data on sleep EEG, circadian physiology (e.g., temperature, autonomic function, rest-activity) and symptoms over multiple days to yield fundamental insights for mental health science.

References

Ancoli-Israel, S., Cole, R., Alessi, C., Chambers, M., Moorcroft, W., & Pollak, C. P. (2003). The role of actigraphy in the study of sleep and circadian rhythms. *Sleep*, 26(3), 342–392.

Ancoli-Israel, S., Martin, J. L., Blackwell, T., Buenaver, L., Liu, L., Meltzer, L. J., ... Taylor, D. J. (2015). The SBSM guide to actigraphy monitoring: clinical and research applications. *Behavioral Sleep Medicine*, 13(sup1), S4–S38.

Baglioni, C., Battagliese, G., Feige, B., Spiegelhalder, K., Nissen, C., Voderholzer, U., ... & Riemann, D. (2011). Insomnia as a predictor of depression: a meta-analytic evaluation of longitudinal epidemiological studies. *Journal of Affective Disorders*, 135(1), 10–19.

Ben-Zeev, D., Ellington, K., Swendsen, J., & Granholm, E. (2011). Examining a cognitive model of persecutory ideation in the daily life of people with schizophrenia: a computerized experience sampling study. *Schizophrenia Bulletin*, 37(6), 1248–1256.

Benca, R. M. (1992). Sleep and psychiatric disorders. *Archives of General Psychiatry*, 49(8), 651.

Borbély, A. A. (1982). A two-process model of sleep regulation. *Human Neurobiology*, 1(3), 195–204.

Bouwmans, M. E., Bos, E. H., Hoenders, H. R., Oldehinkel, A. J., & de Jonge, P. (2017). Sleep quality predicts positive and negative affect but not vice versa. An electronic diary study in depressed and healthy individuals. *Journal of Affective Disorders*, 207, 260–267.

Bower, B., Bylsma, L. M., Morris, B. H., & Rottenberg, J. (2010). Poor reported sleep quality predicts low positive affect in daily life among healthy and mood-disordered persons. *Journal of Sleep Research*, 19(2), 323–332.

Buysse, D. J., Ancoli-Israel, S., Edinger, J. D., Lichstein, K. L., & Morin, C. M. (2006). Recommendations for a standard research assessment of insomnia. *Sleep: Journal of Sleep and Sleep Disorders Research*, 29, 1155–1173.

Carney, C. E., Buysse, D. J., Ancoli-Israel, S., Edinger, J. D., Krystal, A. D., Lichstein, K. L., & Morin, C. M. (2012). The consensus sleep diary: standardizing prospective sleep self-monitoring. *Sleep*, 35(2), 287–302.

Carskadon, M. A., & Dement, W. C. (2011). Normal human sleep: An overview. In M. H. Kryger, T. Roth & W. C. Dement (Eds.), *Principles and Practice of Sleep Medicine* (Fifth Edition) (pp. 16–26). Missouri: Elsevier Saunders.

Colrain, I. M. (2011). Sleep and the brain. *Neuropsychology Review*, 21(1), 1–4.

Cousins, J. C., Whalen, D. J., Dahl, R. E., Forbes, E. E., Olino, T. M., Ryan, N. D., & Silk, J. S. (2011). The bidirectional association between daytime affect and nighttime sleep in youth with anxiety and depression. *Journal of Pediatric Psychology*, 36(9), 969–979.

Czeisler, C. A., Duffy, J. F., Shanahan, T. L., Brown, E. N., Mitchell, J. F., Rimmer, D. W., ... Emens, J. S. (1999). Stability, precision, and near-24-hour period of the human circadian pacemaker. *Science*, 284(5423), 2177–2181.

Davies, G., Haddock, G., Yung, A. R., Mulligan, L. D., & Kyle, S. D. (2016). A systematic review of the nature and correlates of sleep disturbance in early psychosis. *Sleep Medicine Reviews*, 31, 25–38.

Dinges, D. F., Pack, F., Williams, K., Gillen, K. A., Powell, J. W., Ott, G. E., ... & Pack, A. I. (1997). Cumulative sleepiness, mood disturbance and psychomotor vigilance performance decrements during a week of sleep restricted to 4–5 hours per night. *Sleep: Journal of Sleep Research & Sleep Medicine*, 20(4), 267–277.

Edwards, C. J., Cella, M., Tarrier, N., & Wykes, T. (2016). The optimisation of experience sampling protocols in people with schizophrenia. *Psychiatry Research*, 244, 289–293.

Franzen, P. L., & Buysse, D. J. (2008). Sleep disturbances and depression: risk relationships for subsequent depression and therapeutic implications. *Dialogues in Clinical Neuroscience*, 10(4), 473.

Freeman, D., Garety, P. A., Kuipers, E., Fowler, D., & Bebbington, P. E. (2002). A cognitive model of persecutory delusions. *British Journal of Clinical Psychology*, 41(4), 331–347.

Freeman, D., Waite, F., Startup, H., Myers, E., Lister, R., McInerney, J., ... & Foster, R. (2015). Efficacy of cognitive behavioural therapy for sleep improvement in patients with persistent delusions and hallucinations (BEST): a prospective, assessor-blind, randomised controlled pilot trial. *The Lancet Psychiatry*, 2(11), 975–983.

Gorczynski, P., Faulkner, G., Cohn, T., & Remington, G. (2014). Examining strategies to improve accelerometer compliance for individuals living with schizophrenia. *Psychiatric Rehabilitation Journal*, 37(4), 333.

Hall, M., Thayer, J. F., Germain, A., Moul, D., Vasko, R., Puhl, M., ... & Buysse, D. J. (2007). Psychological stress is associated with heightened physiological arousal during NREM sleep in primary insomnia. *Behavioral Sleep Medicine*, 5(3), 178–193.

Hartley, S., Varese, F., Vasconcelos e Sa, D., Udachina, A., Barrowclough, C., Bentall, R. P., ... & Palmier-Claus, J. (2014). Compliance in experience sampling methodology: the role of demographic and clinical characteristics. *Psychosis*, 6(1), 70–73.

Harvey, A. G., Murray, G., Chandler, R. A., & Soehner, A. (2011). Sleep disturbance as transdiagnostic: consideration of neurobiological mechanisms. *Clinical Psychology Review*, 31(2), 225–235.

Hennig, T., & Lincoln, T. M. (in press). Sleeping paranoia away? An actigraphy and experience-sampling study with adolescents. *Child Psychiatry & Human Development*.

Jerome, G. J., Rohm Young, D., Dalcin, A., Charleston, J., Anthony, C., Hayes, J., & Daumit, G. L. (2009). Physical activity levels of persons with mental illness attending psychiatric rehabilitation programs. *Schizophrenia Research*, 108, 252–257.

Jungquist, C. R., Pender, J. J., Klingman, K. J., & Mund, J. (2015). Validation of capturing sleep diary data via a wrist-worn device. *Sleep Disorders*, 2015, 1–6.

Kimhy, D., Myin-Germeys, I., Palmier-Claus, J., & Swendsen, J. (2012). Mobile assessment guide for research in schizophrenia and severe mental disorders. *Schizophrenia Bulletin*, 38 (3), 386–395.

Kratz, A. L., Ehde, D. M., Bombardier, C. H., Kalpakjian, C. Z., & Hanks, R. A. (in press). Pain acceptance decouples the momentary associations between pain, pain interference, and physical activity in the daily lives of people with chronic pain and spinal cord injury. *Journal of Pain*.

Kredlow, M. A., Capozzoli, M. C., Hearon, B. A., Calkins, A. W., & Otto, M. W. (2015). The effects of physical activity on sleep: a meta-analytic review. *Journal of Behavioral Medicine*, 38(3), 427–449.

Meltzer, L. J., Mindell, J. A., & Levandoski, L. J. (2007). The 24-Hour Sleep Patterns Interview: A pilot study of validity and feasibility. *Behavioral Sleep Medicine*, 5(4), 297–310.

Miller, C. B., Kyle, S. D., Melehan, K. L., & Bartlett, D. J. (2014). Methodology for the assessment of sleep. In K. Babson & M. Feldner (Eds.), *Sleep and Affect: Assessment, Theory, and Clinical Implications* (pp. 69–84). San Diego: Elsevier Academic Press Inc.

Mulligan, L. D., Haddock, G., Emsley, R., Neil, S. T., & Kyle, S. D. (2016). High-resolution examination of the role of sleep disturbance in predicting functioning and psychotic symptoms in schizophrenia: a novel experience sampling study. *Journal of Abnormal Psychology*, 125(6), 788.

Murray, G. (2007). Diurnal mood variation in depression: A signal of disturbed circadian function? *Journal of Affective Disorders*, 102(1), 47–53.

Oorschot, M., Kwapil, T., Delespaul, P., & Myin-Germeys, I. (2009). Momentary assessment research in psychosis. *Psychological Assessment*, 21(4), 498.

Palmier-Claus, J. E., Myin-Germeys, I., Barkus, E., Bentley, L., Udachina, A., Delespaul, P. A. E. G., ... & Dunn, G. (2011). Experience sampling research in individuals with mental illness: reflections and guidance. *Acta Psychiatrica Scandinavica*, 123(1), 12–20.

Peeters, F., Berkhof, J., Delespaul, P., Rottenberg, J., & Nicolson, N. A. (2006). Diurnal mood variation in major depressive disorder. *Emotion*, 6(3), 383.

Petrovsky, N., Ettinger, U., Hill, A., Frenzel, L., Meyhöfer, I., Wagner, M., ... & Kumari, V. (2014). Sleep deprivation disrupts prepulse inhibition and induces psychosis-like symptoms in healthy humans. *Journal of Neuroscience*, 34(27), 9134–9140.

Pilcher, J. J., & Huffcutt, A. I. (1996). Effects of sleep deprivation on performance: a meta-analysis. *Sleep*, 19(4), 318–326.

Reeve, S., Sheaves, B., & Freeman, D. (2015). The role of sleep dysfunction in the occurrence of delusions and hallucinations: a systematic review. *Clinical Psychology Review*, 42, 96–115.

Russell, C., Wearden, A. J., Fairclough, G., Emsley, R. A., & Kyle, S. D. (2016). Subjective but not actigraphy-defined sleep predicts next-day fatigue in chronic fatigue syndrome: a prospective daily diary study. *Sleep*, 39(4), 937–944.

Sadeh, A., & Acebo, C. (2002). The role of actigraphy in sleep medicine. *Sleep Medicine Reviews*, 6(2), 113–124.

Short, N. A., Allan, N. P., & Schmidt, N. B. (in press). Sleep disturbance as a predictor of affective functioning and symptom severity among individuals with PTSD: An ecological momentary assessment study. *Behaviour Research and Therapy*.

Snijders, T., & Bosker, R. (2000). *Multilevel Analysis*. Thousand Oaks, CA: Sage Publications.

Tahmasian, M., Khazaie, H., Golshani, S., & Avis, K. T. (2013). Clinical application of actigraphy in psychotic disorders: a systematic review. *Current Psychiatry Reports*, 15(6), 359.

Van Dongen, H. P. A., & Dinges, D. F. (2005). Sleep, circadian rhythms, and psychomotor vigilance. *Clinics in Sports Medicine*, 24(2), 237–249.

Ward, D. S., Evenson, K. R., Vaughn, A., Rodgers, A. B., & Troiano, R. P. (2005). Accelerometer use in physical activity: best practices and research recommendations. *Medicine and Science in Sports and Exercise*, 37(11 Suppl.), S582–S588.

Waters, F., Sinclair, C., Rock, D., Jablensky, A., Foster, R. G., & Wulff, K. (2011). Daily variations in sleep–wake patterns and severity of psychopathology: A pilot study in community-dwelling individuals with chronic schizophrenia. *Psychiatry Research*, 187(1), 304–306.

Werth, E., Dijk, D. J., Achermann, P., & Borbely, A. A. (1996). Dynamics of the sleep EEG after an early evening nap: experimental data and simulations. *American Journal of Physiology-Regulatory, Integrative and Comparative Physiology*, 271(3), 501–510.

Wichniak, A., Skowerska, A., Chojnacka-Wójtowicz, J., Tafliński, T., Wierzbicka, A., Jernajczyk, W., & Jarema, M. (2011). Actigraphic monitoring of activity and rest in schizophrenic patients treated with olanzapine or risperidone. *Journal of Psychiatric Research*, 45 (10), 1381–1386.

Wilson, S. J., Nutt, D. J., Alford, C., Argyropoulos, S. V., Baldwin, D. S., Bateson, A. N., … Wade, A. G. (2010). British Association for Psychopharmacology consensus statement on evidence-based treatment of insomnia, parasomnias and circadian rhythm disorders. *Journal of Psychopharmacology*, 24(11), 1577–1601.

Wulff, K., Dijk, D. J., Middleton, B., Foster, R. G., & Joyce, E. M. (2012). Sleep and circadian rhythm disruption in schizophrenia. *British Journal of Psychiatry*, 200(4), 308–316.

7

EXPERIENCE SAMPLING IN THE STUDY OF DYADS AND FAMILY DYNAMICS

Debora Vasconcelos e Sa, Samantha Hartley and Christine Barrowclough

The Experience Sampling Method (ESM) refers to a research technique in which individuals complete multiple self-report measures in everyday, naturalistic settings to provide an ecologically valid representation of emotional, cognitive, contextual, social, or behavioural events and their interactions. ESM may have an advantage in observing phenomena that occur between individuals, as well as internal states and actions. Specifically, there is an opportunity to capture social interactions as they occur, reducing response bias, and providing directly comparable data from two (or more) participants relating to the same window of real-life experience. The current chapter will seek to: (i) review the existing literature demonstrating the importance of researching social relationships in mental health and outline the existing research that has adapted ESM to the simultaneous study of dyads/multiple participants, (ii) highlight this potential application discussing its merits and challenges, (iii) provide guidance on how ESM could be adapted to study dyadic interactions, and (iv) reflect on implementing this type of research from both a researcher and a participant perspective.

Outline of existing research utilising ESM in social interactions

ESM paradigms have elucidated how social company can impact on an individual's affect and symptoms (Collip et al., 2011; Myin-Germeys, Nicolson, & Delespaul, 2001a; Verdoux, Husky, Tournier, Sorbara, & Swendsen, 2003). However, less is known about how the quality of these social contacts might affect people's experiences. Momentary research with individuals experiencing bulimia nervosa suggests that not only is social contact important in the variation of symptoms and mood, but also the quality of social interactions. For example, Okon and colleagues (2003) studied 20 adolescent girls clinically diagnosed with bulimia nervosa using ESM and found that day-to-day family stressors, such as arguments or disagreements, could be important predictors of bulimic symptom variations among those girls who perceived their family environment to be dysfunctional (that is, perceived as having high conflict and low emotional expressiveness). This study highlights the importance of sampling daily interpersonal interactions within key relationships to elucidate how these might impact on the experience of mood and symptoms.

Social stressors in daily life have also been shown to be key contributors to mood and symptom fluctuations in the field of psychosis research. It has been demonstrated that small daily stressors predict negative emotional reactions both in service users with psychosis and in their first degree relatives (Myin-Germeys, van Os, Schwartz, Stone, & Delespaul, 2001b). Furthermore, minor stresses have been found to predict the intensity of psychotic experiences in service users in a state of clinical remission (Myin-Germeys, Delespaul, & van Os, 2005), and with sub-clinical psychotic experiences in persons who are at risk of developing a psychotic disorder (Lataster et al., 2009; Palmier-Claus, Dunn, & Lewis, 2011). These findings promote the value of ESM and suggest that subtle disturbances in the flow of daily life contribute to the variation of mood and symptom experiences. There is rather less research using daily sampling techniques to help us understand how daily life stressors, particularly those that might occur during interactions within key relationships, might impact on mood and symptoms.

Investigating social context and affect/symptom fluctuations using ESM

The quality of the social environment has been highlighted as an important factor in the course of severe mental health problems (Oorschot, Kwapil, Delespaul, & Myin-Germeys, 2009). Research using daily sampling methodologies has proven to be useful in explaining how contextual differences (such as being alone, at home or in a public place) and specific interpersonal interactions (such as with family members, friends or strangers) may influence symptom variations among individuals experiencing psychosis. In one study by Delespaul and deVries (1987), 11 service users with chronic mental illness were compared with non-psychiatric controls to examine how daily experiences vary between these two groups and how changes in the social context impacted their mental state. Compared to controls, service users spent more time alone or at home, and in these instances they reported more pathological thought content, more daydreams and a greater tendency to drift away from thoughts about current activities. Although daydreaming increased markedly when service users were at home or alone, it shifted to a more focused thinking when they were with others or out of the house. Service users also reported feeling better when away from home and with others, compared to controls. In a similar study, deVries and Delespaul (1989) compared nine service users with a diagnosis of acute schizophrenia with seven non-psychiatric individuals and found that service users tend to spend more time alone than controls. Interestingly, service users felt better when they were in the company of one to three

ES in study of dyads and family dynamics **83**

people, but they felt more 'depressed' when they were alone or with more than three people, suggesting that this may serve as a protective factor for the occurrence of low mood in individuals with psychosis. In contrast, hallucinatory symptoms seem to be an exception to this, as hallucinatory intensity tends to slightly increase if the patient is in the company of others (Delespaul, deVries, & van Os, 2002).

Further studies with more representative samples have shown that even though social engagement, particularly with few people, seems to have a protective effect against the occurrence of psychotic symptoms, this differs according to the type of social company. It has been demonstrated that being in the presence of familiar people, rather than being alone or with strangers, decreased the risk of subsequently experiencing delusions in individuals diagnosed with chronic schizophrenia (Myin-Germeys et al., 2001a). Similarly, Collip and colleagues (2011) found that individuals with medium levels of trait paranoia reported increased paranoid thinking and perceived social threat when in the company of less familiar people. Interestingly, and contrary to earlier findings, for highly paranoid individuals, social company was no longer associated with their paranoid experiences. Studies with at-risk nonclinical populations further showed that the type of social company influences the occurrence of subclinical psychotic experiences in daily life. Individuals at risk of trait paranoia reported higher levels of social threat in the company of less familiar people compared to being with familiar people (Collip et al., 2011). In line with this, being in the presence of unfamiliar people (as opposed to being with familiar company) increased the occurrence of unusual experiences in psychosis-prone individuals (Verdoux et al., 2003). Furthermore, psychosis proneness predicted increases in anxiety and depression scores in situations where the individuals were likely to be confronted with social encounters with people that they did not know well (Husky, Grondin, & Swendsen, 2004).

On the other hand, Verdoux and colleagues (2003) found that in individuals at risk of developing psychosis, change in the social company was a stronger predictor of delusional experiences than social company per se. Specifically, compared to no change in social company, participants' likelihood of experiencing delusions increased when they changed to being with unfamiliar individuals, and decreased by changing to the company of familiar individuals. This contrasts with the finding reported by Myin-Germeys et al. (2001a), which did not find that change in company had any significant effect in predicting delusional moments.

These findings suggest that characteristics of the social context significantly influence the variation of symptoms and affect. Indeed, being in the company of others, especially family members or friends, seems to be beneficial towards preventing the occurrence of psychotic experiences, with the exception of hallucinations. However, for paranoid thinking the social context becomes independent when individuals experience severe symptoms. This highlights the utility of ESM paradigms when investigating social context and affect/symptoms experiences and the interplay between the two. As yet, the research has tended to utilise data from individual participants, who comment on their interactions, rather than mutual perspectives from both parties in the relationship. ESM offers a unique opportunity

The value and challenges of utilising ESM with dyads

ESM is a powerful technique that captures participants' life as it is directly perceived from one moment to the next. This is particularly relevant if the researcher aims to investigate how affect and symptom experiences might be related to social or familial contacts, which by their very nature, occur in real daily life, and not in the laboratory.

The ecological validity of ESM is particularly pertinent in investigating real-time-context perceptions between dyads and in examining how contextual variables, such as being around the family member or experiencing certain behavioural interactions, relate to affect or symptom severity. ESM affords the opportunity to capture dyadic interactions as they naturally occur in the context of daily life (Janicki, Kamarck, Shiffman, & Gwaltney, 2006). Traditional self-report assessments are not momentary or naturalistic in nature, relying heavily on participants' retrospective recollections, and on reports collected in artificial settings, which makes them more susceptible to biases. The prospective and real-time nature of the ESM assessments considerably diminishes the risk of memory and contextual bias. ESM allows for the investigation of these constructs to be carried out in the participants' environment and as part of their everyday routines.

ESM has the benefit of being an inclusive assessment technique, providing not only repeated assessments of internal psychological states, but also of the individuals' context. Thus, ESM is an excellent tool to study reactivity to contextual attributes (Myin-Germeys & van Os, 2007). On the other hand, the multiple moment-to-moment assessments allow not only for between-person investigations to be carried out, but also for the investigation of within-person processes. This is important because within-person analyses have the potential to reveal individual patterns of inner variability that would not become apparent at the mean level of between-person analyses (Scollon, Kim-Prieto, & Diener, 2003). Furthermore, ESM allows examining the temporal order of relationships between variables (Stadler, Snyder, Horn, Shrout, & Bolger, 2012). This is valuable, for instance, if the researcher wants to determine whether a certain variable is a consequence or an antecedent of the patient's symptom experience. In addition, within-person analyses are also sensitive to differences within individuals that emerge over time and across situations, in terms of variability or intensity of behaviour and feelings (Scollon et al., 2003). Mood and symptoms are likely to vary over time so ESM is advantageous to elucidate how these variations relate to situational factors, such as being in the presence or absence of a relative or carer.

Despite the benefits noted above, ESM also has its own pitfalls, particularly its demanding and time-consuming nature. With participants being required to complete repeated self-report questionnaires throughout the day over several days, this methodology becomes heavily reliant on the motivation and self-awareness of the participant. Specifically in relation to dyad research, ESM requires an awareness of the nature of one's interpersonal relationships. Where both members of the dyad participate in the recording of information about the relationship, this could heighten focus on the relationship and result in reactivity or caution in sharing information, despite reassurances about confidentiality. Particular challenges associated with the design and implementation feature are discussed below, with some putative solutions. These reflections and ideas are borne out of a recent study in the context of psychosis (Vasconcelos e Sa, Wearden, Hartley, Emsley, & Barrow-clough, 2016).

Specific design guidelines

The following sections detail specific design issues that should be considered when planning ESM studies with dyads, taking into account the methodological considerations outlined in previous chapters.

Equipment choices and selection

Experience sampling can be implemented in a number of different ways, from a simple pen and paper diary to a handheld computer or an individual's own smartphone. There may be particular considerations relating to equipment when working with pairs of individuals. ESM using computerised or smartphone technologies (ESMc) overcomes some limitations of paper formats and can record precise 'time-stamps' at the moment when the data is actually entered. This feature makes it feasible to investigate the interactions between dyads by synchronising the times of both devices. An additional benefit of ESMc is the capacity to ensure confidentiality with respect to participant responses (Kimhy, Myin-Germeys, Palmier-Claus, & Swendsen, 2012), making it particularly suitable to study dyads and provide reassurance that comments on social interactions are not accessible by the other member of the dyad, thus potentially reducing reactivity or demand characteristics.

Sampling scheme

ESM research guidelines suggest employing the traditional semi-random stratified sampling strategy to investigate dyads (Kimhy et al., 2012; Palmier-Claus et al., 2010). This strategy allows participants to provide their responses at 'unpredictable' time points, where the signal appears to be random to the participant, but is established and therefore known by the researcher. Studies investigating dyads can employ the traditional semi-random stratified sampling strategy prompting participants 10 times per day over six consecutive days, including one weekend (Kimhy et al., 2012; Palmier-Claus et al., 2010). The inclusion of weekends in the sampling scheme is recommended to provide a more inclusive and accurate representation of the dyad's typical weekly activity and to enable potential differences between weekday and weekend routines to be captured. Participants can be aware of the number of prompts per day, but unaware of the sampling scheme, other than that it is 'unpredictable', with prompts occurring at varying intervals (within parameters of 15–90 minutes) from each other. Depending on the baseline information regarding the amount and nature of the contact between the two members of the dyad, the sampling scheme could be tailored to ensure collection of varied data that captures both interactions and periods alone.

In research with dyads the daily sampling assessments can be synchronised for both participants (patient and relative) to ensure that each member is prompted to respond at the same time points. That is, each member of the dyad can be signalled at the same pseudo-random momentary time point to provide independent self-reports about their feelings, experiences, and dyadic interactions multiple times throughout the day. This approach allows for dyadic contact and interactions to be captured as they naturally occur within the context of participants' daily life, and provides an ecologically valid representation of these interactions, overcoming the recall bias and overestimation issues associated with traditional retrospective assessments (Ben-Zeev, McHugo, Xie, Dobbins, & Young, 2012). Synchronised sampling provides shared snapshots of the same moment, providing insight into the interplay between affect and symptom experiences, and behavioural responses within the dyad. Similarly to the traditional semi-random stratified sampling strategy described above, dyads of participants can be made aware of the synchronised approach, but be unaware of the sampling scheme, other than that it would be 'unpredictable'.

In order to facilitate a paired sampling scheme, there is a need to balance the requirements of both individuals, which may result in the scheme being less than ideal for both members of the pair. One solution may be to employ differing schedules for each group, although this would introduce bias and also reduce the amount of time that each dyad may respond to the same events (and thus provide mirrored data). Essentially, dyad research may require that the response opportunities for both parts of the pair do not fully fit their usual individual routines, but this is balanced with maximising the opportunity of capturing contact between the pair, which in some circumstances may mean ensuring weekend days and evenings are captured. Whether this pattern is repeated for the whole of the sample or managed idiosyncratically for each pair is a separate issue, and one that relates to issues of bias, generalisability and also the practicalities of producing tailored schedules. The study reported in Vasconcelos e Sa and colleagues' (2016) paper employed a consistent sampling frame, which ran from 9am to 12pm over six days (therefore always capturing at least one weekend day), which was designed to start later than may be conventional for ESM studies. Feedback relating to the sampling frame was captured using open-ended items (see Tables 7.1 and 7.2).

Historically, in mental health research the sampling scheme has occurred between 7:30 and 22:30, but for research studies with dyads the sampling frame can be adjusted for instance starting at 9:00 and finishing at 24:00. This adjustment

ES in study of dyads and family dynamics **87**

TABLE 7.1 Results of the Likert scale questions

Item	Service user			Relative		
	Mean (standard deviation)	Minimum	Maximum	Mean (standard deviation)	Minimum	Maximum
I was comfortable with completing the project alongside my relative	5.71 (1.33)	3	7	6.42 (0.97)	4	7
The fact that my relative was taking part in the project influenced the way I answered the questions	2.29 (1.60)	1	6	2.00 (1.59)	1	7
I was able to understand the questions	5.93 (1.92)	1	7	6.33 (1.17)	4	7
I found it easy to input my responses in the Palm device	6.04 (1.29)	3	7	6.33 (1.17)	3	7
I found using the Palm device comfortable	5.67 (1.52)	1	7	6.08 (1.21)	4	7
I would like to take part in a similar project in the future	4.63 (1.57)	1	7	5.17 (1.61)	1	7

will ensure that the sampling occurs during times at which dyads are likely to be together, taking into consideration two important aspects: some participants might work and therefore be away during typical working hours (9:00 to 17:00); on the other hand sleep disturbances are a common feature in people mental health difficulties (Jagannath, Peirson, & Foster, 2013; Monti et al., 2013) and medication side effects, such as sleepiness and slowness, also tend to be evident in this population (Monti & Monti, 2004). Thus, it is expected that for some of the participants the typical sleeping and waking hours would differ from those of other populations. In spite of this, all participants should be advised not to change their daily or sleeping routines to fit in the sampling scheme, as this would diminish the validity of the data provided. As far as possible, the sampling scheme should be adapted to suit the dyad's usual waking and sleeping patterns, balancing individual needs with the aim of capturing maximum data relevant to interactions.

TABLE 7.2 Themes arising from content analysis of participant feedback

Major themes (frequency)	Examples
1. Participating was easy/ straightforward/ alright/generally a positive experience (28)	'Straightforward ... You just get on with it, it's part of your everyday life for six days' 'It was easy to use and not too much impact on my everyday life'
2. Using the palm/completing the questions was sometimes difficult/intrusive/ repetitive (20)	'It went off at some awkward times – yesterday it went off when I was at the theatre ... I filled it in but it was a bit irritating' 'Quite tedious doing the same questions over and over'
3. Using the palm/completing the questions was helpful and/or encouraged reflections/understanding (8)	'Made me more aware of my feelings – I stopped and reflected' 'It's positive – gives people an insight into feelings, day-to-day'
4. Using the palm/completing the questions made aware of negative feelings (2)	'Filling it out ... reminded me of my illness' 'Didn't realise what a sad life I had – talk about depressed'
5 Some specific aspects of the question wording/project design were appropriate/related to experiences (6)	'The type of questions were very realistic to the person caring for someone with psychosis' 'The questions were good as I could relate to them'
6. Specific aspects of the questions wording/ project design were inappropriate/ frustrating (8)	'The palm didn't allow you to go back to a page if you had made a mistake' 'Because of the medications, I missed a lot of the morning beeps so it would be good to have the beeps adjusted to your schedule'
7. Participating alongside a relative was positive (1)	'It was fun doing it alongside mum – a joint project, had a laugh about it'
8. Participation based on a desire to help others/increase understanding (4)	'Research might help; got to test things out to make sure things work' 'I hope this information is of future help to both participants and carers'
9. Participation was burdensome (2)	'Filling it in was too much' 'Too much'

Assessment format

Given the strengths outlined above, the computerised assessment format seems to be more suitable than paper assessment for studying dyads. When designing a study with dyads, researchers should keep in mind that some of the self-report questions may probe about sensitive and private topics, such as current distressing experiences or perceptions of behavioural responses on the part of others, and as a consequence participants' answers could be less accurate if there is the potential for confidentiality breaches and data sharing. Therefore, to ensure that participants' confidentiality is maintained a computerised format seems to be more appropriate to deliver the ESM self-assessments.

Dyads briefing and debriefing

It has been highlighted that participants might be deterred from using electronic devices due to concerns about their ability to successfully handle the equipment (Kimhy et al., 2012; Palmier-Claus et al., 2010). To ensure that participants are familiar and feel at ease with the equipment, a detailed standardised briefing procedure should be developed and carried out with each participant individually ensuring that all participants are briefed in the same manner. Briefing procedures should include a brief script and checklist with the topics that ought to be covered during the initial visit. It is advisable that, if appropriate, briefing takes place at the participants' home (except if participants request otherwise or if there is any indication of risk) and it is always conducted separately (with an additional joint discussion) for each member of the dyad. This extra measure ensures that confidentiality between members of the dyad is established from the start and allows participants to raise any concerns freely. The purpose of this briefing visit is to introduce the equipment to participants, explain the ESM self-assessment questions layout and coding system (rating scales and open-ended questions) and to invite participants to have a practice trial. This will ensure that all of the questions are understood and that participants feel confident in using the devices and completing the self-report questions over the sampling procedure.

Throughout the briefing visit a number of key principles relevant to ESM can be highlighted. It is crucial to emphasise that the synchronised sampling requires the self-assessments be provided independently (without conferring) and be kept private. This is one of the main strengths in applying ESM with dyads, and it allows capturing both participants' perspectives of the same moment, whilst preserving participants' confidentiality. Furthermore, it is important to emphasise that the synchronised sampling requires the self-assessments to be completed as soon as possible after participants have heard the signalling prompt. This is imperative, since ESM aims to capture a moment in time, and the emotions, experiences, activities and thought processes concurrent with this. The longer between signal and question completion, the more temporally distant the participant is from the target moment (the moment just before the signal). This may introduce more error and recall bias. Participants should be encouraged to fill the questions out as soon as possible. Hypothetical situations ought to be explored where participants may not be able to respond (for example, if driving or in the shower), and participants should be encouraged to complete the questions at their earliest convenience. At those times where a long period of time has passed since the signal, the participant should discount that question set and wait for the next signal. When working with dyads, it may also be important to emphasise that participants should complete the ESM items whenever they feel able (rather than relying on reminders from the other participant, or following their lead with regards to response completion), which could result in reduced quantity and validity of the data collected. Furthermore, there is a need to encourage individualised responses, not based on discussion or reflection within the dyad, or formulation of a shared perspective (since the divergence is often where the interest lies).

Finally, participants should be reminded of the importance of completing as many self-reports as possible without changing their usual routines. The rationale for this is to acquire psychological phenomena as they naturally unfold in the realm of daily life, increasing the ecological validity of the data. Typically, participants are instructed to start completing the ESM questions the day after the briefing session.

An individual debriefing visit should be arranged for after the ESM phase (usually the six days period) to collect the devices and to conduct any remaining post-ESM phase assessments. If one member of the dyad chooses to discontinue the study prior to the end-point, the research team might still encourage the other participant to continue, as meaningful (although more limited) data on interactions can be garnered from one perspective. Additionally, consideration should be given to whether or not to recognise participants' involvement with a monetary or other reward, especially given the somewhat laborious nature of ESM.

Item development

Within ESM, the design of the items assessment is crucial. As stated above, the value of ESM lies predominantly with its ability to assess changes in phenomena over brief time periods where stressors may occur, and predict these fluctuations. This requires that responses to items will vary sufficiently over the assessment period, and thus should not be too 'extreme' in nature as this would result in more static response patterns and consequently insufficient variance for analysis. This issue may be particularly important in dyads research, where people are asked to respond in relation to the other member of the dyad and, therefore the need to provide socially desirable/acceptable answers may be amplified. For example, a participant may be unlikely to respond variably to the item 'I am criticising the other participant', in contrast to a more moderate item; 'I am nagging the other participant'. Indeed, in Vasconcelos e Sa and colleagues' (2016) study a key target phenomenon was Expressed Emotion (EE) and behaviourally controlling interactions, which are usually elicited in a lengthy semi-structured interview, the Camberwell Family Interview (CFI; Vaughn & Leff, 1976), with criteria imposed by the rater. EE is a robust multi-component measure of family emotional environment, which reflects relatives' critical, hostile and emotionally over-involved attitudes towards a family member with mental illness (Leff & Vaughn, 1985). Assessing these items in the context of daily life using self-report momentary assessments relied heavily on tapping these phenomena in an acceptable way, using concepts such as 'nagging him/her', 'keeping an eye on him/her' and 'encouraging him/her', which use colloquial language to express tempered versions of the relational styles that can cumulatively convey the same phenomena, but which can individually be responded to in a way that is likely to vary over the time period. This can be achieved by piloting the potential items with anonymous participants/stakeholders or consultants or by running focus groups during the initial phase of the study, involving those who are experts by experience. Positively and negatively worded items should also be included to ensure that some variability in the participants' reports is captured over the sampling period. However, if one aim of the research is to differentiate between groups, then more polarising items might be warranted.

Another key aspect of ESM item development is that the items accurately convey the desired meaning to the recipient, and that their structure, tone and content are acceptable to the population they will be used with. The route to achieving this is to involve service users and carers within the design of the ESM items. More generally, service user involvement within mental health services and particularly in research is a key objective, for example, for the UK Department of Health (1999) and the Patient-Centered Outcomes Research Institute in the USA. The potential benefits of service user involvement in research can be reaped by both the service users themselves, the wider population whom they are appointed to represent, the research team, the research field as a whole and the study participants (see for example, Glasby & Lester, 2004). Within ESM specifically, service users can comment on the acceptability and appropriateness of the items. Within dyad research, there should be a concerted effort to involve representatives from 'both sides', consulting carers, relatives and significant others in the lives of service users.

Wherever there are specific areas of interest (e.g. attempts at behavioural control from the carer towards the service user) there might be an opportunity to use mirrored items. For instance, if the service user was asked in the moment to rate 'just before the beep went off [*the other member of the dyad*] was nagging me', the other dyad member (e.g. carer or a relative) can be asked to rate 'just before the beep went off I was nagging him/her'. The use of mirrored items is advantageous in research with dyads as it captures reported and perceived behaviours within dyadic interactions, and provides information on data corroboration and divergence.

To recognise sampling opportunities, participants can be asked to indicate whether or not they had been with the other member of the dyad since the last beep, although this may increase participants' self-awareness biasing their assessments. In past research, authors have defined contact between dyad members as any situation where they were directly spending time or doing things together, including telephone or voice/multimedia over Internet contact (Janicki et al., 2006; Larson, Richards, & Perry-Jenkins, 1994), although if specific types of contact (e.g. touch/ body language) are being investigated, then the definition of contact might need to be adapted. Once contact has been established, questions can then 'branch' to probe more specific aspects of the interaction, such as conversation, perceived control, and influence or encouragement etc.

Analysis

There is a specific chapter in this book that explores the various analysis routes and procedures and therefore the current section will not cover these in detail. However, in particular relevance to work with dyads, researchers should carefully consider their analysis plan prior to any statistical testing or exploratory work. This need arises from the sheer wealth of data produced by ESM dyad research; a dataset that could be mined relentlessly and without clear theoretical oversight in the absence of in-depth planning. Specific areas to consider might be the method of defining relative contact, the source of data in interactions (i.e. the carer's report, the service user's, or both?) and in what ways, using what moderation and mediation formulas, the relationships between variables will be analysed. The analysis strategy can first investigate associations between the predictor and outcome variables, followed by an examination of the moderating effects. For further details please refer to Vasconcelos e Sa et al. (2016).

Participants' experiences of taking part in ESM dyad research

Below we report on participants' experiences of taking part in an ESM dyad study. The full study is reported elsewhere (Vasconcelos e Sa et al., 2016). To summarise, the authors investigated whether contact with high-EE relatives, and relatives' behaviourally controlling interactions related to service users' experiences of psychosis and to both service users' and relatives' levels of affect. Twenty-one service users experiencing psychosis and their closest relatives provided synchronised self-reports of symptoms (service users only), affect, dyadic contact and behavioural controlling interactions over a six-day period. Findings from this study showed that patient reports of relatives taking control of them and helping them were associated with increased patient negative affect and symptoms. Relatives' self-reports of nagging, taking control and keeping an eye on the patient were related to fluctuations in relatives' affect. No evidence was found for the moderating effect of EE status on the association between dyadic contact and affect or, in the case of service users, symptoms. When measured using an ecologically valid methodology, momentary behaviourally controlling interactions within dyads experiencing psychosis can impact on service users' affect and symptoms. As part of this study, we carried out a careful analysis of the acceptability of ESM in dyads, as outlined below.

Retention and engagement

Retention and engagement might be a key indicator of the feasibility and utility of dyad ESM research. In the study discussed here (Vasconcelos e Sa, et al., 2016) there were 29 dyads successfully recruited, of which eight dropped out during the ESM phase mainly due to becoming unwell or not providing enough data reports, although relatives were allowed to remain in the study if they wished to. Clearly this procedure may not be tolerated by all participants and thus considerations will need to be given to the representativeness of the samples analysed. However, engagement in the method was good, with the majority of both patients and relatives completing over half of the 60 assessments ($M = 40.1$, SD $= 10.6$; $M = 45.4$, SD $= 7.9$, respectively). This compares favourably with similar ESM research where relatives were not involved, with a mean completion rate of 24.26 (SD $= 16.98$; Hartley et al., 2013).

Quantitative and qualitative participant feedback

Participants were provided with a post-ESM phase questionnaire, which explored their experience of taking part and impressions of using the technology and answering questions relating to their relative, involving both Likert scale items (scored from 1 – Not at all to 7 – Very much so) and open-ended questions (see Appendix for full questionnaire). The results of the Likert scale questions can be seen in Table 7.1.

Content analysis was applied to the answers to the open-ended questions and then subjected to inter-rater reliability checks by an independent rater, using the coding frame developed by the first two authors, which demonstrated a 90% agreement rate. A list of the major themes emerging from this analysis, and examples thereof, can be seen in Table 7.2. The results of the quantitative items indicate that both service users and relatives were comfortable taking part in the project, and able to engage in the procedures. Although not subject to differential statistical analysis, there appears to be a trend for service users to offer a less positive perspective on the process. In terms of qualitative feedback, the content analysis revealed frequent mention of both the difficult aspects of the procedure alongside the positive aspects of the experience. Of particular relevance to the current discussion, one participant identified completing the research alongside their relative as a positive experience and eight noticed an impact on reflective processes and understanding.

Future directions in research with dyads using ESM

Previous research suggests that dyadic ESM research with those experiencing serious mental health problems and their relatives is feasible and produces valuable insights into interactions in the context of daily life. This research will surely expand, alongside technological advances, to include other problem areas, such as chronic fatigue syndrome or myalgic encephalomyelitis (Band, Barrowclough, Emsley, Machin, & Wearden, 2016), and combine with additional ambulatory assessment methods, such as sleep monitoring (Mulligan, Haddock, Emsley, Neil, & Kyle, 2016) to yield a rich dataset that can be explored in many (hopefully theoretically-driven) ways.

Use of ESM with dyads in the context of mental health problems, and the results of recent research in this area suggest that interactions may be experienced as a stressor although also an opportunity for management. The use of ESM is another potential route for intervention, whereby an immediate intervention could reduce the impact of these stressors on the experience of psychosis. Recently, the role of using ESM to deliver mobile interventions has been emphasised; this would be advantageous, for instance, in providing individualised therapeutic interventions, exercises, tasks or immediate strategies to cope with distressing symptoms (Bucci et al., 2015; Oorschot, Lataster, Thewissen, Wichers, & Myin-Germeys, 2012) and complicated interactions with significant others, possibly in tandem with active family therapy work.

References

Band, R., Barrowclough, C., Emsley, R., Machin, M., & Wearden, A. J. (2016). Significant other behavioural responses and patient chronic fatigue syndrome symptom fluctuations in the context of daily life: An experience sampling study. *British Journal of Health Psychology*, 21(3), 499–514. doi:10.1111/bjhp.12179

Ben-Zeev, D., McHugo, G. J., Xie, H., Dobbins, K., & Young, M. A. (2012). Comparing retrospective reports to real-time/real-place mobile assessments in individuals with schizophrenia and a nonclinical comparison group. *Schizophrenia Bulletin*, 38(3), 396–404.

Bucci, S., Barrowclough, C., Ainsworth, J., Morris, R., Berry, K., Machin, M., ... & Haddock, G. (2015). Using mobile technology to deliver a cognitive behaviour therapy-informed intervention in early psychosis (Actissist): study protocol for a randomised controlled trial. *Trials*, 16(1), 404.

Collip, D., Oorschot, M., Thewissen, V., Van Os, J., Bentall, R., & Myin-Germeys, I. (2011). Social world interactions: How company connects to paranoia. *Psychological Medicine*, 41(5), 911–921. doi:10.1017/S0033291710001558

Delespaul, P., & deVries, M. (1987). The daily life of ambulatory chronic mental patients. *Journal of Nervous and Mental Disease*, 175(9), 537–544.

Delespaul, P., deVries, M., & van Os, J. (2002). Determinants of occurrence and recovery from hallucinations in daily life. *Social Psychiatry and Psychiatric Epidemiology*, 37(3), 97–104.

Department of Health. (1999). *Patient and Public Involvement in the NHS*. London: Department of Health.

deVries, M., & Delespaul, P. (1989). Time, context, and subjective experience in schizophrenia. *Schizophrenia Bulletin*, 15(2), 233–244. doi:10.1093/schbul/15.2.233

Glasby, J., & Lester, H. (2004). Cases for change in mental health: partnership working in mental health services. *Journal of Interprofessional Care*, 18(1), 7–16.

Hartley, S., Varese, F., Vasconcelos e Sa, D., Udachina, A., Barrowclough, C., Bentall, R. P., Lewis, S. N. W., Dunn, G., Haddock, G., & Palmier-Claus, J. (2013). Compliance in experience sampling methodology: the role of demographic and clinical characteristics. *Psychosis*, 1–4. doi:10.1080/17522439.2012.752520

Husky, M. M., Grondin, O. S., & Swendsen, J. D. (2004). The relation between social behavior and negative affect in psychosis-prone individuals: an experience sampling investigation. *European Psychiatry*, 19(1), 1–7.

Jagannath, A., Peirson, S. N., & Foster, R. G. (2013). Sleep and circadian rhythm disruption in neuropsychiatric illness. *Current Opinion in Neurobiology*, 23(5), 888–894.

Janicki, D. L., Kamarck, T. W., Shiffman, S., & Gwaltney, C. J. (2006). Application of ecological momentary assessment to the study of marital adjustment and social interactions during daily life. *Journal of Family Psychology*, 20(1), 168–172. doi:10.1037/0893–3200.20.1.168

Kimhy, D., Myin-Germeys, I., Palmier-Claus, J., & Swendsen, J. (2012). Mobile assessment guide for research in schizophrenia and severe mental disorders. *Schizophrenia Bulletin*, 38 (3), 386–395.

Larson, R. W., Richards, M. H., & Perry-Jenkins, M. (1994). Divergent worlds: The daily emotional experience of mothers and fathers in the domestic and public spheres. *Journal of Personality and Social Psychology*, 67(6), 1034–1046. doi:10.1037/0022–3514.67.6.1034

Lataster, T., Wichers, M., Jacobs, N., Mengelers, R., Derom, C., Thiery, E., Van Os, J., & Myin-Germeys, I. (2009). Does reactivity to stress cosegregate with subclinical psychosis? A general population twin study. *Acta Psychiatrica Scandinavica*, 119(1), 45–53. doi:10.1111/j.1600–0447.2008.01263.x

Leff, J., & Vaughn, C. (1985). *Expressed Emotion in Families*. New York; London: The Guilford Press.

Monti, J. M., BaHammam, A. S., Pandi-Perumal, S. R., Bromundt, V., Spence, D. W., Cardinali, D. P., & Brown, G. M. (2013). Sleep and circadian rhythm dysregulation in schizophrenia. *Progress in Neuro-Psychopharmacology and Biological Psychiatry*, 43, 209–216.

Monti, J. M., & Monti, D. (2004). Sleep in schizophrenia patients and the effects of antipsychotic drugs. *Sleep Medicine Reviews*, 8(2), 133–148.

Mulligan, L., Haddock, G., Emsley, R., Neil, S., & Kyle, S. (2016). High-resolution examination of the relationship between sleep disturbance, functioning and psychotic symptoms in schizophrenia: a novel experience sampling study. *Journal of Abnormal Psychology*, 125(6), 788–797. doi:10.1037/abn0000180

Myin-Germeys, I., Delespaul, P., & van Os, J. (2005). Behavioural sensitization to daily life stress in psychosis. *Psychological Medicine*, 35(5), 733–741.

Myin-Germeys, I., Nicolson, N. A., & Delespaul, P. (2001a). The context of delusional experiences in the daily life of patients with schizophrenia. *Psychological Medicine*, 31, 489–498. doi:10.1017/S0033291701003646

Myin-Germeys, I., & van Os, J. (2007). Stress-reactivity in psychosis: Evidence for an affective pathway to psychosis. *Clinical Psychology Review*, 27(4), 409–424.

Myin-Germeys, I., van Os, J., Schwartz, J. E., Stone, A. A., & Delespaul, P. A. (2001b). Emotional reactivity to daily life stress in psychosis. *Archives of General Psychiatry*, 58(12), 1137–1144. doi:10.1001/archpsyc.58.12.1137

Okon, D. M., Greene, A. L., & Smith, J. E. (2003). Family interactions predict intraindividual symptom variation for adolescents with bulimia. *International Journal of Eating Disorders*, 34(4), 450–457.

Oorschot, M., Kwapil, T., Delespaul, P., & Myin-Germeys, I. (2009). Momentary assessment research in psychosis. *Psychological Assessment*, 21(4), 498–505. doi:10.1037/a0017077

Oorschot, M., Lataster, T., Thewissen, V., Wichers, M., & Myin-Germeys, I. (2012). Mobile assessment in schizophrenia: A data-driven momentary approach. *Schizophrenia Bulletin*, 38(3), 405–413. doi:10.1093/schbul/sbr166

Palmier-Claus, J. E., Dunn, G., & Lewis, S. W. (2011). Emotional and symptomatic reactivity to stress in individuals at ultra-high risk of developing psychosis. *Psychological Medicine*, 42(5), 1003–1012. doi:10.1017/S0033291711001929

Palmier-Claus, J. E., Myin-Germeys, I., Barkus, E., Bentley, L., Udachina, A., Delespaul, P., Lewis, S. W., & Dunn, G. (2010). Experience sampling research in individuals with mental illness: Reflections and guidance. *Acta Psychiatrica Scandinavica*, 123(1), 12–20. doi:10.1111/j.1600–0447.2010.01596.x

Scollon, C. N., Kim-Prieto, C., & Diener, E. (2003). Experience sampling: promises and pitfalls, strengths and weaknesses. *Journal of Happiness Studies*, 4, 5–34.

Stadler, G., Snyder, K. A., Horn, A. B., Shrout, P. E., & Bolger, N. P. (2012). Close relationships and health in daily life: A review and empirical data on intimacy and somatic symptoms. *Psychosomatic Medicine*, 74(4), 398–409.

Vasconcelos e Sa, D., Wearden, A., Hartley, S., Emsley, R., & Barrowclough, C. (2016). Expressed Emotion and behaviourally controlling interactions in the daily life of dyads experiencing psychosis. *Psychiatry Research*, 245, 406–413. doi:10.1016/j.psychres.2016.08.060

Vaughn, C., & Leff, J. (1976). Measurement of expressed emotion in families of psychiatric-patients. *British Journal of Social and Clinical Psychology*, 15(2), 157–165. doi:10.1111/j.2044-8260.1976.tb00021.x

Verdoux, H., Husky, M., Tournier, M., Sorbara, F., & Swendsen, J. D. (2003). Social environments and daily life occurrence of psychotic symptoms: An experience sampling test in a non-clinical population. *Social Psychiatry and Psychiatric Epidemiology*, 38(11), 654–661. doi:10.1007/s00127-00003-0702-0708

8

EXPERIENCE SAMPLING IN THE STUDY OF SELF-HARM

Daniel Pratt and Peter Taylor

Self-harm refers to a range of self-injurious behaviours including both those with and without suicidal motives (e.g. suicide attempts, Royal College of Psyciatrists, 2010; National Collaborating Centre for Mental Health, 2011). It represents one of the extremes of human behaviour and is a substantial health problem affecting individuals and societies around the world. Self-harm is surprisingly common, with an estimated lifetime prevalence of 17% (CI: 8–26%) in adolescents and 13% (CI: 5–22%) in young adults for non-suicidal forms of self-harm (Swannell, Martin, Page, Hasking & St John, 2014), and the rate of suicide in the UK has remained at 10–15 per 100,000 for more than 30 years (Office for National Statistics, 2016). Self-harm is one of the strongest predictors of eventual death by suicide; risk of dying by suicide is 66 times more likely in individuals with medically serious self-harm compared to the general population (Hawton, Zahl, & Weatherall, 2003). Moreover, even though an intent to die may not be present with self-harm, this is a behaviour that still carries a risk of accidental death (Kehrberg, 1997). Those who self-harm are at heightened risk of death by any cause compared to the general population (Bergen et al., 2012). Self-harm is also a marker of significant emotional distress, associated with a range of other psychological difficulties (Bentley, Nock & Barlow, 2014; Bernal et al., 2007; Borges et al., 2010).

Self-harm covers a complex spectrum of behaviours, which vary in form (e.g. overdoses, self-cutting) and suicidal intent. Nonetheless, self-harm is still a behaviour, and as such is amenable to psychological theory and research. Such research is vital in building an understanding of what causes and maintains self-harm, and in supporting the development and evaluation of interventions for those struggling with these behaviours. As noted elsewhere in this book, the Experience Sampling Method (ESM) is a powerful research tool that has the potential to reveal momentary psychological processes as they occur in real-time (Csikszentmihalyi & Larson, 2014; deVries & Delespaul, 1989; Myin-Germeys et al., 2009; Palmier-

98 Daniel Pratt and Peter Taylor

Claus et al., 2011). Within this chapter we begin by defining the subtypes of behaviour and thought that make up self-harm, and introduce some of the controversies around how self-harm is conceptualised. Next, we outline both the advantages and challenges of using ESM in this area. We then provide examples of ESM research that has been undertaken on self-harm, including examples of item design and wording. Lastly, we provide a series of recommendations for future ESM research into self-harm.

Defining self-harm and its subtypes

Within this chapter, we use the term self-harm to broadly refer to the range of self-harming behaviours and cognitions. Problems of definition have beset the study of suicidal and self-injurious behaviour, with varying and inconsistent use of definitions, operationalisations and associated terminology. One of the first papers to provide a detailed description of '*deliberate self-harm*' (Pattison & Kahan, 1983) defined it as a distinctive type of self-destructive behaviour, distinguished by direct and repetitive self-injurious acts with low lethality. Furthermore, self-harm was considered to be accompanied by a personal awareness of the effects of the behaviour, and involve a conscious intent to harm oneself. This definition distinguished self-harm from suicidal behaviours (e.g. suicide attempts) with an emphasis on low lethality and the absence of a conscious intent to die. The prefix 'deliberate' has been largely dropped from self-harm because of concerns that it was judgemental and because the extent to which the behaviour is intentional is not always clear (National Collaborating Centre for Mental Health, 2011). There has been debate around the extent to which self-harming behaviour can be classed as suicidal or non-suicidal (Kapur et al., 2013). These discussions have informed the current usage of the word 'self-harm' to refer to both suicidal and non-suicidal acts (e.g. National Collaborating Centre for Mental Health, 2011; Royal College of Psyciatrists, 2010). This therefore represents a change in the literature from the previous use of self-harm to refer explicitly to non-suicidal behaviours.

In the USA, the past few decades have seen growing use of the term *non-suicidal self-injury* (NSSI) to refer to intentional self-inflicted damage to the surface of the body, that is performed with the expectation that the injury will lead to only minor or moderate physical harm, and in the absence of suicidal intent. Indeed, the suggestion of a potentially distinct NSSI disorder has been made within the 5th edition of the DSM (APA, 2013). Here we use self-harm as an over-arching term encompassing both NSSI and suicide attempts.

Which self-harm thoughts and behaviours are most amenable to ESM approaches?

Clearly, self-harm represents a broad range of different behaviours and cognitions, and ESM may be more applicable to some of these than others. Perhaps the main challenge when applying ESM in this context is the low base rate of some experiences. Suicide attempts, for example, are relatively rare events, even amongst groups of individuals considered to be at particularly high risk. For example, in a review of studies concerning repetition of medically serious self-harm (self-harm requiring hospital attention) just 16% of individuals (median across studies) repeated self-harm in the following year (Owens, Horrocks & House, 2002). This low base rate has an effect on statistical power which is a well-recognised problem in the literature (Goldsmith, Pellmar, Kleinman & Bunney, 2002). Notably, this can be a problem even for longitudinal research with relatively large samples (Borges et al., 2006; Stoep et al., 2011). As ESM focuses on a specified period of time that is typically short in duration (one or two weeks) it would be highly unlikely that infrequent phenomena, such as a suicide attempt, would take place during the study, even with a high-risk sample. There are additional problems with using ESM to study suicide attempts, since the severity of these behaviours (e.g. overdose) create a practical and ethical barrier to any participant continuing to complete an ESM study.

This does not mean, though, that ESM carries no potential for better understanding serious self-harm (e.g. suicide attempts). One possibility is to define groups based on the presence of past, retrospectively assessed, suicide attempts (or subsequent attempts within a longer-term longitudinal design) and to use ESM to compare momentary processes concerning important mechanistic variables between these groups. Husky and colleagues (2014) compared individuals with recent and past suicide attempts to controls using ESM. In this instance, ESM may still provide a valuable window into individuals' lives, and pick up upon mechanisms (e.g. repetitive thinking, unstable affect) that may be better studied through the more focused lens offered by ESM.

Other self-harm phenomena may be better suited to ESM research. Suicidal ideation appears a relatively frequent occurrence. A Europe-wide survey (Casey et al., 2008) identified the prevalence of suicidal ideation in the general population, within a two-week period, as varying between 1.1% (Urban Spain) and 19.8% (Urban Ireland). This prevalence appears higher for similar time frames in clinical populations, such as those at ultra-high-risk of developing psychosis (66%; Taylor, Hutton & Wood, 2015). In one ESM study, 74.2% of depressed inpatients reported suicidal ideation at least once in the week-long ESM period (Ben-Zeev, Young & Depp, 2012). In another study, suicidal ideation was reported for 7.8% of entries in individuals with a recent suicide attempt (Husky et al., 2014). This latter study may have produced a lower prevalence because the ideation question was only asked of those already indicating low mood and because the item did not appear to cover more passive forms of suicidal ideation. In young people with a history of NSSI, suicidal ideation was reported on average once per week within a two-week ESM period (Nock, Prinstein & Sterba, 2009). These suicidal cognitions are still, arguably, clinically important outcomes for research because they may represent a step towards suicidal behaviour within a putative suicidal continuum (O'Connor & Nock, 2014), though the presence of such a continuum remains uncertain (Sveticic & De Leo, 2012). Suicidal ideation is also a marker of distress and impairment in functioning (Reinherz et al., 1995).

Non-suicidal self-injury (NSSI) is typically more frequent than suicide attempts, and is especially prevalent in certain clinical groups such as those diagnosed with Borderline Personality Disorder (Nock, Joiner, Gordon, Lloyd-Richardson & Prinstein, 2006), no doubt in part because it is included as a diagnostic criterion. In a sample of individuals diagnosed with Borderline Personality Disorder an average of one act of NSSI was reported over the 21-day ESM period, with urges to NSSI even more common with a mean endorsement of 2.6 (Zaki, Coifman, Rafaeli, Berenson & Downey, 2013). In another sample diagnosed with personality disorders, 31% of participants reported at least one episode of NSSI over the 21-day ESM period, and 29% reported at least one NSSI urge (Snir, Rafaeli, Gadassi, Berenson & Downey, 2015). Another study in this population identified an average of one NSSI act and 1.5 NSSI urges over a three-week period (Zaki et al., 2013). In this latter study, the low rates necessitated combining urges and acts into a single outcome, suggesting that low rates of NSSI may still be a challenge for researchers. Amongst students and young people with a history of NSSI, 47% (one-week ESM period) to 87% (two week period) reported at least one instance of NSSI (Armey, Crowther & Miller, 2011; Nock et al., 2009). Lower rates of NSSI acts were reported in individuals with an eating disorder, of whom 15% reported at least one NSSI act during the two-week ESM period (Muehlenkamp et al., 2009). In students and young people with a history of NSSI, thoughts or urges were reported on an average of 1.2 days out of 14 (Bresin, Carter & Gordon, 2013) through to an average of five times per week (Nock et al., 2009). Bresin and colleagues reported that the low rate of NSSI acts necessitated the focus on urges instead.

Overall, although NSSI acts and urges have been frequent compared to other forms of self-harm, ESM research into these phenomena has been possible. However, these rates are still low with many studies suggesting a high rate of zero responses (no NSSI within the study period) even within high-risk samples, and some authors have had to combine outcomes or focus on NSSI *urges* rather than *acts* as a consequence of these low incidence rates. These low rates may impact on statistical power in these studies. One solution may be a longer ESM period than the traditional one to two weeks (e.g. five or six weeks). This would likely necessitate fewer daily entries to avoid over-burdening participants, which in turn may result in a greater reliance on retrospective recall (i.e., participants having to think back across longer periods of time), depending on the design of the study.

Notably, the above studies have employed both time-contingent sampling, whereby assessments are completed at time points (often random or pseudo-random, but sometimes fixed) across a day, and event-based sampling that invites participants to complete diary entries immediately following the occurrence of a targeted event (e.g. self-harm episode or suicidal thought). Event-based sampling has the advantage of ensuring important data is captured that relates to the phenomenon of specific interest, but places a requirement on the participant to remember to complete the diary at the correct time-point (which may be challenging given the likely emotional distress experienced by the participant at this time). Of course, time-based and event-based sampling strategies can be combined

Experience sampling in study of self-harm **101**

into perhaps the most comprehensive data collection strategy (e.g. Nock et al., 2009), although participant burden and the acceptability of the diary must also be considered.

Self-harm covers a broad spectrum of behaviour, and there are numerous self-harm-like acts that can also be explored using ESM. For example, ESM has been used to better understanding eating disorder related behaviours including binging and purging (De Young et al., 2013), and to examine predictors of drinking behaviour and problems (Simons, Gaher, Oliver, Bush & Palmer, 2005). As with some forms of self-harm, ESM is well suited to situations where the focus is on discrete, time-limited behaviours and experiences. The question of whether the mechanistic variables, that are more typically associated with self-harm, underlie these other behaviours is an important research question in its own right (there is evidence that thoughts around bingeing/purging co-occur with NSSI-related thoughts; Shingleton et al., 2013).

Why ESM is well suited to studying self-harm

One of the key reasons why ESM might be a useful tool for studying self-harm is that this often concerns discrete and time-limited events. ESM can track these phenomena in real-time, as they occur, in the context of people's daily lives. In the past, the majority of research into self-harm has been cross-sectional and reliant on retrospective accounts. For example, questionnaires will ask people whether they have ever attempted suicide, or engaged in NSSI, over the past year or past month. It is well cited in the literature that such retrospective accounts can be prone to recall bias (see Santangelo, Ebner-Priemer & Trull, 2013). For self-harm, behaviours which are taboo and deemed socially undesirable in many societies, there may be an added pressure towards under-reporting or toning down past behaviours. For example, an urge to self-harm that felt very strong in the moment may, with distance from the event, be later deemed to have been a passing fancy that is not worth troubling the researcher with. Contrary to this possibility, though, Palmier-Claus and colleagues (2013) reported that an ESM assessment of self-harm ideation ('I have had thoughts about harming myself') was associated with retrospective reports of suicidal ideation ($OR = 2.40$), suggesting the two do show some convergence.

The capacity to track the ebb and flow of self-harm in real time provides an opportunity to better understand these phenomena as they naturally occur. In particular, it allows the investigation of moment-to-moment change in variables of interest. An example of this is research concerning changes in mood states in response to self-harm, particularly NSSI (Armey et al., 2011; Muehlenkamp et al., 2009; Nock et al., 2009). These studies have shown that particular emotional states peak prior to episodes of NSSI and then decline afterwards, supporting the theory that such behaviours serve an emotional-regulation function (Hamza & Willoughby, 2015). The capacity to capture change in variables of interest means that ESM can also be applied to investigate how instability (or fluctuation) in variables may contribute to problems like self-harm. One example of this would be variability in mood, which has been positively associated with self-harm ideation (Palmier-Claus, Taylor, Varese & Pratt, 2012b). Whilst self-report questionnaires exist that are designed to assess mood variability, ESM allows variability in mood states to be directly calculated based on momentary ratings of affect (Palmier-Claus et al., 2012b). Palmier-Claus and colleagues (Palmier-Claus, Taylor, Gooding, Dunn & Lewis, 2012a; Palmier-Claus et al., 2013), for example, have demonstrated that daily variability (estimated using the mean-squared successive difference between data points) in negative affect is associated with suicidal ideation and thoughts about self-injury, over and above the average intensity of daily negative affect.

There may be variables hypothesised to cause or maintain self-harm that are better assessed using ESM, particularly those that have a 'state-like' quality and are prone to fluctuations within a short space of time. These include mood states, but also specific cognitive processes, such as self-criticism, which could be studied in this way (Adams, Abela, Auerbach & Skitch, 2009). Dissociation is another state-like variable that has been linked to self-harm and could be explored in the context of self-harm (Armey & Crowther, 2008; Snir et al., 2015). ESM can help to uncover the social and psychological context surrounding such behaviour and thoughts. For example, demonstrating that automatic positive reinforcement motivations are associated with NSSI frequency (Selby, Nock, & Kranzler, 2014) or that thoughts of NSSI are more common when alone (Shingleton et al., 2013).

Ethical challenges and reactivity

We must also pay some attention to the disadvantages of ESM when studying self-harm and suicide, which may include the burdensomeness of the intensive repeated measurement of daily experiences (several times per day over several days or even weeks), and ensuring the security and confidentiality of potentially sensitive data.

Reactivity, the potential for the ESM procedure to actively effect individuals' experiences, is discussed elsewhere in this book (see Chapter 2), but is also a pertinent issue for the study of self-harm. A particular concern is the possibility that using ESM could increase the risk of harm to participants. This is a common trepidation that affects self-harm research more widely, although there does not seem to be strong evidence to support this possibility. The research (though not using ESM specifically) suggests that asking individuals about experiences of self-harm does not increase distress or self-harm risk, and may even reduce these behaviours (Cukrowicz, Smith & Poindexter, 2010; Dazzi, Gribble, Wessely & Fear, 2014). Qualitative research further suggests that many participants experience positive effects of taking part in research (e.g. feeling altruistic, catharsis; Biddle et al., 2013; Taylor et al., 2010), though it is important to note that these potential positive effects may still create a problem for researchers where they bias or obscure effects of interest. However, Husky and colleagues (2014) found no evidence of positive or negative reactive effects in an ESM study of suicide risk, but their small samples (n = 12–42) may have meant that they lacked power to detect such effects. One possible solution to reactivity would be a 'running-in' period to allow participants to acclimatise to the ESM process. However, it is currently unclear to what extent, if it all, this sort of reactivity bias is a problem for self-harm research, and further research is needed.

With improvements in technology it is now possible for electronic devices (e.g. smartphones, mobile devices) used for data collection in ESM studies to transmit data live to the research team. This creates a new ethical challenge for researchers studying self-harm, since information concerning a risk of harm to participants may arrive and require immediate action. Where this issue might occur, a decision needs to be made *a priori* as to at what point the participant is deemed to be at risk and the research team needs to act. In research with individuals with experiences of self-harm, participants are at a heightened risk of harm to themselves, but the actual risk of serious self-harm (e.g. a suicide attempt) within the study period is likely to remain relatively low. Researchers need to be mindful of warning signs that might indicate that a suicide attempt or other serious self-harm is imminent, though the accurate prediction of suicide is not currently possible (Sher, 2011). NSSI presents particular ethical challenges, since individuals may regularly self-harm at a low level of physical damage, and the point at which the research team needs to act upon this is unclear. Within our own research into self-harm, we have developed a risk screening protocol to be used with participants, and have in some instances excluded potential participants from studies where they report an extreme level of acute risk. ESM studies may run across weekends or holidays and this creates a particular problem if a participant is reporting a high suicide risk during this period. Thus, for studies where such data is being collected, it may be preferable to limit the data collection period to week days and work hours, although this may then run the risk of missing data from time points where self-harm is more likely to occur (e.g. late evenings). It may also be helpful to have named members of the research team on call to respond to such concerns as they arise. An alternative strategy may be to have an automated system in place which responds at periods of particular risk with signposting information and encouragements to get support. However, such a system begins to blur the line between observation and intervention.

Compliance rates and missing data

Compliance with the method and high rates of missing entries are a recognised problem in the ESM literature (e.g. Stone, Shiffman, Schwartz, Broderick & Hufford, 2003). Whilst missing data can be managed to some extent through analytic techniques (typically assuming that data are Missing At Random; Snijders & Bosker, 2011), high rates of attrition are still problematic in terms of the impact on power and possibility of systematic bias (i.e., where missing data are Missing Not At Random). Within the context of self-harm there is evidence that ESM can be applied and adequate levels of data collected. Husky and colleagues (2014) required participants to complete five daily entries for one week and reported a 74% completion rate for participants with recent suicide attempts. These authors also noted that compliance increased with time possibly due to increased familiarity with the

ESM research into self-harm: two recent examples

We now offer a few examples of item wordings used in previously reported ESM studies of self-harm and suicide. These examples are not offered as 'correct' or indubitable, but as practical suggestions that seem to be, in our minds at least, in keeping with the established nomenclatures above. 'Recently, have you had any thoughts about suicide or killing yourself?' has been used in multiple ESM studies (Nock et al., 2009; Ben-Zeev, Young & Depp, 2012; Husky et al., 2014). In our own studies, we have found this item to be acceptable to participants and offer sufficient variability within response data from samples at risk of suicide. We are now exploring the possibility of using this item, not only to record the incidence of suicidal ideations, but also as a branching question (within technology enabled data capture, i.e. smart phone apps) whereby additional items regarding the frequency, severity, and accompanying distress/relief are then administered to participants who indicated recent suicidal thoughts. A similarly direct approach has been taken to the assessment of self-harm ideation with items used including 'I want to hurt myself' (Humber et al., 2013) and 'I have had thoughts of harming myself without wanting to die' (Nock et al., 2009).

We now offer brief summaries of two recent studies completed using ESM approaches in the investigation of suicide and self-harm ideation. First, in a sample of 21 prisoners (identified by prison staff to be at high risk of suicide or self-harm), we conducted an ESM study to examine the potential impact of anger on the onset of self-harm ideation (Humber, Emsley, Pratt, & Tarrier, 2013). We were particularly interested in the specific components of anger experience (affective state) and anger expression (e.g. suppression of anger or aggressive behaviour) and the extent to which these components were associated with self-harm ideation. Within the ESM diary, self-harm ideation was measured using the single item 'I want to hurt myself', whilst anger experience and anger expression were measured using composite scores of several items including 'Irritable', 'Wound up', and 'Angry' for anger experience; 'I could hit someone/something', and 'I could snap' for outward anger expression; and 'I'm frustrated more than others know', and 'I'm holding my anger inside' for inward anger expression. All items were rated on a 10-point Likert scale to indicate agreement within the present moment ('Right now, I feel …'). Participants were asked to complete diary entries six times per day for six consecutive days (with optional night-time entries available in the back pages of each diary booklet).

It is worth briefly describing the sample characteristics to provide the reader with an indication of the profile of participants choosing to complete the diary study, and to challenge potential assumptions regarding the unlikelihood of engaging a 'hard-to-reach', severely distressed sample in an ESM study. Over half of study participants were sexual and/or violent offenders, more than half had already been imprisoned for at least 12 months, three-quarters had previously attempted suicide, and more than half had a psychiatric diagnosis. Note that all participants were currently or recently identified by prison staff to be at high risk of self-harm or suicide (this was an eligibility criterion), and mean scores on questionnaire measures indicated severe levels of depression and moderate levels of hopelessness. In terms of recruitment and retention of participants, of all potentially eligible individuals approached, half decided to take part, and all participants that commenced sampling provided sufficient data (>30% item completion) to be included within the analysis (with an average of 27 time-points completed per participant out of a maximum of 36). And so, this was a significantly distressed group of prisoners that, nonetheless, successfully engaged in this potentially demanding methodology.

The results from the study told us that participants' subjective experiences of anger and their outward expressions of anger were significant predictors of concurrent levels of self-harm ideation. These findings remained significant after controlling for levels of depression and hopelessness. Importantly, our study failed to support a hypothesis that anger would predict self-harm ideation at a later time-point. Whilst the association between anger and self-harm ideation had been reported previously (e.g. Chapman & Dixon-Gordon, 2007; Marzano et al., 2011; Rivlin et al., 2011), we concluded that prisoners were more likely to be at risk of self-harm when in an angry state rather than them being angry and then thinking about self-harming at a later point. As such, supporting individuals to resolve experiences of anger states may also confer concurrent protection from self-harm.

Continuing the theme of understanding suicide and self-harm within prisoners, more recently we have investigated the role of self- and situational appraisals in the prediction of self-harm ideation, and found subtly different predictive relationships (Sheehy, 2015). Adopting a similar approach to our Humber and colleagues' (2013) study, we developed an ESM diary containing a range of items measuring situational and self-appraisals, and self-harm ideation. Again, we used the item 'I want to hurt myself' to measure NSSI ideation and, additionally, we reversed the combined score for 'I want to live' and 'life is worth living' to measure passive suicidal ideation.

Of the 65 prisoners identified by staff to be at current or recent risk of self-harm, 42 (65%) agreed to participate and completed a sufficient number of diary entries (>30% item completion) to be included within the data analysis. On average, 27 out of the 36 diary entries were completed. As for our previous study, violent and/ or sexual offences were common amongst participants (43%), as was a history of suicide attempts (79%), with more than half reporting multiple previous attempts. Scores on questionnaire measures indicated clinically severe levels of depression, suicide ideation and hopelessness. This level of participation and engagement provides further support to the acceptability of this research methodology, even within distressed participant groups.

In terms of results, for both suicide and NSSI ideation, appraisals of the present and the future were found to be significant predictors. Appraisals of social support (but not social reciprocity) were also an inverse predictor of NSSI ideation, whilst appraisals of social reciprocity (but not social support) were an inverse predictor of suicide ideation. The contrast within this set of results provides some insight into the potentially differing functions of self-harm behaviours revealed using ESM approaches.

Whilst a discussion of the potential interpretation and implications of the results from these studies is outside the central focus of this chapter, we include these examples to highlight the nuances in phenomenological understanding that can be revealed by the ESM approach. Both of these example studies focused upon the understanding of suicide and self-harm within forensic samples, in line with one of the author's (DP) research interests. As such, these studies highlight the potential of ESM in the face of challenges and demands of a necessarily, restrictive environment within which any methodology would encounter difficulties.

Future directions

Future research should consider the specific strengths and capabilities of ESM and what they can add in exploring self-harm phenomena. As noted, ESM can be used to explore the variability or changing patterns in variables of interest in addition to their overall level and intensity. As such, further research using ESM could explore the temporal pattern, stability and variability of self-harm ideation. Through this approach it may be possible to identify specific self-harm ideation signatures, which might be indicative of greater risk for a particular individual or group of individuals. Relatedly, an important area of investigation in self-harm research has been around understanding what determines the transition from ideation to behaviour (Klonsky & May, 2014). This is important since a large number of people may ideate whilst only a small subset go on to engage in self-harm behaviours. ESM has potential here, particularly with regards to more frequently occurring forms of self-harm like NSSI, to identify the transition points from ideation or urges into behaviour. Lastly, ESM can also be used as a means of evaluating interventions, as part of a wider randomised trial design (Kramer et al., 2014). Specific interventions for self-harm could therefore be evaluated using ESM. This approach may enable researchers to better determine the mechanisms of change underlying interventions in terms of the moment-by-moment processes that ESM can measure.

Conclusion

ESM is a potentially powerful research methodology with the capacity to explore the temporal sequence of events and role of momentary states and mechanisms in the occurrence of self-harm. The discrete nature of many of the thoughts and behaviours associated with self-harm means that ESM is well suited to these phenomena. However, challenges in applying ESM to self-harm exist, specifically with regards to the low base rate of some forms of self-harm and the management of ethical concerns. However, there is evidence of the feasibility of ESM in this context, including acceptable completion rates even in difficult to engage populations, and little evidence of reactivity contributing to risk.

References

American Psychiatric Association (APA). (2013). *Diagnostic and statistical manual of mental disorders, 5th edn*. Washington DC: American Psychiatric Association.

Adams, P., Abela, J. R., Auerbach, R., & Skitch, S. (2009). Self-criticism, dependency, and stress reactivity: an experience sampling approach to testing Blatt and Zuroff's (1992) theory of personality predispositions to depression in high-risk youth. *Personality & Social Psychology Bulletin*, 35(11), 1440–1451. doi:10.1177/0146167209343811

Armey, M. F., & Crowther, J. H. (2008). A comparison of linear versus non-linear models of aversive self-awareness, dissociation, and non-suicidal self-injury among young adults. *Journal of Consulting and Clinical Psychology*, 76(1), 9–14. doi:10.1037/0022-006X.76.1.9

Armey, M. F., Crowther, J. H., & Miller, I. W. (2011). Changes in ecological momentary assessment reported affect associated with episodes of nonsuicidal self-injury. *Behavior Therapy*, 42(4), 579–588. doi:10.1016/j.beth.2011. 01. 00doi:2

Ben-Zeev, D., Young, M. A., & Depp, C. A. (2012). Real-time predictors of suicidal ideation: mobile assessment of hospitalized depressed patients. *Psychiatry Research*, 197(1), 55–59. doi: 10.1016/j.psychres.2011. 11. 025.

Bernal, M., Haro, J. M., Bernert, S., Brugha, T., de Graaf, R., Bruffaerts, R., Lépine, J. P., de Girolamo, G., Vilagut, G., Gasquet, I., Torres, J. V., Kovess, V., Heider, D., Neeleman, J., Kessler, R., Alonso, J. & the ESEMED/MHEDEA Investigators. (2007). Risk factors for suicidality in Europe: results from the ESEMED study. *Journal of Affective Disorders*, 101(1), 27–34. doi:10.1016/j.jad.2006.09.018

Bentley, K. H., Nock, M. K., & Barlow, D. H. (2014). The four-function model of nonsuicidal self-injury: Key directions for future research. *Clinical Psychological Science*. doi:10.1177/2167702613514563

Bergen, H., Hawton, K., Waters, K., Ness, J., Cooper, J., Steeg, S., & Kapur, N. (2012). Premature death after self-harm: A multicentre cohort study. *The Lancet*, 380(9853), 1568–1574. doi:10.1016/S0140-6736(12)61141-6

Biddle, L., Cooper, J., Owen-Smith, A., Klineberg, E., Bennewith, O., Hawton, K., ... & Gunnell, D. (2013). Qualitative interviewing with vulnerable populations: individuals' experiences of participating in suicide and self-harm based research. *Journal of Affective Disorders*, 145(3), 356–362.

Borges, G., Nock, M. K., Abad, J. M. H., Hwang, I., Sampson, N. A., Alonso, J., Andrade, L. H., Angermeyer, M. C., Beautrais, A., Bromet, E., Bruffaerts, R., de Girolamo, G., Florescu, S., Gureje, O., Hu, C., Karam, E. G., Kovess-Masfety, V., Lee, S., Levinson, D., Medina-Mora, M. E., Ormel, J., Posada-Villa, J., Sagar, R., Tomov, T., Uda, H., Williams, D. R., & Kessler, R. C. (2010). Twelve-month prevalence of and risk factors for suicide attempts in the World Health Organization World Mental Health Surveys. *Journal of Clinical Psychiatry*, 71(12), 1617–1628. doi:10.4088/JCP.08m04967blu

Borges, G., Angst, J., Nock, M. K., Ruscio, A. M., Walters, E. E., & Kessler, R. C. (2006). A risk index for 12-month suicide attempts in the National Comorbidity Survey Replication (NCS-R). *Psychological Medicine*, 36(12), 1747–1757. doi:10.1017/S0033291706008786

Bresin, K., Carter, D. L., & Gordon, K. H. (2013). The relationship between trait impulsivity, negative affective states, and urge for nonsuicidal self-injury: A daily diary study. *Psychiatry Research*, 205(3), 227–231. doi:10.1016/j.psychres.2012. 09. 03doi:3

Casey, P., Dunn, G., Kelly, B. D., Lehtinen, V., Dalgard, O. S., Dowrick, C., & Ayuso-Mateos, J. L. (2008). The prevalence of suicidal ideation in the general population: Results from the Outcome of Depression International Network (ODIN) study. *Social Psychiatry & Psychiatric Epidemiology*, 43(4), 299–304. doi:10.1007/s00127-008-0313-5

Chapman, A. L., & Dixon-Gordon, K. L. (2007). Emotional antecedents and consequences of deliberate self-harm and suicide attempts. *Suicide and Life-Threatening Behavior*, 37, 543–552. doi:10.1521/suli.2007.37.5.543

Csikszentmihalyi, M., & Larson, R. (2014). Validity and reliability of the experience-sampling method. In M. Csikszentmihalyi (Ed.) *Flow and the foundations of positive psychology* (pp. 35–54). New York: Springer.

Cukrowicz, K., Smith, P., & Poindexter, E. (2010). The effect of participating in suicide research: does participating in a research protocol on suicide and psychiatric symptoms increase suicide ideation and attempts? *Suicide & Life Threatening Behavior*, 40(6), 535–543. doi:10.1521/suli.2010.40.6doi:535

Dazzi, T., Gribble, R., Wessely, S., & Fear, N. T. (2014). Does asking about suicide and related behaviours induce suicidal ideation? What is the evidence? *Psychological Medicine*, 44(16), 3361–3363. doi:10.1017/s0033291714001299

deVries, M. W., & Delespaul, P. A. (1989). Time, context, and subjective experiences in schizophrenia. *Schizophrenia Bulletin*, 15, 233–244. doi:10.1093/schbul/15.2.233

De Young, K. P., Lavender, J. M., Wonderlich, S. A., Crosby, R. D., Engel, S. G., Mitchell, J. E., ... Le Grange, D. (2013). Moderators of post-binge eating negative emotion in eating disorders. *Journal of Psychiatric Research*, 47(3), 323–328. doi:10.1016/j.jpsychires.2012. 11. 01doi:2

Goldsmith, S. K., Pellmar, T. C., Kleinman, A. M., & Bunney, W. E. (2002). *Reducing suicide: A national imperative*. Washington, DC: The National Academies Press.

Hamza, C. A., & Willoughby, T. (2015). Nonsuicidal self-injury and affect regulation: Recent findings from experimental and ecological momentary assessment studies and future directions. *Journal of Clinical Psychology*, 71(6), 561–574.

Hawton, K., Zahl, D., & Weatherall, R. (2003). Suicide following deliberate self-harm: Long-term follow-up of patients who presented to a general hospital. *British Journal of Psychiatry*, 182(6), 537–542. doi:10.1192/bjp.182. 6. 53doi:7

Humber, N., Emsley, R., Pratt, D., & Tarrier, N. (2013). Anger as a predictor of psychological distress and self-harm ideation in inmates: A structured self-assessment diary study. *Psychiatry Research*, 210(1), 166–173. doi:10.1016/j.psychres.2013. 02. 01doi:1

Husky, M., Olié, E., Guillaume, S., Genty, C., Swendsen, J., & Courtet, P. (2014). Feasibility and validity of ecological momentary assessment in the investigation of suicide risk. *Psychiatry Research*, 220(1), 564–570. doi:10.1016/j.psychres.2014. 08. 01doi:9

Kapur, N., Cooper, J., O'Connor, R. C., & Hawton, K. (2013). Non-suicidal self-injury v. attempted suicide: new diagnosis or false dichotomy? *The British Journal of Psychiatry*, 202(5), 326–328. doi:10.1192/bjp.bp.112.116111

Kehrberg, C. (1997). Self-mutilating behavior. *Journal of Child and Adolescent Psychiatric Nursing*, 10(3), 35–40.

Klonsky, E. D., & May, A. M. (2014). Differentiating suicide attempters from suicide ideators: A critical frontier for suicidology research. *Suicide & Life-Threatening Behaviour*, 44, 1–5. doi:10.1111/sltb.12068

Kramer, I., Simons, C. J. P., Hartmann, J. A., Menne-Lothmann, C., Viechtbauer, W., Peeters, F. S.,...Wichers, M. (2014). A therapeutic application of the experience sampling method in the treatment of depression: A randomized controlled trial. *World Psychiatry*, 13, 68–77. doi:10,1002/wps.20090

Marzano, L., Fazel, S., Rivlin, A., Hawton, K. (2011). Near-lethal self-harm in women prisoners: contributing factors and psychological processes. *Journal of Forensic Psychiatry and Psychology*, 22, 863–884. doi:10.1080/14789949.2011.617465

Muehlenkamp, J. J., Engel, S. G., Wadeson, A., Crosby, R. D., Wonderlich, S. A., Simonich, H., & Mitchell, J. E. (2009). Emotional states preceding and following acts of non-suicidal self-injury in bulimia nervosa patients. *Behaviour Research and Therapy*, 47(1), 83–87. doi:10.1016/j.brat.2008.10.011

Myin-Germeys, I., Oorschot, M., Collip, D., Lataster, J., Delespaul, P., & van Os, J. (2009). Experience sampling research in psychopathology: Opening the black box of daily life. *Psychological Medicine*, 39(9), 1533–1547. doi:10.1017/s0033291708004947

National Collaborating Centre for Mental Health. (2011). *Self-harm: Longer-term management (CG133)*. London: NICE.

Nock, M., Joiner, T., Gordon, K., Lloyd-Richardson, E., & Prinstein, M. (2006). Non-suicidal self-injury among adolescents: Diagnostic correlates and relation to suicide attempts. *Psychiatry Research*, 144(1), 65–72. doi:10.1016/j.psychres.2006. 05. 01doi:0

Nock, M. K., Prinstein, M. J., Sterba, S. K. (2009). Revealing the form and function of self-injurious thoughts and behaviors: a real-time ecological assessment study among adolescents and young adults. *Journal of Abnormal Psychology*, 118, 816–827. doi:10.1037/a0016948

O'Connor, R. C., & Nock, M. K. (2014). The psychology of suicidal behaviour. *The Lancet Psychiatry*, 1(1), 73–85.

Office for National Statistics. (2016). *Statistical bulletin. Suicides in the United Kingdom: 2014 Registrations*. London: ONS.

Owens, D., Horrocks, J., & House, A. (2002). Fatal and non-fatal repetition of self-harm. Systematic review. *British Journal of Psychiatry*, 181, 193–199. doi:10.1192/bjp.181. 3. 19doi:3

Palmier-Claus, J. E., Ainsworth, J., Machin, M., Dunn, G., Barkus, E., Barrowclough, C., ... Lewis, S. W. (2013). Affective instability prior to and after thoughts about self-injury in individuals with and at-risk of psychosis: A mobile phone based study. *Archives of Suicide Research*, 17(3), 275–287. doi:10.1080/13811118.2013.805647

Palmier-Claus, J. E., Myin-Germeys, I., Barkus, E., Bentley, L., Udachina, A., Delespaul, P. A., ... Dunn, G. (2011). Experience sampling research in individuals with mental illness: Reflections and guidance. *Acta Psychiatrica Scandinavica*, 123(1), 12–20. doi:10.1111/j.1600-0447.2010.01596.x

Palmier-Claus, J. E., Taylor, P. J., Gooding, P., Dunn, G., & Lewis, S. W. (2012a). Affective variability predicts suicidal ideation in individuals at ultra-high risk of developing psychosis: An experience sampling study. *British Journal of Clinical Psychology*, 51(1), 72–83. doi:10.1111/j.2044-8260.2011.02013.x

Palmier-Claus, J. E., Taylor, P. J., Varese, F., & Pratt, D. (2012b). Does unstable mood increase risk of suicide? Theory, research and practice. *Journal of Affective Disorders*, 143(1–3), 5–15. doi:10.1016/j.jad.2012. 05. 03doi:0

Pattison, E. M., & Kahan, J. (1983). The deliberate self-harm syndrome. *American Journal of Psychiatry*, 140(7), 867–872. doi:10.1176/ajp.140. 7. 86doi:7

Reinherz, H. Z., Giaconia, R. M., Silverman, A. B., Friedman, A., Pakiz, B., Frost, A. K., & Cohen, E. (1995). Early psychosocial risks for adolescent suicidal ideation and attempts. *Journal of the American Academy of Child & Adolescent Psychiatry*, 34(5), 599–611. doi:10.1097/00004583-199505000-00012

Rivlin, A., Fazel, S., Marzano, L., & Hawton, K. (2011). The suicidal process in male prisoners near-lethal suicide attempts. *Psychology, Crime & Law*, 1, 1–23. doi:10.1080/1068316X.2011.631540

Royal College of Psychiatrists. (2010). *Self-harm, suicide and risk: Helping people who self-harm*. London: Royal College of Psychiatrists.

Santangelo, P. S., Ebner-Priemer, U. W., & Trull, T. J. (2013). Experience sampling methods in clinical psychology. In J. S. Comer & P. C. Kendall (Eds.), *The Oxford handbook of research strategies for clinical psychology* (pp. 188–212). Oxford: Oxford University Press.

Selby, E. A., Nock, M. K., & Kranzler, A. (2014). How does self-injury feel? Examining automatic positive reinforcement in adolescent self-injurers with experience sampling. *Psychiatry Research*, 215(2), 417–423. doi:10.1016/j.psychres.2013. 12. 00doi:5

Sheehy, K. (2015). *Understanding Suicidality in Prisoners*. Unpublished PhD thesis. University of Manchester.

Sher, L. (2011). Is it possible to predict suicide? *Australian and New Zealand Journal of Psychiatry*, 45(4), 341. doi:10.3109/00048674.2011.560136

Shingleton, R. M., Eddy, K. T., Keshaviah, A., Franko, D. L., Swanson, S. A., Jessica, S. Y., ... & Herzog, D. B. (2013). Binge/purge thoughts in nonsuicidal self-injurious adolescents: An ecological momentary analysis. *International Journal of Eating Disorders*, 46(7), 684–689. Rebuilding the tower of Babel: A revised nomenclature for the study of suicide and suicidal behaviors Part 2: Suicide-related ideations, communications, and behaviors. *Suicide and Life-Threatening Behavior*, 37(3), 264–277. doi:10.1521/suli.2007.37.3doi:264

Simons, J. S., Gaher, R. M., Oliver, M. N., Bush, J. A., & Palmer, M. A. (2005). An experience sampling study of associations between affect and alcohol use and problems among college students. *Journal of Studies in Alcohol*, 66(4), 459–469. doi:10.15288/jsa.2005. 66. 45doi:9

Snijders, T. A. B., & Bosker, R. J. (2011). *Multilevel analysis: An introduction to basic & advanced multilevel modeling* (2nd ed.). Thousand Oaks, California: Sage Publishers.

Snir, A., Rafaeli, E., Gadassi, R., Berenson, K., & Downey, G. (2015). Explicit and inferred motives for nonsuicidal self-injurious acts and urges in borderline and avoidant personality disorders. *Personality Disorders: Theory, Research, and Treatment*, 6(3), 267–277. doi:10.1037/per0000104

Stoep, A. V., Adrian, M., McCauley, E., Crowell, S., Stone, A., & Flynn, C. (2011). Risk for suicidal ideation and suicide attempts associated with co-occurring depression and conduct disorders in early adolescence. *Suicide & Life-Threatening Behavior*, 41(3), 316–329. doi:10.1111/j.1943-278X.2011.00031.x

Stone, A. A., Shiffman, S., Schwartz, J. E., Broderick, J. E., & Hufford, M. R. (2003). Patient compliance with paper and electronic diaries. *Controlled Clinical Trials*, 24(2), 182–199. doi:10.1016/S0197-2456(02)00320-3

Sveticic, J., & De Leo, D. (2012). The hypothesis of a continuum in suicidality: A discussion on its validity and practical implications. *Mental Illness*, 4(2), e15. doi:10.4081/mi.2012.e15

Swannell, S. V., Martin, G. E., Page, A., Hasking, P., & St John, N. J. (2014). Prevalence of nonsuicidal self-injury in nonclinical samples: Systematic review, meta-analysis and meta-regression. *Suicide and Life-Threatening Behavior*, 44, 273–303. doi:10.1111/sltb.12070

Taylor, P. J., Awenat, Y., Gooding, P., Johnson, J., Pratt, D., Wood, A., & Tarrier, N. (2010). The subjective experience of participation in schizophrenia research: a practical and ethical issue. *Journal of Nervous and Mental Disease*, 198(5), 343–348.

Taylor, P. J., Hutton, P., & Wood, L. (2015). Are people at risk of psychosis also at risk of suicide and self-harm? A systematic review and meta-analysis. *Psychological Medicine*, 45(5), 911–926. doi:10.1017/s0033291714002074

Zaki, L. F., Coifman, K. G., Rafaeli, E., Berenson, K. R., & Downey, G. (2013). Emotion differentiation as a protective factor against nonsuicidal self-injury in borderline personality disorder. *Behavior Therapy*, 44(3), 529–540. doi:10.1016/j.beth.2013. 04. 00doi:8

9

EMERGING APPLICATIONS OF PREDICTION IN EXPERIENCE SAMPLING

Colin Depp, Christopher N. Kaufmann, Eric Granholm and Wesley Thompson

Introduction

Intensive longitudinal data is increasingly used to predict the future. Outside of mental health research, forecasting outcomes from data on past trends has long been central to various fields, including economics and finance, climatology and disaster prevention, and a vast array of sports. The experience sampling method (ESM) has increasingly opened avenues to modeling trends and temporal sequences and interdependencies of thoughts, feelings and behavior, and could provide a stronger basis for prediction than cross-sectional data. Although many prediction problems in medicine focus on infrequent events that occur over a lengthy time scale, such as the identification of risk factors for the conversion to disease, many challenging questions in mental health research could be addressed by ESM data coupled with prediction models. For example, what unique experiences occur in the days, hours, or minutes before exacerbation in suicidal thinking that might predict future exacerbations? Do the same "early warning signs" herald increased risk for manic and depressive episodes in bipolar disorder? If low mood predicts subsequent cravings for elicit substances, would a "just-in-time" intervention targeting negative affect reduce the likelihood of subsequent drug use? This chapter provides an overview of recent applications of prediction using ESM data, guidance on methods for prediction, and recommendations for future research in this emerging area.

Rationale for ESM versus standard static measures in prediction

This volume showcases many of the potential advantages of ESM over standard point-in-time assessment approaches, such as the diminution of retrospective recall and measurement biases inherent to self-report. ESM could improve the accuracy of prediction over and above standard risk profiling by incorporating information on the sequences and stability of variables over time. At present, prediction of mental health outcomes (e.g. treatment response, crises) is suboptimal, which may, in part, be due to the timing of the variables of interest. Indeed, variables that are measured repeatedly and closer in time to outcome(s) are more likely to generate accurate predictions, whereas those that are distal in time are likely to be inaccurate.

Single point-in-time or retrospective measures generally cannot yield information beyond the presence or severity of a variable, whereas frequently repeated measures provide capability to examine parameters such as trends, intra-individual variability, and other dynamics. Point-in-time measures for prediction generally rely upon a normative comparison group, with risk determined by scores relative to other people's scores. These comparisons might not be appropriate due to confounding and other unmeasured differences in recruitment, study drop outs, and missing data. More importantly, these comparisons might not be meaningful to the individual, and thus repeated individual-level data might provide greater ability to form predictions based on the individual's prior data. As new kinds of intensive longitudinal data become available, such as through sensors, device metadata, and other sources, the ability to model individual level behavior and generate predictions is exponentially increasing.

General applications of prediction using ESM in mental health research

Given that the time frame for ESM research is typically measured in weeks, and in rare cases months, the applications for prediction models with ESM data typically concern events that occur frequently enough to be likely to be captured on a day-to-day or week-to-week basis. As such, ESM approaches might not be useful for prediction of rare (e.g., completed suicide) or infrequent/singular events (e.g., transition from at risk status to diagnosis in psychosis). Moreover, as with ESM research in general, variables that are presumed to be static, such as personality traits, would not likely provide useful fodder for prediction models leveraging intensive longitudinal data.

For constructs that are assumed to be time varying in clinically meaningful ways, frequently gathered data can be used to address a variety of simple or complex questions that are not easily examined in cross-sectional or infrequent panel-type longitudinal data. For example, a single stream of daily mood ratings collected over several months could be extrapolated into the future by projecting a simple linear trend. They could also be based upon more complex patterns including whether mood dynamics over time are best represented by changes in discrete states, by seasonal patterns such as in concordance with circadian rhythms, or towards or away from entropy. ESM data from multiple sources can be used to examine the direction of temporal interdependencies. For instance, combining ratings of sleep duration and mood would allow for analysis of both concurrent (e.g., sleep rating at same time point as mood rating) and time-lagged (sleep rating predicting mood at next time point and vice versa) associations.

Prediction models are increasingly capable of identifying these interdependencies from large networks of variables and updating these predictions based on incoming data using machine learning techniques. Discovery of such temporal inter-dependencies is especially relevant to symptoms that fluctuate over time and have reliable precursors, often referred to as early warning signs. Such early warning signs might be in the form of behaviors or symptoms (e.g., hypersomnia heralding bouts of increased depression), which could be nested in various time periods (e.g., seasons of the year; periods after hospitalization) or contexts (e.g., periods of social isolation). Thus, prediction models using ESM could be employed to identify when and where clinically meaningful changes are most likely to occur for which people with which risk factors. In this context, prediction models might be particularly useful to validate or disconfirm theoretical targets for interventions, informing the mechanisms of experimental interventions delivered during the sampling frame. Finally, and perhaps most excitingly, should accurate predictions linking modifiable warning signs to outcomes be achieved, it is possible to intervene at the time when early warning signs are first reported or detected in ESM paradigms so as to attempt to prevent problems. Such a "closed loop" system could help individuals manage chronic recurrent illnesses. In the next section, we discuss the capabilities of ESM using examples of recent work that has employed prediction models.

Capabilities of ESM in prediction research for mental health

Examination of trajectories in single variables over time

One of the most common purposes of ESM data is to characterize longitudinal patterns within a single stream of data (e.g. a single variable). Examples in mental health research may include ratings of positive and negative affect (Hamaker, Grasman, & Kamphuis, 2016), and mood symptoms (Bonsall, Geddes, Goodwin, & Holmes, 2015). One can use results from analyzing these streams to identify clinically important points of high or low risk for mental health outcomes, for example, the persistence of certain states (longer durations of positive affect) (Hohn et al., 2013), and fluctuations in rating variability (e.g. see Bonsall and colleagues (2012) who characterized trajectories of mood instability in bipolar disorder).

Examination of lagged associations between two or more variables

A more complex predictive approach involves examining the effect of time-lagged associations between variables. As discussed above, one of the limitations of cross-sectional and panel studies is the inability to ascertain temporal ordering, and ESM provides a way to examine possible mechanisms that may underlie associations. For example, Langguth and colleagues (2016) examined the impact of daytime physical activity on evening and next-morning depressed affect in adolescents. They found that in women, moderate-to-vigorous physical activity, greater than the indivi-dual's average norm, yielded substantially lower next-morning depressed affect.

Similarly, Kaufmann and colleagues (2016) assessed whether nightly sleep duration predicted abnormalities in same- and next-day positive and negative affect in outpatients diagnosed with bipolar disorder and found that fewer than 7–8 hours of sleep predicted next morning lower positive affect and higher negative affect. Analysis of more complex processes including mediation between variables is also possible with examples ranging from impulsivity mediating affective states in bipolar disorder (Depp et al., 2016) to various mechanisms in bulimia nervosa (Lavender et al., 2016).

Using ESM to identify potential early warning signs

The nature of frequent inquiries of experience also fosters the exploration of specific precursors and warning signs for imminent mental health events (e.g., psychotic episodes, panic attacks, or even suicide ideation/attempts). This not only allows investigators to identify the type of experience preceding an event, but also the time period for which prediction can be made. Thompson and colleagues (2014), for example, found that trends in negative affect, but not positive affect, predicted suicidal ideation up to two weeks prior to a clinician visit. Spaniel and colleagues (2016) identified early warning signs for relapse in schizophrenia two months prior to hospitalization. These studies indicate the power of identifying temporally precise points of increased risk to potentially urgent psychiatric events. Identifying these risk points provides an opportunity for personalized real-time prevention, and demonstrates the usefulness of ESM data in this context.

ESM data for theory development

Modern technology facilitating ESM is also a powerful tool to test theoretical models, and even contribute to the development of new models. Specifically, ESM allows one to test whether theoretically specified conditions (e.g., emotions, contexts) predict the likelihood of target behaviors in real time. For example, the self-medication theory of alcoholism suggests that individuals may be driven to alcohol use by underlying symptoms/feelings/states. Possemato and colleagues (2015) studied veterans with Post-Traumatic Stress Disorder (PTSD) and found that greater PTSD symptomatology was associated with near-term increased drinking, and this was moderated by avoidance coping and lower self-efficacy. In addition, another study among patients with schizophrenia (Swendsen, Ben-Zeev, & Granholm, 2011), showed strong within-day prospective associations in both directions between substance use and negative psychological states or psychotic symptoms, but considerable variation by substance type (e.g., alcohol, cannabis, etc.).

ESM as assessment in interventions

ESM can also be used as an assessment tool to evaluate interventions in clinical trials. For example, in studies evaluating smoking cessation interventions, ESM has highlighted that negative affect predicts short-term (Shiffman et al., 2007), as well as longer-term (Brodbeck, Bachmann, Brown, & Znoj, 2014), smoking relapses. Brodbeck and colleagues (2014) found that these long-term outcomes are mediated by negative affect during quit attempts leading to increased smoking urges and lower self-efficacy (hence resulting in lower likelihood of abstaining from smoking). Lam and colleagues (2014) also showed that after a quit attempt, several factors (including alcohol consumption, being around other smokers, and personal negative affect) separately and together yielded increased risk for smoking relapses.

ESM prediction with large groups of indicators

Exciting recent studies have begun exploring the use of ESM techniques in complex data from large sets of indicators (e.g., sensors in modern smartphones (Burns et al., 2011) (Asselbergs et al., 2016), home sensors (Lopez-Guede, Moreno-Fernandez-de-Leceta, Martinez-Garcia, & Grana, 2015)). Given the ubiquity of devices and passive data collectors in daily life, as well as the attractiveness of objective data collected without the need for participant adherence, passive data collection offers inherent promise. The challenge in such data is determining how to synthesize it into meaningful indicators that are interpretable by stakeholders.

ESM in long-term longitudinal studies

While ESM provides detail in the collection of highly frequent data, its collection can take up technological resources and lead to participant burden if used for a long duration. To that end, ESM data collection, as a part of long-term cohort studies, may seek to have multiple short "bursts" of ESM assessments over time (e.g., disparate waves), enabling inferences in larger follow-up periods without the threat of drop outs. An example of such methodology is Wichers and colleagues (2010) research on a woman with history of major depression using ESM over the course of five separate waves. They found that reward experiences and instability in negative affect predicted depressive symptoms in subsequent waves suggesting that information obtained by ESM may provide useful information on risk for major depression recurrence.

Methods used and guidance for research

The methods for implementing prediction models into ESM protocols are quite diverse. The implementation of statistical models with intensive longitudinal data is complex and beyond the scope of this chapter, with excellent resources available (Walls & Schafer, 2006). However, we synthesize key areas to consider and potential barriers to prediction.

Missing data and adherence

Missing data is common in ESM research. It is likely to be more a problem in predictive modeling than in approaches that focus on average values, given that patterns of missing data may be linked to the nature of the predictor(s), outcomes(s), or both. Firstly, predictions typically involve modeling of trends rather than means aggregated over time. Reliably estimating trends requires more data than when considering averages. Furthermore, indices of intra-individual variability necessitate at least 50 observations per person in order to be reliable (Jahng, Wood, & Trull, 2008). Secondly, unless the focal outcome is a daily occurrence, the duration of sampling is typically longer for predictive modelling which yields a greater chance for missing data. The risk of fading, or the tendency for participants to reduce responding over time, might increase with the duration of the sampling protocol. As such, identifying effective strategies to promote longer-term engagement in mobile health data collection is critical. Strategies such as the use of participants' own devices, gamification, incorporation of intervention elements, and graded compensation for sampling based on adherence levels have been utilized to enhance longer term adherence (Brown et al., 2016; Scollon, Prieto, & Diener, 2009).

Duration and intensity of the sampling

Although some work has been completed to determine the validity of varying intensities of sampling (e.g., number of times per day) (Christensen, Barrett, Bliss-Moreau, Lebo, & Kaschub, 2003), little is understood about how frequently data need to be gathered in the context of prediction algorithms. The rate of data collection depends substantially upon the expected dynamics of the construct being measured. In one study, Piette and colleagues examined the incremental value of weekly vs. monthly measures of depression in predicting subsequent ratings, and found that the added benefit of the daily assessment was minimal (Piette et al., 2013). Given the tension between adherence/missingness and temporal resolution, more research aimed at understanding the amount of expected "noise" in intra-individual variation in both predictors and outcomes is warranted. In addition to identifying the relationship between predictors and outcomes, predictive approaches may also be used in the future to alter sampling rates. For example, sampling rates might increase upon recognition of high risk states (e.g. an individual with a history of depression who reports being alone for several consecutive surveys may be surveyed more frequently) or decrease if the incremental value of more frequent assessments is marginal (Piette et al., 2013).

Statistical approaches for predictive modeling

There are two important distinctions when selecting statistical approaches to prediction problems. Firstly, approaches vary depending upon whether predictors are pre-specified as part of testing a theory-driven hypothesis or whether their selection is exploratory. Secondly, approaches differ depending on whether extensions of inferential statistics are used to quantify the accuracy of prediction or whether emerging models of statistical learning are employed to optimize prediction as new data accumulates. Typically, theoretical model testing uses lagged models in which theorized predictors are entered as independent variables predicting "future" outcomes, with temporal sequencing indicative of potential causal influences (see Kaufmann et al., 2016 and Langguth et al., 2016 for examples). In such models, a key challenge is accounting for and disentangling autoregressive relationships (e.g., the relationship of the predictor/outcome with itself across time points) as well as concurrent relationships between predictors and outcomes. Structural equation models can be used to simultaneously examine these relationships (Lavender et al., 2016). An important extension of this kind of modeling is Time Varying Effect Models, which allow for variation in the effect of the predictor on outcome. Here, instead of assuming a constant association between a predictor and outcome as in standard modeling, it is assumed that this association can vary as a function of time or other moderators. For example, Mason and colleagues (2015) modeled trajectories of stress and its association with cravings over time using intensive longitudinal data as part of a randomized control trial on smoking cessation; the trajectory of associations between stress and cravings was substantially stronger for control subjects compared to the treatment group two to three months after start of the intervention. Conversely, Shiyko et al. (2012) examined trajectories of associations between negative affect, self-efficacy, and smoking urges among successful and unsuccessful quitters of smoking. They found that over time there was a "decoupling" of negative affect with smoking urges among successful quitters, whereas this was less evident in unsuccessful quitters. Self-efficacy was associated with a lower likelihood of smoking urges among successful quitters, but this association was less strong for unsuccessful quitters.

Turning to exploratory analyses, a common problem with ESM data is the large number of potential predictors that are interdependent. As the number of variables in prediction models increases, techniques for variable selection are needed. Ordinary least squares approaches, such as stepwise regression, frequently result in models that do not replicate to new data. Such models suffer from the problem of "overfitting" in which models are overly influenced by noise. Techniques for variable selection that may reduce the potential for overfitting include the Least Absolute Shrinkage and Selection Operator (LASSO) (Tibshirani, 1996), which constrains predictors to make for simpler models that can enhance accuracy.

Industrial and computer science applications of predictive modeling often focus less on actual content and drawing causal inferences, and more on prediction efficiency and optimization. The latter approach is frequently associated with machine learning and predictive algorithms, with specific techniques including neural networks, support vector machines, and Bayesian methods. Future approaches to predictive modeling with ESM might involve application of machine learning in real time in which algorithms are updated based on the accumulating data, perhaps becoming more personalized to the individual by virtue of greater information on that individual. As such, the panoply of statistical options for ESM and prediction problems is rapidly increasing and frequently requires the input of data scientists familiar with these emerging approaches.

Validation

Prediction models are often gauged in terms of their accuracy, as measured by the area under of the curve, a statistical metric indicating how optimal a measurement discerns a positive or negative result based on a "gold-standard." To generate reliable estimates of accuracy, validation is required and this can be accomplished in a variety of techniques. Separating data into training and validation sets is the prototypical approach, yet frequently ESM samples are not large and such separation of subjects is infeasible. Leave-one-out cross validation examines the performance of a model within the training dataset. Another approach to validation of the specificity of the predictor is the use of case-crossover designs (Bagge et al., 2013), which examines the contrasts in the dynamics of predictors in the presence or absence of the outcome. This uses cases as their own controls, and could be used to examine the specificity of predictors on outcomes.

Future directions

As this burgeoning area of research is in its early stages, there are many opportunities to leverage the strengths of ESM for prediction in mental health research and clinical practice. ESM can build upon pre-existing models for prediction by providing highly detailed context yielding precise predictions. This section will review these unique opportunities.

Data integration beyond self-report

With the recent explosion of "Big Data," there are numerous prospects to use ESM to enrich and give context to information from multiple sources, including mobile devices (e.g., phone metadata), linked sensors (e.g., activity monitors), social media (e.g., Twitter and Facebook), administrative records (e.g., electronic health records), medical devices (e.g., neuroimaging), and even publicly available data (e. g., open city initiatives, public transit, police arrests, housing prices, regional pollution). Challenges to incorporating such data include the "volume, velocity, and variety" (Laney, 2001) of data types and structures, and require complex data management platforms to enable analyses. Relatedly, using these data in consort could yield tremendous insights about the progression of mental health and well-being over time and their interaction with elements from the individual, interpersonal, community, and societal levels. For example, a study on seasonal affective disorder may combine local weather data to identify weather (e.g., temperature, sunlight, cloudiness) precursors for mood trajectories. However, challenges still remain as to how to merge and synthesize these data in statistically appropriate

Emerging applications of prediction in ES **119**

ways. Additionally, logistics of data access and integration are dependent on settling issues related to data access policies, ownership of data, and privacy expectations (Mittelstadt & Floridi, 2016).

Development of systems for real-time prediction

With passive collection of data and increasing computer processing power and speed, there are promising opportunities to manifest real-time predictions. For example, accelerometers matched with computer programming may provide opportunities to assess whether certain patterns of change in activity levels are predictive of feelings of wellbeing (see Zhang et al., 2016 as an example) – such real-time prediction may assist in identifying "critical points" of increased risk for possible events. Other possibilities include identifying when an individual is alone and whether that leads to altered affect in the near and short-term.

Testing mechanisms of change in interventions

There is increasing interest in identifying the processes by which interventions exert impact on outcomes. As described by Reininghaus and colleagues (2016), predictive modeling in ESM is well suited to testing theoretical models that specify relationships between mechanism and outcomes. This is largely due to its capacity to identify changes in mechanisms that exert subsequent impact on outcomes and under what conditions. With pre-post designs in which ESM is repeated (or if continuously delivered), it is possible to examine if theoretical processes or hypothetical mechanisms of change did indeed alter. A successful example is the examination of the decoupling of negative affect in mobile-phone based data (Toscos, Connelly, & Rogers, 2013).

Providing real-time feedback in interventions

Coupled with real-time prediction, there are opportunities to create interventions that target the development of abnormal states. These interventions could possibly be delivered through biosensors and mobile technology while an individual is in their natural environment – a "nudge" can be made through text or other means to consider taking specific action (like exercise, get out of the house, or to contact a friend). There are exciting efforts currently being made to assess the feasibility of using real-time data in interventions – researchers in the UK are studying how sensor data can be used to identify the points to intervene before a psychotic episode (Clark, 2015). Research by Bucci et al. (2015) is currently evaluating the use of smartphone delivered cognitive behavioral therapy for early psychosis. Efforts are being made to utilize GPS data to identify locations for where recovering drug-users may be at greater risk for relapse (Epstein et al., 2014). However, the appropriate means by which

Incorporation of consumer stakeholders in all phases of defining prediction problems, participatory data collection, and defining ethics of predictive analytics

The ultimate goal of predictive modeling is to enhance the understanding of health and capacity to control illnesses. As data collection tools and analysis platforms become accessible, an impressive number of service users have begun to engage in self-tracking in order to understand their difficulties. The Quantified Self movement, whose followers seek to gain "self-knowledge through numbers," is one example of this growing interest (Quantified Self Labs, 2015).

Service users and other stakeholders are particularly vital to shaping prediction with ESM as it becomes embedded in clinical services or interventions. When considering a future in which predictions about near term risks become accurate and accessible (e.g., "early warning systems"), it is possible that predictions could do harm by increasing anxiety or bringing attentional focus on illness rather than other life domains. This could be particularly problematic to the individual if they are unprepared to act on the prediction. Moreover, clinicians who are made aware of predicted outcomes may be concerned about their capacity to allocate efforts, particularly when balanced against the needs of patients with *known and present* concerns. Therefore, real-time predictive feedback would need to be carefully designed alongside service users and other stakeholders to enable, and not bog down, effective self-management of illnesses.

A second area in which service users' input and preferences are vital is in the issues surrounding privacy and data security. A counter balance to the excitement regarding big data sources (e.g. sensors, medical records) is that service users frequently experience a lack of control and understanding about what information is accessible, how it is transmitted, and which parties own and manage its access. Few patients are aware of the potential losses of privacy upon agreeing to "terms and conditions" of modern internet applications. Encroachment into sensitive information such as mental health symptoms without evidence of informed consent is a recipe for diminishing the trustworthiness of the public regarding health research. Solutions to incorporating consumer feedback include providing users of ESM applications granular control over the kinds of data that they are willing and unwilling to make available and to whom, as well as providing feedback about what uses are made of their individual data and by whom.

Conclusions

As this volume highlights, ESM enhances the capacity to form predictions about the future, which is impossible to obtain through data collected at a single point. There are many opportunities to integrate ESM approaches with other existing data sources to yield richer predictive insights. However, many challenges still remain to fully capitalize on predictive modelling in ESM including further development of data analysis and real-time computing methodology, management protocols for large and complex data, and ethical issues for communicating findings from prediction models in intervention paradigms. Despite these challenges, ESM provides us with the opportunity to identify potentially important patterns in mental health conditions and to predict subsequent outcomes. This can enable us to determine when, where, and how symptoms change, and use this information to identify and deliver appropriate treatments "just in time."

References

Asselbergs, J., Ruwaard, J., Ejdys, M., Schrader, N., Sijbrandij, M., & Riper, H. (2016). Mobile phone-based unobtrusive ecological momentary assessment of day-to-day mood: An explorative study. *Journal of Medical Internet Research*, 18(3), e72. doi:10.2196/jmir.5505

Bagge, C. L., Lee, H. J., Schumacher, J. A., Gratz, K. L., Krull, J. L., & Holloman, JrG.. (2013). Alcohol as an acute risk factor for recent suicide attempts: a case-crossover analysis. *Journal of the Study of Alcohol and Drugs*, 74(4), 552–558.

Bonsall, M. B., Geddes, J. R., Goodwin, G. M., & Holmes, E. A. (2015). Bipolar disorder dynamics: affective instabilities, relaxation oscillations and noise. *Journal of Research into Social Interface*, 12(112). doi:10.1098/rsif.2015.0670

Bonsall, M. B., Wallace-Hadrill, S. M., Geddes, J. R., Goodwin, G. M., & Holmes, E. A. (2012). Nonlinear time-series approaches in characterizing mood stability and mood instability in bipolar disorder. *Proceedings: Biological Sciences*, 279(1730), 916–924. doi:10.1098/rspb.2011.1246

Brodbeck, J., Bachmann, M. S., Brown, A., & Znoj, H. J. (2014). Effects of depressive symptoms on antecedents of lapses during a smoking cessation attempt: an ecological momentary assessment study. *Addiction*, 109(8), 1363–1370. doi:10.1111/add.12563

Brown, M., O'Neill, N., van Woerden, H., Eslambolchilar, P., Jones, M., & John, A. (2016). Gamification and adherence to web-based mental health interventions: A systematic review. *Journal of Medical Internet Research: Mental Health*, 3(3), e39. doi:10.2196/mental.5710

Bucci, S., Barrowclough, C., Ainsworth, J., Morris, R., Berry, K., Machin, M., … Haddock, G. (2015). Using mobile technology to deliver a cognitive behaviour therapy-informed intervention in early psychosis (Actissist): study protocol for a randomised controlled trial. *Trials*, 16, 404. doi:10.1186/s13063-015-0943-3

Burns, M. N., Begale, M., Duffecy, J., Gergle, D., Karr, C. J., Giangrande, E., & Mohr, D. C. (2011). Harnessing context sensing to develop a mobile intervention for depression. *Journal of Medical Internet Research*, 13(3), e55. doi:10.2196/jmir.1838

Christensen, T. C., Barrett, L. F., Bliss-Moreau, E., Lebo, K., & Kaschub, C. (2003). A practical guide to experience-sampling procedures. *Journal of Happiness Studies*, 4(1), 53–78.

Clark, L. (2015). Fitbit data could help schizophrenia sufferers avoid relapse. Retrieved from http://www.wired.co.uk/article/schizophrenia-relapse-alert-system-fitbit

Depp, C. A., Moore, R. C., Dev, S. I., Mausbach, B. T., Eyler, L. T., & Granholm, E. L. (2016). The temporal course and clinical correlates of subjective impulsivity in bipolar disorder as revealed through ecological momentary assessment. *Journal of Affective Disorders*, 193, 145–150. doi:10.1016/j.jad.2015. 12. 01doi:6

Epstein, D. H., Tyburski, M., Craig, I. M., Phillips, K. A., Jobes, M. L., Vahabzadeh, M., ... Preston, K. L. (2014). Real-time tracking of neighborhood surroundings and mood in urban drug misusers: application of a new method to study behavior in its geographical context. *Drug and Alcohol Dependency*, 134, 22–29. doi:10.1016/j.drugalcdep.2013. 09. 00doi:7

Hamaker, E. L., Grasman, R. P., & Kamphuis, J. H. (2016). Modeling BAS dysregulation in bipolar disorder: Illustrating the potential of time series analysis. *Assessment*. doi:10.1177/ 1073191116632339

Hohn, P., Menne-Lothmann, C., Peeters, F., Nicolson, N. A., Jacobs, N., Derom, C., ... Wichers, M. (2013). Moment-to-moment transfer of positive emotions in daily life predicts future course of depression in both general population and patient samples. *PLoS One*, 8(9), e75655. doi:10.1371/journal.pone.0075655

Jahng, S., Wood, P. K., & Trull, T. J. (2008). Analysis of affective instability in ecological momentary assessment: Indices using successive difference and group comparison via multilevel modeling. *Psychological Methods*, 13(4), 354–375. doi:10.1037/a0014173

Kaufmann, C. N., Gershon, A., Eyler, L. T., & Depp, C. A. (2016). Clinical significance of mobile health assessed sleep duration and variability in bipolar disorder. *Journal of Psychiatric Research*, 81, 152–159. doi:10.1016/j.jpsychires.2016. 07. 00doi:8

Lam, C. Y., Businelle, M. S., Aigner, C. J., McClure, J. B., Cofta-Woerpel, L., Cinciripini, P. M., & Wetter, D. W. (2014). Individual and combined effects of multiple high-risk triggers on postcessation smoking urge and lapse. *Nicotine & Tobacco Research*, 16(5), 569–575. doi:10.1093/ntr/ntt190

Laney, D. (2001). 3-D data management: Controlling data volume, variety and velocity. Retrieved from https://blogs.gartner.com/doug-laney/files/2012/01/ad949-3D-Data-Ma nagement-Controlling-Data-Volume-Velocity-and-Variety.pdf

Langguth, N., Schmid, J., Gawrilow, C., & Stadler, G. (2016). Within-person link between depressed affect and moderate-to-vigorous physical activity in adolescence: An intensive longitudinal approach. *Applied Psychological Health & Well Being*, 8(1), 44–63. doi:10.1111/ aphw.12061

Lavender, J. M., Utzinger, L. M., Cao, L., Wonderlich, S. A., Engel, S. G., Mitchell, J. E., & Crosby, R. D. (2016). Reciprocal associations between negative affect, binge eating, and purging in the natural environment in women with bulimia nervosa. *Journal of Abnormal Psycholology*, 125(3), 381–386. doi:10.1037/abn0000135

Lopez-Guede, J. M., Moreno-Fernandez-de-Leceta, A., Martinez-Garcia, A., & Grana, M. (2015). Lynx: Automatic elderly behavior prediction in home telecare. *BioMed Research International*, 2015, 201939. doi:10.1155/2015/201939

Mason, M., Mennis, J., Way, T., Lanza, S., Russell, M., & Zaharakis, N. (2015). Time-varying effects of a text-based smoking cessation intervention for urban adolescents. *Drug& Alcohol Dependence*, 157, 99–105. doi:10.1016/j.drugalcdep.2015. 10. 01doi:6

Mittelstadt, B. D., & Floridi, L. (2016). The ethics of big data: Current and foreseeable issues in biomedical contexts. *Science & Engineering Ethics*, 22(2), 303–341. doi:10.1007/s11948-015-9652-2

Piette, J. D., Sussman, J. B., Pfeiffer, P. N., Silveira, M. J., Singh, S., & Lavieri, M. S. (2013). Maximizing the value of mobile health monitoring by avoiding redundant patient reports: prediction of depression-related symptoms and adherence problems in automated health assessment services. *Journal of Medical Internet Research*, 15(7), e118. doi:10.2196/jmir.2582

Possemato, K., Maisto, S. A., Wade, M., Barrie, K., McKenzie, S., Lantinga, L. J., & Ouimette, P. (2015). Ecological momentary assessment of PTSD symptoms and alcohol use in combat veterans. *Psychology of Addictive Behaviours*, 29(4), 894–905. doi:10.1037/ adb0000129

Quantified Self Labs. (2015). Quantified self: self knowledge through numbers. Retrieved from http://quantifiedself.com

Reininghaus, U., Depp, C. A., & Myin-Germeys, I. (2016). Ecological interventionist causal models in psychosis: Targeting psychological mechanisms in daily life. *Schizophrenia Bulletin*, 42(2), 264–269. doi:10.1093/schbul/sbv193

Scollon, C. N., Prieto, C.-K., & Diener, E. (2009). Experience sampling: promises and pitfalls, strength and weaknesses. In E. Diener (Ed.), *Assessing well-being* (pp. 157–180). Dordrecht, Netherlands: Springer.

Shiffman, S., Balabanis, M. H., Gwaltney, C. J., Paty, J. A., Gnys, M., Kassel, J. D., ... Paton, S. M. (2007). Prediction of lapse from associations between smoking and situational antecedents assessed by ecological momentary assessment. *Drug & Alcohol Dependence*, 91(2–3), 159–168. doi:10.1016/j.drugalcdep.2007. 05. 01doi:7

Shiyko, M. P., Lanza, S. T., Tan, X., Li, R., & Shiffman, S. (2012). Using the time-varying effect model (TVEM) to examine dynamic associations between negative affect and self confidence on smoking urges: differences between successful quitters and relapsers. *Prevention Science*, 13(3), 288–299. doi:10.1007/s11121-011-0264-z

Spaniel, F., Bakstein, E., Anyz, J., Hlinka, J., Sieger, T., Hrdlicka, J., ... Hoschl, C. (2016). Relapse in schizophrenia: Definitively not a bolt from the blue. *Neuroscience Letters*. doi:10.1016/j.neulet.2016. 04. 04doi:4

Swendsen, J., Ben-Zeev, D., & Granholm, E. (2011). Real-time electronic ambulatory monitoring of substance use and symptom expression in schizophrenia. *American Journal of Psychiatry*, 168(2), 202–209. doi:10.1176/appi.ajp.2010.10030463

Thompson, W. K., Gershon, A., O'Hara, R., Bernert, R. A., & Depp, C. A. (2014). The prediction of study-emergent suicidal ideation in bipolar disorder: a pilot study using ecological momentary assessment data. *Bipolar Disorder*, 16(7), 669–677. doi:10.1111/bdi.12218

Tibshirani, R. (1996). Regression shrinkage and selection via the lasso. *Journal of the Royal Statistical Society. Series B (Methodological)*, 58(1), 267–288.

Toscos, T., Connelly, K., & Rogers, Y. (2013). Designing for positive health affect: Decoupling negative emotion and health monitoring technologies. Paper presented at the Proceedings of the 7th International Conference on Pervasive Computing Technologies for Healthcare.

Walls, T. A., & Schafer, J. L. (2006). *Models for intensive longitudinal data*. New York: Oxford University Press.

Wichers, M., Peeters, F., Geschwind, N., Jacobs, N., Simons, C. J., Derom, C., ... van Os, J. (2010). Unveiling patterns of affective responses in daily life may improve outcome prediction in depression: a momentary assessment study. *Journal of Affective Disorders*, 124 (1–2), 191–195. doi:10.1016/j.jad.2009. 11. 01doi:0

Zhang, Z., Song, Y. Y., Cui, L., Liu, X., & Zhu, T. (2016). Emotion recognition based on customized smart bracelet with built-in accelerometer. *PeerJ PrePrints*, 4, e1650v1651.

10

THE DEVELOPMENT OF ECOLOGICAL MOMENTARY INTERVENTIONS

Henrietta Steinhart, Inez Myin-Germeys and and Ulrich Reininghaus

Introduction

Ideas for complex interventions can arise from a variety of sources, one of which is new technological developments (Craig et al., 2008). Recent years have seen major technological advances, particularly in *mobile* communication technology, opening up innovative possibilities for the delivery of healthcare. The use of mobile devices within clinical services is commonly referred to as mHealth (mobile Health). mHealth offers new possibilities for shifting the focus of treatment out of the consultation room and into patients' everyday lives. This novel approach to health care delivery is most prominently exemplified by Ecological Momentary Interventions (EMIs; Heron & Smyth, 2010; Versluis, Verkuil, Spinhoven, van der Ploeg, & Brosschot, 2016). These interventions utilize mHealth in order to deliver real-world and real-time treatments in natural environments (*ecological* treatment delivery) at those *moments* when people need them the most (Myin-Germeys, Klippel, Steinhart, & Reininghaus, 2016; Pop-Eleches et al., 2011). EMI thus differs from ESM in that ESM is a *data assessment method* aimed at measuring experiences in real life whilst causing the least possible disruption or reactivity in the individual's behavior, mood etc., whereas EMIs are a *treatment* delivered in real life, hence specifically aimed at introducing change. Types of EMIs vary from unstructured reminders (i.e. not following a specific schedule tailored to the individual; Pop-Eleches et al., 2011) to more structured interventions that are personalized to the current needs of the patient (Ben-Zeev et al., 2014). They can involve content delivery, self-monitoring, and interaction with the device (Doherty, Coyle, & Matthews, 2010). However, the one characteristic that links all of the different EMIs is the direct application of intervention strategies into patients' everyday routines (Heron & Smyth, 2010).

Although researchers and clinicians increasingly acknowledge the many benefits of EMIs, the approach is still fairly new and rarely developed in a structured manner. The current chapter aims to provide the reader with a set of guidelines for the development of EMIs. Earlier work by Doherty, Coyle, and Matthews (2010) advises on the design and evaluation of all mental health technologies, and Bakker and colleagues (2016) make 16 evidence-based recommendations for the development of mental health applications more generally. The current chapter, however, will specifically focus on the development of EMIs and the role of the experience sampling methodology (ESM).

The first part of the chapter will address the advantages and pitfalls of EMIs for the delivery of mental health care. Subsequently, the authors introduce a set of guidelines for the development and evaluation of EMIs. Within this, they will discuss a series of questions that need to be asked in the process of developing an EMI (see Table 10.1 at the end of the chapter). The guidelines described in this chapter aim to facilitate the generation of interventions that extend the scope of therapy into patients' daily lives and intervene at those times when therapeutic input is most needed, thus attuning to the user's fluctuating needs.

Advantages of EMIs

EMIs are an attractive new treatment modality. The following section will give a short overview of the most important benefits of EMIs compared to classical approaches exclusively involving face-to-face contact.

1. Provision of health-related information at relevant moments. Health-related information may be much more effective when provided at times where it is relevant and needed. For example, information on behavioral sleep management techniques presented at the doctor's office may quickly be forgotten, whereas providing this information in the evening, close to the time of sleep, may better prompt the recommended strategies.

2. Translation of skills into patients' everyday lives and formation of habits. Patients may fail to generalize new skills, learnt at the doctor's office, to their personal, ever-changing life and environment (also known as the therapy-real world gap; Kelly et al., 2012). Conversely, Versluis and colleagues (2016) point out that EMIs might result in faster formation of associations between behaviors and relevant contexts. Patients can be asked to apply new skills several times a day throughout different environments, thereby more easily forming an association between their own daily contexts and new strategies. Being able to draw on a range of adaptive habits is crucial, particularly in stressful situations where people tend to switch from goal-directed to more habitual behavior (Schwabe & Wolf, 2009). Habitual behavior, in this sense, is defined as behavior that is more readily accessible as it has been carried out several times before. Newly acquired coping strategies thus require some practice before being the first thing that comes to mind in stressful situations.

3. Tackling complaints via underlying mechanisms. ESM-derived insights into interactions between complaints and context, as well as the potential to access information on the temporal order of events, may help to elucidate the *causal mechanisms* that underlie certain complaints (Reininghaus, Depp, & Myin-Germeys, 2015). Take the example of an intervention for paranoia. It has been found that a drop in self-esteem predicts paranoid ideation (Thewissen, Bentall, Lecomte, van Os, & Myin-Germeys, 2008). An EMI may detect and counteract such a drop in self-esteem, which, if a causal relationship existed, would reduce the paranoid ideation itself (Myin-Germeys, Birchwood, & Kwapil, 2011).

4. Personalized treatment. By assessing the patient's current status and context, EMIs allow for tailoring of interventions to their current needs. It can also provide the right intervention at the most appropriate time and setting, based on the available data. This individualization aims at bridging the knowledge-practice gap, hence the difference between the individual client and the generic evidence-based treatment protocol (Kelly et al., 2012).

5. Accessibility of services. Accessibility of mental health care services can be limited by several factors, including regional unavailability, financial constraints or stigma (Collin et al., 2011; Corrigan, 2004). On the other hand, many people endorse the idea of using their mobile phones as a medium for intervention (Mitchell, Bull, Kiwanuka, & Ybarra, 2011). Access to mental health care services via mobile phones can thus reach individuals who would not otherwise be able to use services.

6. Decrease in costs. As EMIs aim for truly sustainable change by directly targeting the underlying causal mechanisms of a complaint (Reininghaus et al., 2015), they have the potential to be more effective in the long run, providing users with a new set of skills that will be adaptive to the many novel situations that they might encounter in their daily lives. This may reduce costs considerably. Moreover, other benefits of this approach could involve a reduction in contact hours and maximization of clinical resources (e.g. reduced clinician travel time, ability to treat more patients at the same time). Finally, use of technology to fill in questionnaires and carry out between-appointment assignments would support a paper-light environment.

7. Empowerment of the patient. With EMIs, patients receive a treatment tool that they can use to help themselves (Wichers et al., 2011). This can increase perceived control and feelings of empowerment (Groot, 2010; Wichers et al., 2011). Improved access to information, easier communication with clinicians and convenience have all been noted as factors that increase patients' sense of responsibility for their treatment (Mirza, Norris, & Stockdale, 2008).

Potential pitfalls of EMIs

Besides the many possibilities the EMI approach offers, it may also involve some pitfalls. These should also be taken into account when developing an EMI.

1. Less face-to-face treatment contact. One of the concerns that is often expressed is that the use of EMIs would result in decreased interpersonal contact between therapist and patients and hence poorer working alliance, which has been argued to play an important role in the recovery process (Gaston, 1990). One qualitative study of the feasibility and acceptability of a smartphone-based intervention for depression involving a maximum of 20 minutes of therapist-contact per week found that most participants wished for more contact with the therapist and would not want to be treated by a stand-alone smartphone intervention (Ly, Janni, et al., 2015). On the other hand, evidence from another study comparing a pure face-to-face behavioral activation treatment for depression (consisting of ten sessions) with a combined approach (consisting of four face-to-face sessions + smartphone app) did not suggest any differences on working alliance between the two conditions after three weeks of treatment (Ly, Topooco, et al., 2015). Stand-alone EMIs such as *Actissist* (Bucci et al., 2015) have also demonstrated positive treatment outcomes. Hence, at the moment there is no convincing evidence that the introduction of EMIs impairs treatment outcome or reduces the therapeutic alliance between patients and their clinicians.

2. Increased engagement in mobile phone. Another concern may involve the fact that an EMI will inherently lead to an increase in mobile phone related activity, which in turn has been found to be associated with increased stress (Thomée, Härenstam, & Hagberg, 2011). However, we do not assume that the use of mobile phones for the delivery of an intervention will have the same effect as heavy private mobile phone use. Moreover, the ultimate goal of an EMI is not to be integrated in the users' lives permanently, but to help them learn to use the techniques independently of the app. Hence, mobile phone use within an EMI will only be increased for a confined period of time.

3. Intrusive character. One final concern that has been expressed is that EMIs might be considered intrusive. However, from our experience with ecological momentary assessment in the research context, we are confident that only a minor proportion of users will consider this to be an issue. Again, since EMIs aim at teaching users to ultimately apply the strategies independently of the application, the period in which the EMI truly intrudes in the users' everyday lives is rather short. Moreover, nowadays the use of mobile phone applications involving notification systems is so common that most users are not expected to be concerned about the use of an app for treatment. Studies on the feasibility and acceptability of smartphone-based interventions demonstrate generally good acceptability of this treatment modality, thus supporting the assumption that users in general do not consider the use of EMIs to be too intrusive (Allen, Stephens, Dennison Himmelfarb, Stewart, & Hauck, 2013; Ben-Zeev et al., 2014; Stephens & Allen, 2013).

Guidelines

The following section provides guidelines on how researchers and clinicians might develop EMIs. First, the authors highlight the importance of identifying appropriate theory and evidence before intervening. Subsequently, they will address issues concerning the design and development of EMIs, as well as the role of ESM for the personalization of treatment. The authors will then discuss the potential impact of the target population and the choice of technology on EMI design. The final section will reflect on the importance of user-friendliness and acceptability, and the evaluation of EMIs. For each section, we provide helpful relevant key questions that readers should ask at each stage of the development process. These can be found in Table 10.1 at the end of the chapter.

Is an EMI the best approach to tackle the complaint in question?

Readers should ask themselves why an EMI would be preferred over other intervention techniques. How can the effectiveness of an intervention be enhanced through integration into the daily lives of patients? EMIs operate on the assumption that change (e.g. in behaviors, cognitions, well-being, symptom intensity etc.) can be achieved most successfully by intervening in those situations and at those moments when the complaints and/or the underlying mechanisms occur. This assumption, however, does not necessarily apply to every target. In order to pick the most adequate treatment, we need a thorough understanding of the day-to-day dynamics between individuals and their environments.

Similarly, we need to understand in what context symptoms occur and how we could best intervene in those moments when they are occurring. Take the example of stress sensitivity, i.e. the increase of negative affect as a reaction to a stressor in real life (Myin-Germeys & van Os, 2007; Wichers et al., 2009). According to theory and empirical evidence, would it be enough to teach patients about the factors that influence stress sensitivity in the form of a psychoeducation lesson or would patients benefit from more targeted information on how to deal with stress that is attuned to their recent behaviors and current context? To answer this question, we need knowledge of the *mechanisms* underlying these complaints. As most of the current health behavior theories are not based on daily-life mechanisms, they may be inadequate to inform this type of intervention (Riley et al., 2011). Therefore, it is advisable to start with a literature search that focuses on investigations of the target complaints *in daily life*, such as that studied with ESM. It is crucial to obtain a thorough understanding of these complaints before starting development of an EMI. Modelling and pre-clinical evaluation of the process and outcome of the EMI will be useful in order to establish a causal association between the intervention and outcome (Craig et al., 2008). Without a thorough model, it will be difficult to establish why the intervention is effective (or not) and how effective it is (see section on evaluation). Methods that can be used for modelling may include systematic reviews, expert meetings with researchers and practitioners, focus groups and interviews with the target population, and/or economic modelling for estimating the cost-effectiveness of the intervention (Torgerson & Byford, 2002; Torgerson & Campbell, 2000).

What do you need to keep in mind when designing an EMI?

After establishing whether the EMI approach is the most appropriate method, the next step is to think about the design of the intervention.

Content of EMIs

Most EMIs developed to date have involved components that are closely linked to specific face-to-face interventions. One example is the ACT in Daily Life (ACT-DL) training, an adjunct to in-person Acceptance and Commitment Therapy (ACT) (Steinhart et al., submitted; Tim Batink et al., 2016). ACT-DL has been developed to activate modules that are relevant to the work already completed within face-to-face ACT therapy. Although the use of mHealth interventions is sometimes recommended as an adjunct to in-person contact (Donker et al., 2013; Labrique, Vasudevan, Kochi, Fabricant, & Mehl, 2013), EMIs may also consist of a stand-alone treatment (Neff & Fry, 2009). One example for such a stand-alone treatment is the so-called *Actissist* application (Bucci et al., 2015). Actissist is an EMI that builds on the cognitive maintenance model of psychotic disorders. It emits a number of prompts each day for the user to engage in the app. After each prompt, users are asked to fill in a short questionnaire and to choose one or more of the target treatment domains (perceived criticism; socialization; cannabis use; paranoia; and distressing voice-hearing). Depending on the user's response, normalizing messages and cognitive-behavioral suggestions are provided. While Actissist and ACT-DL follow a rather similar structure, they differ in their interrelationship with in-person therapy sessions.

Other possibilities involve the implementation of the ESM as a therapeutic tool in itself, either as a mere self-monitoring aid (Ainsworth et al., 2013) or as a means to inform the subsequent therapeutic steps (Depp et al., 2010). One can also develop entirely new EMI treatments, specifically targeting day-to-day mechanisms. For example, a study in people with depression improved insight into the daily life associations between context and the experience of positive affect by feeding back their resultant ESM data. This resulted in a reduction in depression (Kramer et al., 2014) and a change in behavior (Snippe et al., 2016).

The type and severity of intervention targets and the type of target population may play a crucial role in deciding the content of your EMI. So for example, the presence of severe symptoms or a patient's need for personal contact may contradict the use of EMI as a stand-alone treatment, whereas this form of treatment delivery might be preferable for targeting mildly elevated stress sensitivity in response to daily hassles in the general population.

Interrelationship of EMI components

EMI designs may include components that are closely interconnected or completely independent from each other. An independent EMI design implies that components of the intervention are not inter-related or do not gradually build on each other. For example, the FOCUS system employs five independent modules concentrating on different domains of mental health (e.g. sleep or medication adherence; Ben-Zeev et al., 2014; Ben-Zeev et al., 2013). Before the start of the therapy, the therapist and patient decide which modules best fit the patient's presenting difficulties or complaints. Access to the treatment modules does not therefore depend on completion of previous work, but rather on the patient's current needs. Other EMI designs involve closely interconnected components that may gradually build on each other, as was done in the ACT-DL training (Steinhart et al., submitted; Tim Batink et al., 2016). These allow users to choose exercises from modules that they have previously encountered. Other EMI designs do not involve different components at all but rely on only one treatment principle and hence a single component (e.g. self-monitoring EMIs).

Event-based, time-based and combined EMI delivery schemes

Different EMI delivery schemes can be deployed. Event-based delivery procedures imply that the intervention is triggered by a specific incident. For instance, patients may be asked to request mobile support when experiencing symptoms of panic. This delivery scheme requires patients to take the initiative to access support when they recognize predefined problematic events. Fixed time-based delivery schemes involve the provision of the intervention at predefined moments in time. This might include shift workers receiving advice for sleep hygiene prior to or at the end of work (Patterson et al., 2014). A third option is a *random* time-based sampling scheme, in which the intervention is offered at random time-points throughout the day (Ben-Zeev et al., 2014). This last option ensures delivery of EMIs in a representative sample of contexts and is preferable over other delivery schemes if the intervention aims to help the recipient to generalize the newly acquired skills across different situations.

Different delivery schemes can also be combined. One option is to introduce a random time-based delivery scheme alongside an event-based delivery scheme. Here, in addition to receiving prompts at random time points throughout the day, users may choose to engage with the device whenever they feel that they need support. This *on-demand* function may increase a sense of empowerment and the individualization of treatment.

The frequency and timing of prompts in time-based EMI delivery schemes, the number of days per week that prompts are offered, and the length of the intervention are based on the type and severity of problems being targeted and the population. For example, individuals with depression tend to demonstrate diurnal variations in their mood, with more negative and less positive affect early in the

Ecological momentary interventions **131**

day (Gordijn, Beersma, Bouhuys, Reinink, & Van den Hoofdakker, 1994; Leibenluft, Noonan, & Wehr, 1992; Peeters, Berkhof, Delespaul, Rottenberg, & Nicolson, 2006). If the aim of the EMI is to improve mood, this knowledge of diurnal variation may be used to inform the timing of prompts so that more prompts are offered in the morning. Investigations using ESM have given us some insights about the importance of finding a balance in the number of prompts offered (Palmier-Claus et al., 2011). If too few prompts are provided, the sampled situations may not be representative. On the other hand, too many prompts may constitute a burden to the user. This, in turn, would decrease the acceptability and user-friendliness of the intervention, leading to reduced motivation and engagement. To our knowledge, no systematic investigation of the delivery rate and timing appropriate for different target groups has been carried out (except for some evidence indicating that prompts delivered once a week are more useful than prompts delivered every three weeks; Lombard, Lombard, & Winett, 1995). Therefore, hypotheses concerning these factors should be tested in the modelling stage (see section on theoretical background and empirical evidence). Moreover, in line with tailoring the treatment to the individual, the feasibility of the sampling rate should also be discussed with each individual patient (Palmier-Claus et al., 2011).

Issues regarding the personalization of EMI

One of the greatest benefits of EMIs is the potential to tailor the intervention to the individual. This feature is aided by the inclusion of ESM in the design. Assessment of the user's current experience and context is necessary to offer a treatment that is relevant to a given moment, context and experience. While the inclusion of an on-demand function (i.e. the possibility to turn on the device whenever users feel the need) is recommended, this function will most probably not cover all relevant moments, since it will be accessed according to the users' *subjectively* perceived need (which may not always be consistent with what is clinically indicated). With the inclusion of ESM, one introduces an assessment of the current mental state and context at random moments in time, which may then guide and inform the delivery of the EMI. This could either mean that treatment is delivered only at those moments when the targeted symptoms are present or reach a certain severity threshold. Alternatively, it could provide the users with the opportunity to engage in the intervention within a wide range of moments, contexts, and experiences of their daily life, thus supporting the integration of taught strategies in the ever-changing environment.

Another advantage of including ESM is the potential to intervene at the level of the underlying mechanisms. With ESM, the interaction between psychological processes and the real world can be investigated, thereby helping to establish the point of action for an intervention (Myin-Germeys et al., 2011; Myin-Germeys et al., 2009; Shiffman, Stone, & Hufford, 2008). Furthermore, according to the ecological interventionist causal model approach, the combination of ESM and EMI

Issues pertaining to EMI feedback

In order to give users direct insights to their personal needs, one option is to include a feedback function that illustrates users' ESM data. Although the mere act of filling in ESM questionnaires increases the users' awareness of their inner states and emotions, this process is even further facilitated by providing feedback on these reports to the user. This awareness in itself can have a therapeutic effect, building the foundation for behavioral change (Kramer et al., 2014; Vago & David, 2012).

Feedback functions do not need to be restricted to the mere depiction of averages or moment-to-moment variation, but can outline *associations* between mechanisms and complaints. For instance, individuals with depression may spend much time alone and express a preference for solitude (Myin-Germeys et al., 2009). However, their experience sampling data may reveal only a short-term benefit of being alone, whilst indicating an overall long-term increase in unhappiness, which might prompt them to become more proactive in seeking out social contact. Hence, *awareness* of such an association between social context and mood, supported by *their own data*, might motivate users to change their behavior in a direction that benefits their general well-being (Kramer et al., 2014). Depending on the outcome of interest, another possibility for feedback involves illustrating the user's past performance and levels of improvement (Ramanathan et al., 2012). For example, if the aim of the EMI is to increase positive affect, feedback to the user could involve a depiction of the user's average positive affect at the end of each week, including the scores of all previous weeks. This might help users to track their own improvement more easily.

The format of feedback is crucial to its acceptability. Whilst illustrations in the form of feedback graphs might be an acceptable format for researchers and clinicians, patients might require a less scientific depiction of their data or guidance on how to interpret their results. ESM-derived feedback may be illustrated in the form of pictures or augmented by a few direct statements, which may help users to better understand their results.

The decision on whether the ESM data should be fed back to the user or the clinician (or both) depends on the target population and the extensiveness of the intervention. Some individuals might find this feedback useful, whereas others might consider it stressful or confusing. Moreover, if the intervention already includes a great number of components, developers should be careful not to overburden patients by introducing additional elements.

It is useful to consider when best to present feedback to the user. Patients may receive feedback after each assessment, at the end of the day, at the end of the week, on demand, or in consultation with a clinician. If feedback is given after each assessment, it is easier for the user to learn from this feedback (as it is given

Ecological momentary interventions   **133**

after a shorter interval) and to apply it to the situation at hand. Moreover, fluctuations throughout the day are made explicit. Conversely, through repeated daily provision of their data, patients might become desensitized to the information provided (i.e. they might lose interest in the feedback). Further, provision of feedback, especially if it is depicted in a graph that requires active interpretation by the patient, will prolong the time required to engage in the prompt. It is important to find a balance between usefulness and burden to the patient when deciding on the timing and amount of feedback.

Issues pertaining to interactive EMI components

Another way by which an intervention can be personalized is through the use of interactive EMI components, which are based on ESM-derived information, thus offering exercises tailored to the user's current experience and situation. For such components, it is important to identify those ESM questions that would provide us with the information needed to facilitate the appropriate exercise in a given moment. For some interventions, information on generic positive and negative affect may be enough in order for the system to decide which exercise should be offered to the user. Other therapies might try to tackle more specific symptoms (such as cravings or anxiety) or mechanisms (such as stress reactivity or motivation for physical activity) and will have to obtain information on these variables to provide the appropriate intervention. iRTT (intelligent Real Time Therapy) is a concept developed by Kelly and colleagues in 2012 (Kelly et al., 2012), which aims at more effectively bridging the knowledge–practice and the therapy–real world gaps. iRTT uses machine and reinforcement learning to distinguish between multiple pathways that may lead to mental health issues. This, in turn, facilitates the delivery of the most appropriate intervention for that specific individual at that particular time. iRTT begins by using probabilistically effective strategies (i.e. based on population data), which are then fine-tuned to the individual based on his or her real-life ESM data. This way the intervention will be truly individualized to the patient's current needs.

Choosing hardware and software for EMI

In addition to working out the content of the intervention, another important consideration concerns the necessary hard- and software.

Device

Letting patients use their own mobile phones for EMIs has several advantages. These include lower costs, not needing to carry an additional device, and that engagement in the intervention will attract less attention from others. Moreover, patients are familiar with their own mobile phones and will therefore require less assistance (Doherty et al., 2010). The drawback is that programming of the app becomes much more complicated since the EMI needs to run on different operating systems, different versions of the operating systems, and on different devices. Moreover, whenever new versions of operating systems are released, compatibility with these new versions needs to be examined (Ben-Zeev et al., 2015). Another caveat is that interactions between the EMI and other apps might cause errors in the execution of the EMI. Hence, for every user, compatibility of the EMI with his or her individual device would need to be assessed to assure error-free operation. Depending on the required level of interaction with the EMI, a possible solution for these potential difficulties is to use text messages instead of a smartphone application. Although native smartphone applications (i.e. an application that is installed on the device itself) have been found to be generally preferred over an SMS text-only implementation, text messages have been reported to be a valuable tool in this respect (Ainsworth et al., 2013).

If patients are provided with a device (and a native application is used, see next section), developers of the intervention need to decide on the operating system they want to use. Since most of the market is currently covered by iOS and Android, one of these operating systems should typically be selected. Moreover, since Android is used by a wider range of user populations and iOS prevents some potentially important features of EMIs, it is generally suggested to use Android over iOS (Ben-Zeev et al., 2015).

Data storage

There are several possibilities to save and retrieve data when operating an EMI. Information used and collected by the EMI (e.g. exercises or psychoeducational content and ESM data) may be transferred via an external server or online resource on the one hand (web-based applications), or could be stored via the app on the device itself (native application; Ben-Zeev et al., 2015). Native applications have higher processing speed and run independently from an internet connection. Web-based applications, on the other hand, are more easily programmed due to relatively simple programming languages such as HTML or JavaScript and can run across different operating systems (i.e. for example iOS and Android; Ben-Zeev et al., 2015).

Choosing the right target population

As we have seen in previous sections, during all stages of development, when developing EMIs the specific characteristics of the target population need to be taken into account (Ben-Zeev et al., 2013). For example, it has been shown that individuals diagnosed with schizophrenia may encounter difficulties with websites designed for the general population, potentially due to cognitive deficits and/or less experience with computers (Brunette et al., 2012). It is important to consider such population-specific difficulties. These considerations should be based on empirical evidence. Modern mental health applications often lack experimental evidence (Bakker et al., 2016), but clinical experience and anecdotal evidence do not always lead to correct assumptions. For instance, a common concern by clinicians is that investigation and treatment of psychotic symptoms with modern technology will exacerbate suspicious thoughts (Depp et al., 2010). However, many studies using ESM in this patient group have demonstrated little reactivity to these approaches, with only a minority of patients expressing such concerns. Screening the literature and contacting relevant investigators can help to take a more evidence-based approach and allay such fears.

Another patient characteristic that might hinder compliance with EMI is severe motivational problems (Scollon, Prieto, & Diener, 2009). In such cases, the addition of a preparatory session (e.g. applying motivational interviewing) may be useful. The question of IQ, reading level, and age of the target group may define the complexity of the intervention and the willingness to engage in EMI. There is a notion that older individuals or those with lower IQ may experience more difficulties handling newer technology. On the other hand, a meta-analysis on patient preferences indicated that the elderly actually prefer using electronic diaries over paper-and-pencil (Shiffman et al., 2008). Again, searching the literature for empirical evidence concerning assumptions about the potential interactions between patient characteristics and ability to operate an EMI is crucial.

User-friendliness and acceptability

Since personalized approaches such as EMIs rely heavily on the willingness of users to engage with the intervention, a simple and intuitive design and interface is key to its potential success (Bakker et al., 2016). In addition to taking into account the specific characteristics of the target group, it is essential to test the system in order to ensure acceptability (Ramanathan et al., 2012; van der Krieke, Wunderink, Emerencia, de Jonge, & Sytema, 2014). Moreover, involving different wordings and variations in the sequence of exercises prevents repetitiveness and predictability, which, in turn, will decrease the likelihood of users disengaging from the intervention (Ben-Zeev et al., 2014).

Evaluation of EMIs

A thorough evaluation of the EMI is necessary before implementation into clinical practice. There are two types of evaluation, *outcome* and *process evaluation*. Outcome evaluation refers to the effect of the intervention on the pre-defined target(s). Since EMIs are supposed to target complaints and mechanisms in daily life, outcome evaluation should involve inspection of changes in the daily lives of patients (i.e. measured with ESM). Of course, not all targets need to involve outcomes that fluctuate in daily life, but may also include other measurements such as retrospective questionnaires. Hypothesized outcomes of the EMI should be defined in the modelling phase.

A process evaluation considers how the intervention was implemented, including compliance with the protocol, satisfaction of users and clinicians, who was reached by the intervention and barriers that prevented its success. In the case of an EMI, protocol compliance on the part of the user can be assessed by tracking engagement in the exercises. If the EMI is used as an adjunct to in-person treatment, there should be a measure of the extent to which the therapist complied with the protocol (e.g. through checklists that the therapist can fill in at the end of

TABLE 10.1 Summary of key questions and considerations researchers and clinicians should bear in mind across the EMI development process

Is an EMI the best approach to tackle the complaint in question?

- What outcome are you aiming for and why would an EMI be helpful in this respect? Does the problem that you are trying to tackle happen *in the moment*, i.e. does it fluctuate throughout the day and across different situations?
- Does your intervention have a coherent theoretical basis?
- Is there any empirical evidence for the assumption that maintenance factors can be tackled in the *daily life* of patients?

What do you need to keep in mind when designing an EMI?

- Should the intervention be an adjunct to in-person treatment or can it function as stand-alone therapy? If you consider it an adjunct to in-person treatment, should it be offered during or after the period of the in-person treatment?
- What should the general structure of the intervention look like? Do the exercises build up on each other or can they be carried out independently?
- How many prompts should be provided on a given day and how many days a week should prompts be offered?
- Which ESM items do you need to include?
- What threshold on the ESM scales should trigger an exercise?
- Could intervention benefit from feedback function?

Choosing hardware and software for EMI

- Will the device be provided or will patients use their own mobile phone? In case of the latter, does the app run on different operating systems (iOS vs. Android), different versions, and different phones?
- How is data saved and retrieved (native vs. web-based application)?

Choosing the right target population

- What is your target population? Does this population have any characteristics that need to be taken into account when designing the EMI?
  - → type of complaints? (e.g. social anxiety, motivational complaints, paranoid thinking)
  - → severity of complaints?
  - → age group?
  - → IQ/reading capabilities?

User-friendliness and acceptability

- Is the interface clearly arranged and user-friendly? Will users need training in order to use the system properly?
- Can sound/notifications be modified by the user?
- Is there enough variation in wordings/exercises to prevent repetitiveness?

Evaluation of EMIs

- Which design do you want to evaluate your EMI? Is an experimental design feasible?
- Which outcomes do you need to assess to test effectiveness of the intervention?
- Did patients (and therapists) comply with the protocol?
- Were users and therapists satisfied? Why/why not?
- Who was reached by the EMI?
- What were the barriers that prevented success of the EMI?

the session or by recording treatment sessions for later independent scoring of protocol compliance).

As mentioned before, active engagement in EMIs depends to a large extent on a simple design and intuitive interface. Process evaluation of an EMI should involve questions on how easily users (and clinicians) could handle the EMI and whether technical difficulties prevented proper engagement in the intervention. Also, it is important to establish whether the EMI can be navigated by different subgroups of patients and, if not, which factors caused these differences.

In order to evaluate the effectiveness of an EMI, different designs can be used. As for the evaluation of other interventions, randomized designs will avoid most biases. Craig and colleagues (2008) provide a helpful overview of the different designs, their advantages and disadvantages, and methods on how to deal with drawbacks of non-randomized designs.

Development and evaluation of an intervention form an iterative process. New insights about the effectiveness and potential barriers to effectiveness of the EMI should lead to modifications of its design, which, in turn, should be integrated into a new model that will subsequently be re-evaluated. Only if evaluation of the EMI demonstrates its effectiveness should it be implemented into clinical practice.

Conclusion

The current chapter describes a set of guidelines for the development of EMIs; interventions that are taking place in patients' natural environment and at those *moments* when help is needed the most. It addresses important issues, including identifying the evidence base and appropriate theoretical basis, different EMI designs, and components and approaches. It also considers how to develop EMIs with advice on hardware, software, selecting a target population, acceptability, user-friendliness and evaluation. The key questions and issues that researchers and clinicians should consider when developing an EMI are summarized in Table 10.1.

Continuous advances in technological developments in combination with growing numbers in smartphone ownership both in the general and psychiatric populations have established many new possibilities for mental health research and interventions. This is reflected in the increasing numbers of ESM studies and EMIs on the market (Luxton, McCann, Bush, Mishkind, & Reger, 2011). While there are well-established guidelines on the development of in-person treatments, recommendations for the development of an EMI are distinct. Use of mobile technology and expansion of treatment into users' daily lives pose novel challenges that must be overcome. This chapter is not so much aimed to provide a complete overview of all aspects of the EMI development process but rather a range of possibilities that the EMI approach offers, as well as examples of potential constraints. However, it is a very exciting time to be developing innovative treatments such as EMIs, making possible what was previously out of reach.

Acknowledgements

This work was supported by a Veni grant from the Netherlands Organisation for Scientific Research (451-13-022) to Ulrich Reininghaus and by an ERC consolidator grant to Inez Myin-Germeys (ERC-2012-StG, project 309767 – INTERACT).

References

Ainsworth, J., Palmier-Claus, J. E., Machin, M., Barrowclough, C., Dunn, G., Rogers, A., ... Wykes, T. (2013). A comparison of two delivery modalities of a mobile phone-based assessment for serious mental illness: native smartphone application vs text-messaging only implementations. *Journal of Medical Internet Research*, 15(4), e60.

Allen, J. K., Stephens, J., Dennison Himmelfarb, C. R., Stewart, K. J., & Hauck, S. (2013). Randomized controlled pilot study testing use of smartphone technology for obesity treatment. *Journal of Obesity*, 2013. doi:10.1155/2013/151597

Bakker, D., Kazantzis, N., Rickwood, D., & Rickard, N. (2016). Mental health smartphone apps: Review and evidence-based recommendations for future developments. *JMIR Mental Health*, 3(1), e7.

Ben-Zeev, D., Brenner, C. J., Begale, M., Duffecy, J., Mohr, D. C., & Mueser, K. T. (2014). Feasibility, acceptability, and preliminary efficacy of a smartphone intervention for schizophrenia. *Schizophrenia Bulletin*, 40(6), 1244–1253. doi:10.1093/schbul/sbu033

Ben-Zeev, D., Kaiser, S. M., Brenner, C. J., Begale, M., Duffecy, J., & Mohr, D. C. (2013). Development and usability testing of FOCUS: A smartphone system for self-management of schizophrenia. *Psychiatric Rehabilitation Journal*, 36(4), 289.

Ben-Zeev, D., Schueller, S. M., Begale, M., Duffecy, J., Kane, J. M., & Mohr, D. C. (2015). Strategies for mHealth research: Lessons from 3 mobile intervention studies. *Administration and Policy in Mental Health and Mental Health Services Research*, 42(2), 157–167.

Brunette, M. F., Ferron, J. C., Devitt, T., Geiger, P., Martin, W. M., Pratt, S., ... McHugo, G. J. (2012). Do smoking cessation websites meet the needs of smokers with severe mental illnesses? *Health Education Research*, 27(2), 183–190.

Bucci, S., Barrowclough, C., Ainsworth, J., Morris, R., Berry, K., Machin, M., ... Buchan, I. (2015). Using mobile technology to deliver a cognitive behaviour therapy-informed intervention in early psychosis (Actissist): study protocol for a randomised controlled trial. *Trials*, 16(1), 404.

Collin, P. J., Metcalf, A. T., Stephens-Reicher, J. C., Blanchard, M. E., Herrman, H. E., Rahilly, K., & Burns, J. M. (2011). ReachOut. com: The role of an online service for promoting help-seeking in young people. *Advances in Mental Health*, 10(1), 39–51.

Corrigan, P. (2004). How stigma interferes with mental health care. *American Psychologist*, 59 (7), 614.

Craig, P., Dieppe, P., Macintyre, S., Michie, S., Nazareth, I., & Petticrew, M. (2008). Developing and evaluating complex interventions: the new Medical Research Council guidance. *British Medical Journal*, 337, a1655.

Depp, C. A., Mausbach, B., Granholm, E., Cardenas, V., Ben-Zeev, D., Patterson, T. L., ... Jeste, D. V. (2010). Mobile interventions for severe mental illness: design and preliminary data from three approaches. *Journal of Nervous and Mental Disease*, 198(10), 715.

Doherty, G., Coyle, D., & Matthews, M. (2010). Design and evaluation guidelines for mental health technologies. *Interacting with Computers*, 22(4), 243–252.

Donker, T., Petrie, K., Proudfoot, J., Clarke, J., Birch, M.-R., & Christensen, H. (2013). Smartphones for smarter delivery of mental health programs: a systematic review. *Journal of Medical Internet Research*, 15(11), e247.

Gaston, L. (1990). The concept of the alliance and its role in psychotherapy: Theoretical and empirical considerations. *Psychotherapy: Theory, Research, Practice, Training*, 27(2), 143.

Gordijn, M., Beersma, D., Bouhuys, A., Reinink, E., & Van den Hoofdakker, R. (1994). A longitudinal study of diurnal mood variation in depression; characteristics and significance. *Journal of Affective Disorders*, 31(4), 261–273.

Groot, P. C. (2010). Patients can diagnose too: how continuous self-assessment aids diagnosis of, and recovery from, depression. *Journal of Mental Health*, 19(4), 352–362.

Heron, K. E., & Smyth, J. M. (2010). Ecological momentary interventions: incorporating mobile technology into psychosocial and health behaviour treatments. *British Journal of Health Psychology*, 15(1), 1–39.

Kelly, J., Gooding, P., Pratt, D., Ainsworth, J., Welford, M., & Tarrier, N. (2012). Intelligent real-time therapy: Harnessing the power of machine learning to optimise the delivery of momentary cognitive–behavioural interventions. *Journal of Mental Health*, 21(4), 404–414.

Kramer, I., Simons, C. J., Hartmann, J. A., Menne-Lothmann, C., Viechtbauer, W., Peeters, F., ... Delespaul, P. (2014). A therapeutic application of the experience sampling method in the treatment of depression: a randomized controlled trial. *World Psychiatry*, 13(1), 68–77.

Labrique, A. B., Vasudevan, L., Kochi, E., Fabricant, R., & Mehl, G. (2013). mHealth innovations as health system strengthening tools: 12 common applications and a visual framework. *Global Health: Science and Practice*, 1(2), 160–171.

Leibenluft, E., Noonan, B. M., & Wehr, T. A. (1992). Diurnal variation: reliability of measurement and relationship to typical and atypical symptoms of depression. *Journal of Affective Disorders*, 26(3), 199–204.

Lombard, D. N., Lombard, T. N., & Winett, R. A. (1995). Walking to meet health guidelines: the effect of prompting frequency and prompt structure. *Health Psychology*, 14 (2), 164.

Luxton, D. D., McCann, R. A., Bush, N. E., Mishkind, M. C., & Reger, G. M. (2011). mHealth for mental health: Integrating smartphone technology in behavioral healthcare. *Professional Psychology: Research and Practice*, 42(6), 505.

Ly, K. H., Janni, E., Wrede, R., Sedem, M., Donker, T., Carlbring, P., & Andersson, G. (2015). Experiences of a guided smartphone-based behavioral activation therapy for depression: A qualitative study. *Internet Interventions: The Application of Information Technology in Mental and Behavioural Health*, 1(2), 60–68.

Ly, K. H., Topooco, N., Cederlund, H., Wallin, A., Bergström, J., Molander, O., ... Andersson, G. (2015). Smartphone-supported versus full behavioural activation for depression: A randomised controlled trial. *Plos One*, 10(5).

Mirza, F., Norris, T., & Stockdale, R. (2008). Mobile technologies and the holistic management of chronic diseases. *Health Informatics Journal*, 14(4), 309–321.

Mitchell, K. J., Bull, S., Kiwanuka, J., & Ybarra, M. L. (2011). Cell phone usage among adolescents in Uganda: acceptability for relaying health information. *Health Education Research*, 26(5), 770–781.

Myin-Germeys, I., Birchwood, M., & Kwapil, T. (2011). From environment to therapy in psychosis: a real-world momentary assessment approach. *Schizophrenia Bulletin*, 37 (2), 244–247.

Myin-Germeys, I., Klippel, A., Steinhart, H., & Reininghaus, U. (2016). Ecological momentary interventions in psychiatry. *Current Opinion in Psychiatry*, 29(4), 258–263.

Myin-Germeys, I., Oorschot, M., Collip, D., Lataster, J., Delespaul, P., & van Os, J. (2009). Experience sampling research in psychopathology: opening the black box of daily life. *Psychological Medicine*, 39(9), 1533.

Myin-Germeys, I., & van Os, J. (2007). Stress-reactivity in psychosis: evidence for an affective pathway to psychosis. *Clinical Psychology Review*, 27(4), 409–424.

Neff, R., & Fry, J. (2009). Periodic prompts and reminders in health promotion and health behavior interventions: systematic review. *Journal of Medical Internet Research*, 11(2), e16.

Palmier-Claus, J. E., Myin-Germeys, I., Barkus, E., Bentley, L., Udachina, A., Delespaul, P., ... Dunn, G. (2011). Experience sampling research in individuals with mental illness: reflections and guidance. *Acta Psychiatrica Scandinavica*, 123(1), 12–20.

Patterson, P. D., Moore, C. G., Weaver, M. D., Buysse, D. J., Suffoletto, B. P., Callaway, C. W., & Yealy, D. M. (2014). Mobile phone text messaging intervention to improve alertness and reduce sleepiness and fatigue during shiftwork among emergency medicine clinicians: study protocol for the SleepTrackTXT pilot randomized controlled trial. *Trials*, 15(1), 1.

Peeters, F., Berkhof, J., Delespaul, P., Rottenberg, J., & Nicolson, N. A. (2006). Diurnal mood variation in major depressive disorder. *Emotion*, 6(3), 383.

Pop-Eleches, C., Thirumurthy, H., Habyarimana, J. P., Zivin, J. G., Goldstein, M. P., De Walque, D., ... Sidle, J. (2011). Mobile phone technologies improve adherence to antiretroviral treatment in a resource-limited setting: a randomized controlled trial of text message reminders. *AIDS (London, England)*, 25(6), 825.

Ramanathan, N., Alquaddoomi, F., Falaki, H., George, D., Hsieh, C.-K., Jenkins, J., ... Selsky, J. (2012). Ohmage: an open mobile system for activity and experience sampling. Paper presented at the 2012 6th International Conference on Pervasive Computing Technologies for Healthcare (PervasiveHealth) and Workshops.

Reininghaus, U., Depp, C. A., & Myin-Germeys, I. (2015). Ecological interventionist causal models in psychosis: targeting psychological mechanisms in daily life. *Schizophrenia Bulletin*, 42(2), 264–269.

Riley, W. T., Rivera, D. E., Atienza, A. A., Nilsen, W., Allison, S. M., & Mermelstein, R. (2011). Health behavior models in the age of mobile interventions: are our theories up to the task? *Translational Behavioral Medicine*, 1(1), 53–71.

Schwabe, L., & Wolf, O. T. (2009). Stress prompts habit behavior in humans. *The Journal of Neuroscience*, 29(22), 7191–7198.

Scollon, C. N., Prieto, C.-K., & Diener, E. (2009). Experience sampling: promises and pitfalls, strength and weaknesses. In E. Diener (ed.), *Assessing well-being* (pp. 157–180). Dordrecht, Netherlands: Springer.

Shiffman, S., Stone, A. A., & Hufford, M. R. (2008). Ecological momentary assessment. *Annual Review of Clinical Psychology*, 4, 1–32.

Snippe, E., Simons, C. J., Hartmann, J. A., Menne-Lothmann, C., Kramer, I., Booij, S. H., ... Wichers, M. (2016). Change in daily life behaviors and depression: Within-person and between-person associations. *Health Psychology*, 35(5), 433.

Steinhart, H., Vaessen, T., Batink, T., Klippel, A., Reininghaus, U., & Myin-Germeys, I. (submitted). Act in daily life: A momentary intervention approach.

Stephens, J., & Allen, J. (2013). Mobile phone interventions to increase physical activity and reduce weight: a systematic review. *Journal of Cardiovascular Nursing*, 28(4), 320.

Thewissen, V., Bentall, R. P., Lecomte, T., van Os, J., & Myin-Germeys, I. (2008). Fluctuations in self-esteem and paranoia in the context of daily life. *Journal of Abnormal Psychology*, 117(1), 143.

Thomée, S., Härenstam, A., & Hagberg, M. (2011). Mobile phone use and stress, sleep disturbances, and symptoms of depression among young adults: a prospective cohort study. *BMC Public Health*, 11(1), 66.

Tim Batink, J. B., Vaessen, T., Kasanova, Z., Collip, D., van Os, J., Wichers, M., Myin-Germeys, I., & Peeters, F. (2016). The ACT in Daily Life Training; a feasibility study of a mHealth intervention. *Journal of Medical Internet Research mHealth and uHealth*, 4(3), e103.

Torgerson, D. J., & Byford, S. (2002). Economic modelling before clinical trials. *British Medical Journal*, 325(7355), 98.

Torgerson, D. J., & Campbell, M. K. (2000). Cost effectiveness calculations and sample size. *British Medical Journal*, 321(7262), 697.

Vago, D. R., & David, S. A. (2012). Self-awareness, self-regulation, and self-transcendence (S-ART): a framework for understanding the neurobiological mechanisms of mindfulness. *Frontiers in Human Neuroscience*, 6, 296.

van der Krieke, L., Wunderink, L., Emerencia, A. C., de Jonge, P., & Sytema, S. (2014). E-mental health self-management for psychotic disorders: state of the art and future perspectives. *Psychiatric Services*, 65(1), 33–49. doi:10.1176/appi.ps.201300050

Versluis, A., Verkuil, B., Spinhoven, P., van der Ploeg, M. M., & Brosschot, J. F. (2016). Changing mental health and positive psychological well-being using ecological momentary interventions: a systematic review and meta-analysis. *Journal of Medical Internet Research*, 18(6).

Wichers, M., Barge-Schaapveld, D., Nicolson, N., Peeters, F., De Vries, M., Mengelers, R., & Van Os, J. (2009). Reduced stress-sensitivity or increased reward experience: the psychological mechanism of response to antidepressant medication. *Neuropsychopharmacology*, 34(4), 923–931.

Wichers, M., Simons, C., Kramer, I., Hartmann, J., Lothmann, C., Myin-Germeys, I., ... van Os, J. (2011). Momentary assessment technology as a tool to help patients with depression help themselves. *Acta Psychiatrica Scandinavica*, 124(4), 262–272.

11

MOBILE COGNITIVE TESTING USING EXPERIENCE SAMPLING

Joel Swendsen, Pierre Schweitzer and and Raeanne C. Moore

Over the past two decades, considerable progress has been observed in diverse scientific domains thanks to the increasing use of mobile technologies. These applications and devices have advanced research through the real-time assessment of subjective states such as the experience of symptoms, emotions or events, as well as through collecting objective data concerning activity, physical health status and other variables (Cain et al., 2009; Shiffman et al., 2008; Depp et al., 2016; Swendsen, 2016; Swendsen & Salamon, 2012). While the technological revolution assures us that progress will continue to provide many innovative applications in the years to come, the newest of these developments involve in-vivo assessments of human cognition. These tests are often administered through smartphones and can assess memory, attention, executive functions, and a wide range of other cognitive capacities that are necessary for everything from basic autonomous living to performance in more challenging circumstances. The capacity of applications to train and enhance these cognitive functions is also being increasingly explored, and there is a growing commercial market for "serious games" and other applications with the objective of improving cognitive capacities or performance.

In light of interest from researchers, clinicians and the general public, this chapter provides a review of the state of mobile cognitive assessments as they are currently applied in the fields of mental health and neurology. However, in order to fully understand the unmet needs to which mobile cognitive assessments respond, it is important to first examine the principal limitations of traditional neuropsychological testing that can at least partially be overcome by mobile assessments. A review of the literature will then describe the research to date using different forms of mobile cognitive testing, followed by a discussion of drawbacks and potential risks associated with this approach.

Barriers and limitations of traditional neuropsychological testing

Validated neuropsychological tests with established normative data are essential to evaluating an individual's cognitive capacities and to detect eventual areas of difficulty or decline. A major limitation of traditional neuropsychological tests, however, is that they are most often administered only punctually; the patient is assessed by a clinician on a single given day and at a specific time. The potential problem with such punctual assessments is that the obtained scores may not be representative of the individual's functioning on "most days" or "most times." It is possible that on the day of testing, for example, the patient did not have his or her usual two cups of coffee, or that he or she was distracted by thoughts of an upcoming medical procedure. Such circumstances may reasonably be thought to detrimentally impact on the patient's performance at the moment of testing. In the same way, it can also be argued that other events or circumstances may help to improve performance momentarily relative to what is "typical" for that patient, such as being particularly well-rested or having recently received very positive news. Such variance is quite common, as an individual's cognitive performance scores fluctuate as a function of daily rhythms, stress and many other state-dependent influences. For this reason, traditional clinical instruments used for characterizing cognitive functioning or for detecting deficits are characterized by a "margin of error" that may range from very small to very large. Due to this variance, subtle but clinically-relevant dysfunction may be undetectable at the time of examination. The impact that this margin of error has on research is that the detection of some signs of cognitive decline or deficits, especially those associated with the early onset of disorders, would often require the recruitment of very large samples of individuals. Large-scale studies are very expensive and the reality of the scientific literature is that they are few in number compared to investigations of more moderate sizes, which are limited in their statistical power to detect minor cognitive deficits.

Fortunately, an important alternative to increasing the number of participants enrolled in a study is to increase the number of observations acquired for each participant. This approach is often not feasible for traditional neuropsychological protocols due to the time and expense associated with clinician-administered tests. However, mobile technologies can readily provide brief but repeated assessments of cognitive functions, behavior and emotion in real-time and across the different contexts of daily life. The repeated daily assessment of these variables may reduce the margin of error associated with traditional clinical tools and provide high-resolution data concerning cognitive functions in daily life contexts. This is illustrated in Figure 11.1, where the circle represents the hypothetic point at which cognitive decline can be detected using traditional instruments. The remaining uncircled part of the blue line represents those cases that are "under the radar" of neuropsychological tests but that may nonetheless represent the earliest stages of dementia, which begin more than a decade before a diagnosis can be given (Amieva et al., 2008). Yet, one of the most coveted goals in aging research is to identify the earliest stages of cognitive decline in the hope that the overall

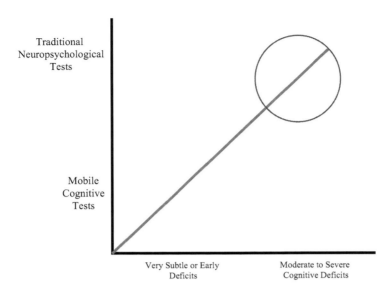

FIGURE 11.1 Cognitive decline in dementia and matching assessment methods

trajectory might be altered or slowed if interventions can be provided long before the development of dementia.

As an example of research using mobile tests to examine the aforementioned question, Allard and colleagues (2014) used both the Isaac Set Test (IST), a traditional neuropsychological test of semantic memory and verbal fluency, as well as repeated mobile assessments of these same cognitive capacities. Even though poorer IST performance was previously shown to be associated with hippocampal atrophy in a sample of more than 300 individuals (Bernard et al., 2014), Allard and colleagues found no statistically significant association between these variables in their sample of 60 participants. This is not surprising given the link between the size of the margin of error and reduced statistical power associated with their smaller sample. However, when using repeated test scores administered through the experience sampling method in this study, a highly significant association was observed between semantic memory performance and hippocampal atrophy. Moreover, should experience sampling have been used in the sample of 300 subjects (e.g. Bernard et al., 2014), one can expect that particularly subtle associations could have been identified, thereby facilitating detection of the earliest stages of the cognitive decline and dementia.

A second major limitation of neuropsychological testing concerns the fixed environmental contexts in which the assessments occur. The provision of testing in one environment can provide information only about the overall state of the individual or, at best, only suggest potential correlations for which the causes cannot be verified. This second issue is illustrated in Figure 11.2. In the left panel of the figure, we can see the general type of correlations frequently reported in the

Mobile cognitive testing using ES   145

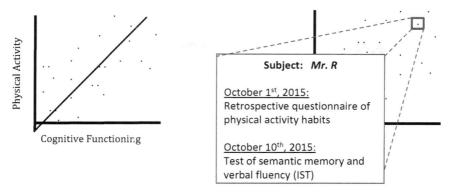

FIGURE 11.2 Nature of clinical and epidemiologic data demonstrating a correlation between physical activity and cognitive functioning

literature that have linked the risk of Alzheimer's disease and other forms of dementia to specific variables including physical activity, diet and other lifestyle characteristics. However, in the right panel one can observe that the type of data collected for each participant was based on a general and retrospective assessment of activity preferences as well as on a one-time administration of the IST. We are therefore unable to conclude whether increased physical activity actually improves sematic memory, or if those with declining semantic memory perform less exercise, or again if additional factors may explain the link between these two variables in the sample.

In order to examine such daily-life correlations, as well as to determine their directionality and causality, highly dynamic data, adapted to the natural life cycle of each variable, are needed. An example of one such protocol is presented in Figure 11.3, based on five electronic interviews per day over a week-long period as used by the Allard and colleagues (2014) study.

In this investigation, a range of daily life experiences, behaviors and events were assessed at each electronic Experience Sampling Method (ESM) interview and a mobile test of semantic memory performance was administered. Allard and

9:22 am	Emotion, Activity, Diet, Sleep, Stress, Social Contact	Cognition
12:11 pm	Emotion, Activity, Diet, Sleep, Stress, Social Contact	Cognition
2:11 pm	Emotion, Activity, Diet, Sleep, Stress, Social Contact	Cognition
4:37 pm	Emotion, Activity, Diet, Sleep, Stress, Social Contact	Cognition
8:07 pm	Emotion, Activity, Diet, Sleep, Stress, Social Contact	Cognition

FIGURE 11.3 Assessment of lifestyles and cognitive functioning

146 Swendsen, Schweitzer and Moore

colleagues were able to demonstrate that intellectually-stimulating activities (such as playing scrabble, reading or crossword puzzles) increased semantic memory performance in the subsequent hours of the same day, while no association was found for other candidate variables (i.e., physical activity, social interaction, daily chores). Moreover, each arrow represented in Figure 11.3 represents the prospective link of these activities with later-memory performance, controlling for the state of memory at the previous assessment and thereby allowing for directionality to be assessed. This method also allows for such relationships to be examined in the reverse direction (i.e. cognitive performance predicting intellectually-stimulating activities), thereby overcoming the circularity of many correlations that have been identified with traditional research methods.

Current state of publications using mobile cognitive testing

Examiner-administered vs. self-administered tests

While our focus in this chapter is on studies that employed self-administered mobile cognitive tests within an ESM paradigm, it is worth noting that several studies have developed and tested mobile (e.g., PDAs, smartphones, tablets) assessments designed to be administered by examiners in naturalistic settings and which, depending on the study question, can have advantages over laboratory-based assessments. While examiner-administered tests require more resources, a benefit of this approach is that the testing conditions can be verified and responses can be more readily interpreted in light of environmental or personal factors (distraction, motivation, etc.). For example, to enhance battlefield concussion assessment for active duty U.S. service members in field-deployed settings, a series of examiner-administered mobile cognitive test batteries, varying in composition and duration, were recently developed (Lathan et al., 2013). Deployment feasibility was demonstrated in several "operationally relevant environments" (desert, jungle, mountain, arctic, and shipboard). Thus, these assessment procedures hold promise to aid the rapid assessment of brain injury, facilitate prompt referrals for treatment, and monitor recovery over time. They also present an exciting opportunity to examine the impact of extreme physical environments and contexts on real-time cognitive function.

Other investigators have utilized examiner-administered mobile cognitive tests for the detection of cognitive change over time in hospitalized inpatients (Zalon et al., 2010), studying the effects of alcohol on cognition in naturalistic settings (i.e., bars; Scholey et al., 2012), pre-surgical sedation (Thomson et al., 2009), and detecting cognitive changes in response to sleep deprivation (Peters et al., 2009; Lamond et al., 2008; Thorne et al., 2005). In addition, several cognitive assessments on iPads and other tablet devices have been developed for at-home self-administration. There are several tablet-based batteries and tests that hold promise for use in clinical trials (e.g. Rentz et al., 2016; Moore et al., 2015); however, these have not been administered within an ESM paradigm and thus detailed consideration falls outside the scope of this chapter. Upon review of the current literature, very few studies to-date have used an ESM paradigm to objectively assess cognitive ability; these studies are summarized below.

Self-administered mobile cognitive tests: data capture methods and cognitive functions tested

We identified thirteen studies that utilized self-administered, mobile cognitive tests within an ESM paradigm (Allard et al., 2014; Sliwinski et al., 2016; Waters & Li, 2008; Veasey et al., 2015; Keenan et al., 2014; Kennedy et al., 2011; Tiplady et al., 2009; Timmers et al., 2014; Schweitzer et al., 2016; Schuster et al., 2015; Riediger et al., 2014; Frings et al., 2008; Brouillette et al., 2013). At this time, mobile cognitive tests have mostly been used in non-clinical samples of healthy volunteers. One exception was a study by Frings and colleagues (2008) in which real-time working memory performance of patients with epilepsy (who were being titrated with levetiracetam) was compared to a control group of patients on stable treatment with antiepileptic drugs. Participants in these studies ranged in age from 14 to 83 years old (mean weighted by sample size: 47 years). Most studies cited above were administered on a mobile phone provided to the participants, with the exception of four studies employing Personal Digital Assistants (PDAs; Allard et al., 2014; Waters et al., 2008; Schuster et al., 2015; Frings et al., 2008). Timing and duration of studies ranged from one assessment per day for one day (Brouillette et al., 2013) to five assessments per day for fourteen days (Sliwinski et al., 2016). On average, studies deployed 3.4 assessments per day for 6.6 days. This variance is attributable to differences in specific study objectives and whether investigators chose to link mobile cognitive test scores to other momentary assessments or retrospective data.

Few studies have reported information concerning potential biases or convergent validity between neuropsychological scores and mobile tests attempting to assess the same functions. However, Schweitzer and colleagues (2016) developed ESM tests to assess semantic and episodic memory, as well as executive functioning. They demonstrated that a learning or "practice" effect can be observed for the number of correct items generated during the majority of memory tests (Table 11.1). The within-subject coefficients when pooled across the sample therefore demonstrate that performance generally improves for a given type of memory test as a function of the number of times it was administered to the subject and despite the fact that the actual content of each test was unique for each administration. One notable exception was seen for the delayed recognition for a list-learning task, whereby performance actually decreased by the number of tests administered. This same investigation examined a mobile letter-word generation task that relies more directly on executive capacities and found strong support for its feasibility and concurrent validity, but no evidence of practice effects (Schweitzer et al., 2016). A separate mobile executive test developed by this team (a stroop-like, color-word interference task) was also characterized by a high level of compliance (80.3% of

148 Swendsen, Schweitzer and Moore

TABLE 11.1 Practice effects associated with the repetition of mobile cognitive tests

Test	Coeff.	T ratio	P value
Semantic memory and verbal fluency	0.420	2.851	0.005
Semantic category generation	0.430	1.425	0.155
List-learning immediate free-recall	0.090	1.285	0.200
List-learning immediate recognition	0.266	2.331	0.021
List-learning delayed free-recall	0.328	2.339	0.020
List-learning delayed recognition	−0.958	−10.064	0.000
Letter-word generation	−0.094	−0.592	0.554

tests were completed among participants meeting minimal adherence with the ESM protocol), by a lack of fatigue effects, and by convergent validity between the Weschler code score and both the number of correct answers (coefficient = 0.045, t = 2.011, p < .05) and test duration (coefficient = −1.500, t = −4.659, p < .001). However, the test was also characterized by strong practice effects in that the number of correct responses increased (coefficient = 0.306, t = 3.429, p < .001) and test duration decreased (coefficient = −1.610, t = 5.001, p < .001) as a function of the number of tests administered. These findings clearly show that practice effects can be observed using repeated ESM testing of certain cognitive functions. For this reason, it is recommended researchers should adjust analyses for the number of times that a given test had previously been administered (and not just for the overall number of tests that were administered during the ESM assessment period).

Even when controlling for biases, Schweitzer and colleagues (2016) found moderate to strong associations between scores for traditional neuropsychological tests and the mobile tests designed to assess the same cognitive functions. Table 11.2 demonstrates these analyses confirming their convergent validity. It may also

TABLE 11.2 Association of neuropsychological tests with mobile cognitive test scores.

Neuropsychological Test	Mobile Cognitive Test	Covariates	Coeff.	T ratio	p value
Isaacs set test	Semantic memory and verbal fluency	test number, age, sex	0.088	5.673	0.000
Grober and Buschke free recall	List-learning free recall	test number, age, sex	0.059	2.524	0.014
Grober and Buschke free recall	List-learning recognition	test number, age, sex	0.082	2.275	0.026
Grober and Buschke delayed free recall	List-learning delayed free recall	test number, age, sex	0.226	2.316	0.024
Wechsler symbol coding	Letter-word generation	test number, age, sex	0.182	4.834	0.000

be expected that very high correlations would be unlikely given the differences between the two types of tests, both in terms of mode of administration and due to the incomplete overlap of testing content.

Concerning the diversity of functions tested, seven of the thirteen studies administered a single mobile cognitive test (Allard et al., 2014; Moore et al., 2015; Timmers et al., 2014; Schuster et al., 2015; Riediger et al., 2014; Frings et al., 2008; Brouillette et al., 2013), while the other six administered anywhere from two to five tests over the duration of the study (Sliwinski et al., 2016; Veasey et al., 2015; Tiplady et al., 2009; Schweitzer et al., 2016). Seven studies reported adherence ratings to the study protocol, with a mean adherence rating across the multiple cognitive tests (weighted by sample size) of 79.2%. We did not observe associations between age, duration of the study, or frequency of mobile cognitive tests with study adherence.

Each research team in the identified investigations developed a unique test(s) for their study. Overall, tests were developed in the following cognitive domains: working memory, attention/reaction time, processing speed, semantic memory, short-term memory, delayed memory, and executive functions. To our knowledge, none of these tests are currently publically available. Touch screens were the most common mode of responding with scoring completed automatically. However, one study (Schweitzer et al., 2016), had participants' respond orally; responses were recorded on the smartphones for later scoring. While automatic scoring has clear advantages over manual scoring, these researchers did report that they identified probable "cheating" (e.g., help from someone else) on the audio recording for a small portion of their participants.

Self-administered mobile cognitive tests: psychometrics

The psychometric properties of studies completed to-date are encouraging. In addition to Schweitzer and colleagues (2016), several studies have examined the convergent validity between standard in-lab tests and the mobile versions of tests of similar constructs. While we were unable to concatenate the correlations between the laboratory-based and mobile versions of tests, concordance with in-lab tests generally had medium effects (Allard et al., 2014; Sliwinski et al., 2016; Waters & Li, 2008; Schuster et al., 2015; Brouillette et al., 2013). We note, however, that these concordance rates may be reduced due to difficulties in fully duplicating neuropsychological tests with a corresponding mobile version, and that some studies (Allard et al., 2014) compared distinct cognitive tests presumed to assess the same cognitive capacity. Additionally, two studies directly examined whether significant associations existed between their mobile cognitive tests and in-lab measures of different constructs, and found evidence in support of the mobile test's discriminant validity (Schuster et al., 2015; Brouillette et al., 2013).

As previously discussed, a unique advantage of ESM cognitive tests is the ability for repeated sampling, both within and between days. Studies to-date have

150 Swendsen, Schweitzer and Moore

demonstrated good test-retest reliability (Timmers et al., 2014; Brouillette et al., 2013), adequate internal reliability (Waters & Li, 2008), and excellent between-person reliability and within-person variability (Sliwinski et al., 2016) for various mobile cognitive tests.

Self-administered mobile cognitive tests: usefulness over and above traditional laboratory-based testing

Five studies have directly examined the usefulness of ESM cognitive assessments beyond traditional in-lab testing. In addition to the research previously described by Allard and colleagues (2014), Riediger and colleagues (2014) examined the association between ESM assessed nervousness, momentary heart rate, and concurrent working memory performance. They found an interaction effect with increased nervousness and stress was associated with poorer working memory test performance in older, rather than younger, adults. A third study examined the relationship between self-reported alcohol consumption and real-world attention and working memory scores (Tiplady et al., 2009). The authors detected expected diurnal changes on the ESM attention tasks throughout the day and participants' performance on the ESM tests were worse on days when participants had consumed alcohol.

The final two studies examined the lagged effect of caffeine and eating breakfast, respectively, on future real-world cognitive performance. Keenan and colleagues (2014) evaluated the effects of bedtime caffeine use on next-day working memory in a randomized controlled trial. Blind to treatment allocation, participants took one week of caffeine or placebo pills. Despite disrupted sleep when taking bedtime caffeine, next-day working memory performance was significantly higher throughout the caffeine week than the placebo week. Veasey and colleagues (2015) were interested in the effect of breakfast size prior to morning exercise on working memory performance later in the day. Participants included 24 young, healthy, and habitually active females. Results indicated that consuming a larger breakfast was associated with mid-afternoon working memory decrements, which were not observed when participants consumed a smaller breakfast.

In summary, the research to-date has demonstrated that EMA-based cognitive assessments are feasible and generally well accepted among research participants. In addition, there is good support for the psychometric properties of these tests concerning both reliability and convergent validity. Studies are only beginning to demonstrate applications for repeated, mobile cognitive testing in clinical research, and the expansion of these applications over the next few years is certain to provide new sources of information for understanding human cognitive functioning in real-world settings.

Decisions for researchers

As previously mentioned, the choice of sampling schedules depends largely on the research questions of the given investigation. For example, a single cognitive assessment per day over multiple days may be sufficient if the researcher is interested in acquiring repeated performance scores, such as in the goal of reducing variance associated with traditional neuropsychological tests. However, more intensive sampling schedules are required in order to examine within-day associations of cognitive performance with mood or behavior. Studies that have examined compliance rates demonstrate no salient fatigue effects with repeated assessments conducted up to five times per day, or every three to four hours on average (Schweitzer et al., 2016).

As for number of days of assessment, many ESM researchers have applied a one-week design in order to acquire information across the natural rhythms of work and leisure that are common in society, but multiple-week assessments have also been successfully employed (Sliwinski et al., 2016). Although these choices depend on the specific scientific questions at hand, researchers should apply care in the timing of cognitive assessments, whilst considering test type. Unless they are used at every within-day assessment, mobile cognitive tests should be counterbalanced across the day in order to avoid systematic time biases (as would be the case when assessing memory or attention only in the morning or evening).

The investigations presented in the previous review also involved study-specific "in-house" programming that presents certain difficulties for the broader diffusion of mobile cognitive tests. New technology requires pilot testing on a study-to-study basis. While establishing the acceptability and feasibility of these tests is possible with relatively small sample sizes, their convergent or discriminant validity can often only be examined after a larger sample has been collected. For this reason, the selection of neuropsychological tests to accompany a mobile testing protocol are of importance, and careful matching should be used relative to the specific cognitive functions being tested. This objective often requires creativity on behalf of researchers in order to respect the copyright of any test that is not in the public domain, whilst waiting for the field to permit the availability of mobile cognitive test "batteries" to its scientific community that would avoid the replication of unnecessary validation efforts.

Finally, researchers can apply a range of strategies to increase subjects' compliance to mobile cognitive tests, most often in the form of financial or psychological incentives. Financial incentives may include a "bonus" for a particular level of compliance (such as completion of 75% of all programmed assessments), and psychological incentives have included providing a progressive "counter" that shows subjects how many assessments were completed to date or that administer positive feedback through messages on the mobile device. However, these strategies are not a substitute for a motivated verbal explanation of the importance of the project to the participant; the researcher should carefully explain why mobile technologies help them to understand their daily experiences, or their personal "story," in a way that is not possible with other methods.

Limitations and difficulties associated with mobile cognitive testing

In concluding this chapter, it is important to appreciate the limitations of mobile cognitive tests that distinguish them from traditional neuropsychological instruments. First, at no point in this chapter did the authors use the phrase "mobile neuropsychological testing." This intentional caution in the use of vocabulary is necessary given the differences between the two testing types. Clinical or laboratory-based neuropsychological testing is completed by technicians or expert clinicians that are trained in the interpretation of test performance in order to elucidate the individual's physical and psychological status at the time of testing, as well as motivation in performing the test itself. Such information is essential for clinical diagnosis and cannot be achieved through isolated self-administered mobile cognitive tests. For this reason, the latter can never replace the former. Instead, the information provided by mobile tests must be considered a different source of data concerning cognitive functioning. This also applies to the nature of testing contexts, where neuropsychological tests are administered in quiet and distraction-free environments and after establishing a specific appointment time with the patient. They are therefore best adapted to characterizing the overall cognitive capacities of the patient. In turn, mobile cognitive tests may occur at any time in daily life, whether or not the television is on, the person has just awoken from a nap, or the individual is in the middle of gardening. Such data are therefore best adapted to characterizing the "typical" cognitive functioning of the patient in daily life, with all of its distractions and constraints.

It is also important to note that mobile cognitive tests are limited by the technologies that are used in their administration and by the ESM methodology itself. A smartphone may be easily capable of administering certain tests such as the IST, but the small screen may render the administration of many other tests unfeasible. ESM also requires relatively brief assessments, which mean that extensive cognitive testing may also be inappropriate for this methodology. As previously noted, while the repeated assessment of cognitive functions is a strength for many reasons, it introduces potential biases that clinical researchers must acknowledge and control for in their study designs.

Finally, a word of caution is necessary concerning the proliferation of smartphone applications for clinical populations because they are not without risk. To use one salient illustration, there are currently hundreds of smartphone applications to aid individuals with different forms of addiction, but not all were developed using prudent clinical judgment. For example, among the numerous applications that exist for alcohol dependence, some encourage full and immediate abstinence. This approach fully ignores the danger that going "cold turkey" off alcohol poses for some patients due to seizures or other medical complications. In the same line of reasoning, the mass diffusion of mobile cognitive tests may be counterproductive for some patients with cognitive difficulties who would otherwise have directly sought expert advice and diagnosis, but who do not do so because of the assumption that their problem has been adequately assessed. The rapid advances in mobile technologies may therefore, to some extent, have progressed too quickly and it is the responsibility of researchers and clinicians alike to inform individuals of the appropriate place that such tools may have in their lives.

In conclusion, the caution that one may have about the use of mobile cognitive tests is offset by the quite extraordinary promise that they provide in advancing research as a complement to neuropsychological testing and other clinical tools. The development of these tests is still in its infancy, but the existing data underscores the feasibility and convergent validity of this form of assessment. Ideally, a repository of validated tests can be constructed in order to provide wider access to researchers and reduce the heterogeneity associated with the development of unique tests by different academic fraternities for the purpose of specific investigations. It is now necessary to progress, develop and refine this novel approach through further careful validation studies.

References

Allard, M., Husky, M., Catheline, G., Pelletier, A., Dilharreguy, B., Amieva, H., … Swendsen, J. (2014). Mobile technologies in the early detection of cognitive decline. *PLoS One*, 9(12), e112197. doi:10.1371/journal.pone.0112197

Amieva, H., Le Goff, M., Millet, X., Orgogozo, J. M., Pérès, K., Barberger-Gateau, P., … & Dartigues, J. F. (2008). Prodromal Alzheimer's disease: successive emergence of the clinical symptoms. *Annals of Neurology: Official Journal of the American Neurological Association and the Child Neurology Society*, 64(5), 492–498.

Bernard, C., Helmer, C., Dilharreguy, B., Amieva, H., Auriacombe, S., Dartigues, J. F., … & Catheline, G. (2014). Time course of brain volume changes in the preclinical phase of Alzheimer's disease. *Alzheimer's & Dementia*, 10(2), 143–151.

Brouillette, R. M., Foil, H., Fontenot, S., Correro, A., Allen, R., Martin, C. K., … Keller, J. N. (2013). Feasibility, reliability, and validity of a smartphone based application for the assessment of cognitive function in the elderly. *PLoS One*, 8(6), e65925. doi:10.1371/journal.pone.0065925

Cain, A. E., Depp, C. A., & Jeste, D. V. (2009). Ecological momentary assessment in aging research: a critical review. *Journal of Psychiatric Research*, 43(11), 987–996.

Depp, C. A., Moore, R. C., Perivoliotis, D., & Granholm, E. (2016). Technology to assess and support self-management in serious mental illness. *Dialogues in Clinical Neuroscience*, 18 (2), 171–183.

Frings, L., Wagner, K., Maiwald, T., Carius, A., Schinkel, A., Lehmann, C., & Schulze-Bonhage, A. (2008). Early detection of behavioral side effects of antiepileptic treatment using handheld computers. *Epilepsy & Behavior*, 13(2), 402–406. doi:10.1016/j.yebeh.2008.04.022

Keenan, E. K., Tiplady, B., Priestley, C. M., & Rogers, P. J. (2014). Naturalistic effects of five days of bedtime caffeine use on sleep, next-day cognitive performance, and mood. *Journal of Caffeine Research*, 4(1), 13–20. doi:10.1089/jcr.2011.0030

Kennedy, D. O., Veasey, R. C., Watson, A. W., Dodd, F. L., Jones, E. K., Tiplady, B., & Haskell, C. F. (2011). Vitamins and psychological functioning: a mobile phone assessment of the effects of a B vitamin complex, vitamin C and minerals on cognitive performance and subjective mood and energy. *Human Psychopharmacology*, 26(4–5), 338–347. doi:10.1002/hup.1216

Lamond, N., Jay, S. M., Dorrian, J., Ferguson, S. A., Roach, G. D., & Dawson, D. (2008). The sensitivity of a palm-based psychomotor vigilance task to severe sleep loss. *Behavior Research Methods*, 40(1), 347–352.

Lathan, C., Spira, J. L., Bleiberg, J., Vice, J., & Tsao, J. W. (2013). Defense Automated Neurobehavioral Assessment (DANA)-psychometric properties of a new field-deployable neurocognitive assessment tool. *Military Medicine*, 178(4), 365–371. doi:10.7205/milmed-d-12-00438

Moore, R. C., Fazeli, P. L., Patterson, T. L., Depp, C. A., Moore, D. J., Granholm, E., ... Mausbach, B. T. (2015). UPSA-M: Feasibility and initial validity of a mobile application of the UCSD Performance-Based Skills Assessment. *Schizophrenia Research*, 164(1–3), 187–192. doi:10.1016/j.schres.2015.02.014

Peters, J. D., Biggs, S. N., Bauer, K. M., Lushington, K., Kennedy, D., Martin, J., & Dorrian, J. (2009). The sensitivity of a PDA-based psychomotor vigilance task to sleep restriction in 10-year-old girls. *Journal of Sleep Research*, 18(2), 173–177. doi:10.1111/j.1365-2869.2008.00716.x

Rentz, D. M., Dekhtyar, M., Sherman, J., Burnham, S., Blacker, D., Aghjayan, S. L., ... Sperling, R. A. (2016). The feasibility of at-home iPad cognitive testing for use in clinical trials. *The Journal of Prevention of Alzheimers Disease*, 3(1), 8–12. doi:10.14283/jpad.2015.78

Riediger, M., Wrzus, C., Klipker, K., Muller, V., Schmiedek, F., & Wagner, G. G. (2014). Outside of the laboratory: Associations of working-memory performance with psychological and physiological arousal vary with age. *Psychology and Aging*, 29(1), 103–114. doi:10.1037/a0035766

Scholey, A. B., Benson, S., Neale, C., Owen, L., & Tiplady, B. (2012). Neurocognitive and mood effects of alcohol in a naturalistic setting. *Human Psychopharmacology*, 27(5), 514–516. doi:10.1002/hup.2245

Schuster, R. M., Mermelstein, R. J., & Hedeker, D. (2015). Acceptability and feasibility of a visual working memory task in an ecological momentary assessment paradigm. *Psychological Assessment*, 27(4), 1463–1470. doi:10.1037/pas0000138

Schweitzer, P., Husky, M., Allard, M., Amieva, H., Peres, K., Foubert-Samier, A., ... Swendsen, J. (2016). Feasibility and validity of mobile cognitive testing in the investigation of age-related cognitive decline. *International Journal of Methods in Psychiatric Research*, 26(3), e1521.

Shiffman, S., Stone, A. A., & Hufford, M. R. (2008). *Ecological momentary assessment. Annu. Rev. Clin. Psychol.*, 4, 1–32.

Sliwinski, M. J., Mogle, J. A., Hyun, J., Munoz, E., Smyth, J. M., & Lipton, R. B. (2016). Reliability and validity of ambulatory cognitive assessments. *Assessment*, 25(1), 14–30. doi:10.1177/1073191116643164

Swendsen, J. (2016). Contributions of mobile technologies to addiction research. *Dialogues in Clinical Neuroscience*, 18(2), 213–221.

Swendsen, J., & Salamon, R. (2012). Mobile technologies in psychiatry: providing new perspectives from biology to culture. *World Psychiatry*, 11(3), 196–198.

Thomson, A. J., Nimmo, A. F., Tiplady, B., & Glen, J. B. (2009). Evaluation of a new method of assessing depth of sedation using two-choice visual reaction time testing on a mobile phone. *Anaesthesia*, 64(1), 32–38. doi:10.1111/j.1365-2044.2008.05683.x

Thorne, D. R., Johnson, D. E., Redmond, D. P., Sing, H. C., Belenky, G., & Shapiro, J. M. (2005). The Walter Reed palm-held psychomotor vigilance test. *Behavior Research Methods*, 37(1), 111–118.

Timmers, C., Maeghs, A., Vestjens, M., Bonnemayer, C., Hamers, H., & Blokland, A. (2014). Ambulant cognitive assessment using a smartphone. *Applied Neuropsychology Adult*, 21(2), 136–142. doi:10.1080/09084282.2013.778261

Tiplady, B., Oshinowo, B., Thomson, J., & Drummond, G. B. (2009). Alcohol and cognitive function: assessment in everyday life and laboratory settings using mobile phones. *Alcoholism, Clinical and Experimental Research*, 33(12), 2094–2102. doi:10.1111/j.1530-0277.2009.01049.x

Veasey, R. C., Haskell-Ramsay, C. F., Kennedy, D. O., Tiplady, B., & Stevenson, E. J. (2015). The effect of breakfast prior to morning exercise on cognitive performance, mood and appetite later in the day in habitually active women. *Nutrients*, 7(7), 5712–5732. doi:10.3390/nu7075250

Waters, A. J., & Li, Y. (2008). Evaluating the utility of administering a reaction time task in an ecological momentary assessment study. *Psychopharmacology*, 197(1), 25–35. doi:10.1007/s00213–00007–1006–1006

Zalon, M. L., Sandhaus, S., Valenti, D., & Arzamasova, U. (2010). Using PDAs to detect cognitive change in the hospitalized elderly patient. *Applied Nursing Research*, 23(3), e21–27. doi:10.1016/j.apnr.2009.10.002

INDEX

Note: Page references for figures are in *italics*. Page numbers for tables are **bold**.

Acceptance and Commitment Therapy (ACT) 129
actigraphy 69, 73
ACT in Daily Life (ACT-DL) 129, 130
Actissist 129
adherence 115–16
administrative records 118
affect: negative 39, 42, 68, 70, 111, 113–14, 115, 117, 119, 130; positive 42, 68, 113–14, 129, 130; unstable 99
alcohol use: alcohol consumption 150; alcohol dependence 152; alcoholism 114; drinking behavior and problems 101
anger 105
antipsychotic medication 3
anxiety disorder 69
Asperger's Syndrome (AS) 54–5, 57, 61–4
assessment development 11; chronological organisation of momentary and interval ES items *12*; ESM item wording 12–13; overall duration of self-assessment forms and internal ordering 13–14
assessments: interviews 2, 44; microlongitudinal 3–4; questionnaires 2, 44; retrospective 44; of trait-like variables 11; *see also* mobile cognitive testing; neuropsychological testing
associations, temporal 3–4
attention//reaction time 149
auditory hallucinations 39–40, 46–7, 48, 49

autism spectrum disorders (ASD) 53, 63–4; acceptability of ESM 55; benefits of using ESM 54; compliance to ESM 55; executing the procedure 62–3; feasibility of ESM 54; methodology 56–61; reliability and validity of ESM data 56; research in 54; time schedules 62
automated text solutions 1
autonoetic functioning 54
autonomic regulation 42
autoregressive relationships 117

big data 118
binging and purging 101
bipolar disorder 68, 113, 114
Borderline Personality Disorder 100
briefing sessions 15–16, 74–5, 89–90
Brief Screen for Sleep Disorders 77
British Picture Vocabulary Scale II (BPVS II) 61
bulimia nervosa 81–2, 114

Camberwell Family Interview 90
centring 25
circadian rhythm disturbances 69, 76
cognitive behavioral therapy (CBT) 119
cognitive biases, controlling for 148
cognitive decline **144**
cognitive function 147–9, 152; assessment of lifestyles and **145**; and physical activity **145**
cognitive testing *see* mobile cognitive testing

Index 157

compliance to ESM 75–6, 103–4
confidentiality 85
confounders 30
Consensus Sleep Diary (CSD) 71
contextual attributes 84
contextual bias 84
continuous sampling 11
coping strategies 125
cortisol 42
cravings 117

data analysis 30–1, 32; for autism spectrum disorders 56; centring 25; concurrent relationship between negative affect and paranoia **35**; data coding 20; data set up 25, 27; data structure 18–19; in dyad research 92; managing and entering data 19–20; in mental health research 112–13; missing data considerations 28–9; models with measurements at different levels 26–7; moderation 26; multilevel models 20–5; negative affect by gender interaction **35**; in predictive modeling 116–18; results 34–5; statistical analysis plan 30–1; summarizing multilevel data 27–8; for theory development 114; worked example 31–6
data capture methods 147–9
data coding 20
data hoarding 10
data set-up 25, 27
data storage 134
daydreaming 82
debriefing sessions 16, 75, 89–90
delusional experiences 49, 83
dementia **144**
depression and depressed mood 3, 40, 68–9, 83, 105, 115, 129, 130–1
diary studies, 10, 105; *see also* sleep diaries
drinking behaviour and problems *see* alcohol use
dyads 81; value and challenges of ESM 84–5
dyad study design: analysis 92; assessment format 88–9; briefing and debriefing 89–90; equipment choices and selection 85; item development 90–1; Likert scale questions **87**; participants' experiences 92–3; sampling scheme 85–8; themes arising from content analysis of feedback **88**
dysfunction 4

eating disorders 101; *see also* bulimia nervosa
ecological momentary interventions (EMIs) 124–5; advantages of 125–6; compared to other intervention techniques 128–9; content of 129; data storage 134; delivery schemes 130–1; evaluation of 135–6; feedback issues 132–3; guidelines for 128–37; interactive components 133; interrelationship of components 130; key questions and considerations **136**; personalization of 131–2; potential pitfalls of 126–7; selection of devices 133–4; target population 134–5; user-friendliness and acceptability 135
electronic sampling devices 1, 4, 14, 38, 42, 55, 56–7, 85, 89, 103, 118, 133–4, 146, 151
emotional granularity 41
emotion functioning 40–2
engagement 92–3
equipment and technology 14–15, 45, 49, 85; *see also* technology
ethical challenges in predictive analysis 120
evaluation: outcome 135; process 135–7; *see also* assessments
event-based delivery procedures 9, 100, 130
event-contingent sampling 9
examiner-administered tests 146–7
executive function 147, 149
experimental design studies 3

family dynamics 81, 90
family therapy 94
feedback: from ecological momentary interventions (EMIs) 132–3; qualitative 93; quantitative 93; real-time 119–20
fixed effects 25
fixed time-based delivery procedures 130
FOCUS system 130

gender differences 35–6, **35**, 41, 47

hallucinatory experiences 39–40, 83
high-functioning autism (HFA) 54–5, 57, 61–4
hippocampal atrophy 144
hippocampal volume 42
hopelessness 105
hypersomnia 69

illicit substance use 3
incentives 151
inner voices 63; *see also* auditory hallucinations
inpatient settings 48
insomnia 68, 76
internal ordering 13–14
interval-contingent sampling 9–10

158 Index

interventions 111, 114–15, 117; mechanisms of change in 119; real-time feedback in 119–20; *see also* ecological momentary interventions; mental health (mHealth) interventions
interview assessments 2, 44
iRTT (intelligent Real Time Therapy) 133
Isaac Set Test (IST) 144

lagged associations 113–14
Likert scale questions **87**
linked sensors 118
longitudinal studies, long-term 115

MAR (missing at random) data 29, 103
margin of error 143
maximum likelihood estimation (MLE) 29
MCAR (missing completely at random) data 29
measurement bias 111
mediation 26
medical devices 118
medication side effects 87
memory: autobiographical 54; delayed 149; episodic 147; semantic 144, 145–6, 147, 149; short-term 149; working 149, 150
mental health: and sleep 67–8, 76–7; and social environment 82; *see also* dyad study design
mental health (mHealth) interventions 44, 124, 129
mental health events 114
mental health research: capabilities of ESM 113–15; ESM methods and guidance 115–18; general applications of prediction using ESM 112–13
mental illness 2; *see also* mental health; psychosis
methodology: choosing methods and equipment 45, 56–7; item development for ASD 57–61; missing data and adherence 115–16; for prediction models 115–18; questionnaire development 45–6
microlongitudinal assessment 3–4
missing data considerations 28–9, 32–3, 103–4, 115–16; approaches to analysis 29; mechanism 29; missing at random (MAR) 29, 103; missing completely at random (MCAR) 29; missing not at random (MNAR) 29, 103; proportion of missing data for each beep *34*
MLE (maximum likelihood estimation) 29
MNAR (missing not at random) data 29, 103

mobile cognitive testing: association of neuropsychological tests with mobile cognitive test scores **148**; cognitive functions tested 147–9; data capture methods 147–9; decisions for researchers 150–1; diversity of functions tested 149; examiner-administered vs. self-administered tests 146–7; limitations and difficulties associated with 151–3; practice effects associated with **148**; psychometrics 149–50; publications using 146–50; self-administered 147–9
mobile phones 43–4, 57
moderation 26
motivation 135
multilevel data structures 18–19, 36; centring 25; for concurrent analysis 21; database structure with three paranoia items and baseline measure **19**; data coding 20; data management and entry 19–20; data set up 25, 27; for lagged analysis 24–5; models with measurements at different levels 26–7; random coefficient models 22–4; random intercept model, three-level *21*; random intercept models 20, 21–2, *23*; summarizing multilevel data 27–8; within-day and between-day variation 27–8

negative affect 39, 42, 68, 70, 111, 113–14, 115, 117, 119, 130
neurobiology, 42–43
neurocognitive functioning, 41
neuroimaging 118
neuropsychological testing 143–6, 149, 151–2; cognitive decline in dementia **144**; lifestyles and cognitive functioning **145**; nature of clinical and epidemiologic data **145**
non-suicidal self-injury (NSSI) 98, 100, 101, 102, 105–6

outpatient settings 48
overdoses 97
overnight polysomnography (PSG) 73, 77

panic attacks 114
paranoia 40, 83
paranoid personality traits 38
parasomnia 76
parasympathetic activity 42
Participation in Everyday Life Survey Application (PIEL App.) 55

pathological thought content 82
Patient-Centered Outcomes Research Institute 91
patient empowerment 126
Patient Reported Outcome (PRO) Diary 73
periodic limb movement disorder 76
persecutory delusions 40
polysomnography (PSG) 73, 77
positive affect 42, 68, 113–14, 129, 130
Positive and Negative Affect Scale for Children (PANAS-C) 57, 61
Post-Traumatic Stress Disorder (PTSD) 114
prediction 111, 120–1; capabilities of ESM in mental health research 113–15; of early warning signs 114; ESM vs. standard static measures 111–12; examination of lagged associations 113–14; examination of trajectories 113; future directions 118–20; with large groups of indicators 115; methods used and guidance for research 115–18; real-time 119; using ESM in mental health research, 112–13
predictive modeling: capabilities of ESM 113–15; consumer stakeholders in 120; data integration beyond self-report 118–19; duration and intensity of sampling 116; general applications of, 112–13; missing data and adherence 115–16; rationale for 111–12; statistical approaches to 116–18; validation 118
privacy issues 120
processing speed 149
profile plots *33*
psychometrics 149–50
psychopathology 2, 4
psychosis 83; assessment of 38–9; auditory hallucinations 39–40, 46–7, 48, 49; cognitive behavioral therapy for 119; delusions 49; paranoia 40; persecutory delusions 40; and self-harm 99; and sleep 69–70; and social stressors 82; subclinical 38–9
psychotic episodes 114, 119
p values 31

qualitative feedback 93
Quantified Self movement 120
quantitative feedback 93
questionnaires 2, 44; development of ESM items and assessment batteries 45–6; examples of questions **46**; question

framework **59**–**60**; sample questions for ASD **58**

random coefficient models 22–4; with positive/negative covariance *23*; with two subject-specific effects *23*
random effect models 20, 21–2
random effects 25
random intercept models **35**; graph, *23*
randomised trial design 106
random time-based delivery procedures 130
reactivity bias 102–3
recruitment 15–16, 47, 105
reliability 150
repetitive thinking 99
retention 15–16, 47, 92–3, 105
retrospective recall bias 2, 5, 44, 111

sampling strategy 8–9; continuous 11; event-contingent 9; interval-contingent 9–10; signal-contingent 9, 10–11; time-contingent 9, 100
schizoid personality features 38
schizophrenia 41, 46, 82, 114; incorporating ESM into treatment 43–4; neurobiology of 42–3
schizophrenia-spectrum diagnosis 69–70
schizotypal personality features 38
seasonal affective disorder 118
self-administered tests 146–7
self-assessment 9–10, 13–14, 89
self-criticism 102
self-cutting 97; *see also* self-harm
self-efficacy 117
self-harm 97, 101; defined 98; interventions for 106; medically serious 99; in prisoners 104–6; subtypes of, 98
self-harm ideation 101–2, 104, 105, 106
self-harm studies: ethical challenges 102–3; reactivity 102–3
self-knowledge 54
self-medication theory 114
self-monitoring129
self-report questions 1, 9, 10, 38, 84, 89–90, 111
semi-random stratified sampling 85–6
signal contingent sampling 9, 10–11
sleep 67; and depression 68–9; designing study for 70–3; and ESM 67–8; and mental health 76–7; practical

160 Index

considerations of studying using ESM 70; and psychosis 69–70
sleep apnea 69, 76
sleep diaries 69, 71
sleep disturbance 67
sleep efficiency (SE) 71, 73
sleep fragmentation (SF) 73
sleep onset latency (SOL) 71, 73
sleep pressure 67
sleep quality 71
sleep studies: briefing 74–5; challenges 75–6; choosing methods and equipment 73–4; daytime level variables 70; debriefing 75; executing the procedure 74–7; follow-up calls 75; list of sleep-wake/circadian rhythm variables and definitions, **72**; night-time level variables 71; objective sleep methods 73; subjective sleep methods 71; time schedules 74
smartphone applications 1, 14–15, 45, 85, 103, 118, 119, 127, 133–4, 142, 146, 151, 152
smoking urges 117
social context 3
social engagement 83
social interactions 81–2
social media 118
social stressors 81–2
social withdrawal 41
software: development of 4–5; multilevel 20; smartphone applications 45; statistical, 20, 29
somatic complaints 39
sporadic symptoms 5
standard risk profiling 111–12
statistical analysis plan 30–31; convert research question into statistical models 30, 32; data analysis 30–1, 32; identify research question 30, 32
statistical power 76
statistical software 20, 29
stress 117; family-induced 81–2
stressful events ideation 3
stress induction 67
stress reactivity 42
stress sensitivity 128, 129
substance abuse 3; *see also* alcohol use

suicidal ideation 2, 99, 114
suicidal intent 97
suicide 97, 102, 112; risk of, 103, 104
suicide attempts 97, 98, 99, 103, 105, 114
survey research 11
suspicious thoughts 135
sympathovagal balance 42

tablet devices 146
technology 14–15, 49, 114; and mobile cognitive testing 142, 151–2; mobile communication 124; *see also* electronic sampling devices; smartphone applications
temporal associations 3–4
text message systems 15, 43–4
thought disorder 47
time-contingent sampling 9, 100
time-lagged analysis 24–5
time schedules 47, 62, 74
time spent in bed (TIB) 71, 73
Time Varying Effect Models 117
total sleep time (TST) 71, 73
trait paranoia 83
traumatic events 5
treatment effects 3

UK Department of Health 91
unstable affect 99

validation 118
validity of mobile cognitive testing 149–50
variability 4, 101–2, 147; controlling for 44–5; intra-individual 116; within-day and between-day 27–8; within-person 150
verbal fluency 144
visual imagery 59, 63

wakefulness 67
wake-time after sleep onset (WASO) 71, 73
Woodcock Reading Mastery Test – Third Edition (WRMT-III) 61